SPIRIT OF TRUTH

Spirit of Truth

ECUMENICAL PERSPECTIVES ON THE HOLY SPIRIT

Papers of
THE HOLY SPIRIT CONSULTATION
Commission on Faith and Order, NCCCUSA
October 24-25, 1985 — Brookline, Massachusetts

Edited by

Theodore Stylianopoulos and S. Mark Heim

Holy Cross Orthodox Press
Brookline, Massachusetts 02146

We are extremely pleased to acknowledge the generosity of His Eminence Archbishop Iakovos who generously provided the funds for the publication of this volume.

The essays that appear in this volume were first published in *The Greek Orthodox Theological Review,* Vol. 31 (1986), Nos. 3 and 4.

Published by Holy Cross Orthodox Press
50 Goddard Avenue
Brookline, Massachusetts 02146

Cover design by Mary C. Vaporis

Library of Congress Cataloging-in-Publication Data

Holy Spirit Consultation (1985: Brookline, Mass.)
Spirit of truth.
Published also as v. 31, nos. 3 and 4 of the Greek Orthodox theological review
Bibliography: p.
1. Holy Spirit—Congresses. 2. Holy Spirit—Procession—Congresses. I. Heim, S. Mark II. Stylianopoulos, Theodore G. III. National Council of the Churches of Christ in the United States of America. Commission on Faith and Order. IV. Title.
BT121.2.H65 1985   231'.3   86-27682
ISBN 0-917651-39-1 (pbk.)

Contents

CONTRIBUTORS

Dr. Roberta Bondi is Associate Professor of Church History, Candler School of Theology, Emory University.

Dr. Francine Cardman is Associate Professor of Historical Theology, Weston School of Theology.

Dr. Donald W. Dayton is Professor of Theology and Ethics, Northern Baptist Theological Seminary.

Dr. S. Mark Heim is Associate Professor of Christian Theology, Andover Newton Theological School.

Dr. Lauree Hersch Meyer is Associate Professor of Biblical Theology, Bethany Theological Seminary.

Dr. Richard Lovelace is Professor of Church History, Gordon-Conwall Theological Seminary.

Dr. Lloyd G. Patterson is Professor of Historical Theology, Episcopal Divinity School.

Dr. Gerald T. Sheppard is Associate Professor of Old Testament Literature and Exegesis, Emmanuel College of Victoria University, University of Toronto.

Dr. Martha Ellen Stortz is Associate Professor of Historical Theology and Ethics, Pacific Lutheran Theological Seminary.

V. Rev. Dr. Theodore G. Stylianopoulos is Professor of New Testament and of Orthodox Spirituality, Hellenic College/Holy Cross Greek Orthodox School of Theology.

The Holy Spirit Consultation
An Introduction

S. MARK HEIM

THE CONSULTATION ON THE HOLY SPIRIT, the papers of which
are presented in this volume, is one small part of a much larger ecumenical project. Like any single part of a fuller conversation, its true
value and worth can be seen only in the context of the whole. Nor
is this larger context simply the long argument—often much more
like conflict—between the Christian East and the Christian West over
the insertion of the *filioque* clause into the Nicene Creed. Central
as this issue is to the discussion, it is set within the even broader
contemporary search of the churches for unity in the trinitarian apostolic faith.

Within the Faith and Order Commission of the World Council
of Churches, there has been general agreement that the path to full
Christian unity (and perhaps to a general ecumenical council) would
necessarily include three major steps: agreement on the church-
dividing issues of baptism, eucharist, and ministry; common confession
of the apostolic faith; and common ways of deciding and acting together.

The 1982 World Council of Churches Faith and Order document
Baptism, Eucharist and Ministry represents a major contribution toward
the first condition of Christian unity.[1] This document is now before

---

[1]Jeffrey Gros, ed., *The Search for Visible Unity* (New York, 1984); *Baptism,
Eucharist and Ministry,* Faith and Order Paper No. 111, (Geneva, 1982); Max
Thurian and Geoffrey Wainwright, eds., *Baptism and Eucharist: Ecumenical
Convergence in Celebration,* (Geneva, 1983); Jeffrey Gros, "Baptism, Eucharist
and Ministry," *One World* (January 1985).

[1]

the churches for their possible reception.

From the time of the 1975 World Council Assembly at Nairobi, the World Council's Faith and Order Commission has engaged in a second major study: "Towards the Common Expression of the Apostolic Faith Today."[2] This study process addresses itself to another of the major conditions of Christian unity: the common recognition and expression of fundamental Christian faith.

On the world level, this study has gathered significant confessional material from WCC member churches and has sponsored a series of consultations focused on the Nicene Creed.[3] The study has chosen to focus on the Nicene Creed as the most common *confession* shared by Christians, seeking to have the various traditions find a common *explication* of the creed's meaning; a common *recognition* of the creed; and finally common *confession* of the faith of the creed. Consultations have taken place in Africa, Asia and Europe, dealing with the creed's articles on God, Christ, and the Holy Spirit.

The Faith and Order Commission of the National Council of Churches of Christ in the U.S.A. has participated in the work of the Apostolic Faith study, working on its own related but independent agenda. The Commission has sponsored six consultations in addition to the one reported in this volume: Creeds and the Churches, Language and the Creeds, Scripture and Creeds, The Apostolic Faith in Relation to the Jewish Faith, Christology, and Black Witness to the Apostolic Faith.[4] The U.S. Faith and Order Commission

---

[2]David Paton, ed., *Breaking Barriers,* Nairobi 1975 (London, 1976); *The Ecumenical Review* 26 (April 1974); Michael Kinnamon, ed., *Towards Visible Unity,* Vols. 1 and 2, Faith and Order Papers No. 112, 113 (Geneva, 1982); Faith and Order Paper No. 121, Minutes, Standing Commission of Faith and Order, Crete (Geneva, 1984).

[3]C. S. Song, ed., *Confessing Our Faith Around the World,* Vol. 1, Faith and Order Paper No. 104 (Geneva, 1980), Hans-Georg Link, ed., *Confessing Our Faith Around the World,* Vol. 2, Faith and Order Paper No. 120 (Geneva, 1983), Vol. 3 (Faith and Order Paper No. 123 (Geneva, 1984). Hans-Georg Link, ed., *The Roots of Our Common Faith: Faith in the Scriptures and in the Early Church* (Geneva, 1984).

[4]Some of these consultations have published documentation and others may find publication in the future. See, for instance, Mark Heim, "Gender and Creed: Confessing a Common Faith," *Christian Century,* 102 (1985) 379-81; *Union Seminary Quarterly Review,* Vol. 40, No. 3 (August 1985), special issue on Language and the Creeds; *Mid-Stream,* Vol. 24, No. 4 (October 1985), special issue on Black Witness to the Apostolic Faith.

attempts to bring a contribution to the larger study which will reflect the North American context: the pluralism of traditions, the strength of non-creedal churches, the perspectives of minority communities, the importance of issues of language and gender. At the same time, it focuses on the ways in which our various churches confess the same apostolic faith.

The background for this particular consultation on the Holy Spirit includes the work within the larger Apostolic Faith study which has focused on the Spirit, as well as the labors of individual scholars and bilateral dialogues which have prepared the ground for that work. Most particularly, we must refer to the World Council consultations issuing in the "Klingenthal Memorandum."[5] These meetings focused on the long controversy over the insertion of the *filioque* clause into the Niceno-Constantinopolitan Creed. The fruitful work of Klingenthal suggested that healing of this vexing controversy might be soon at hand for the churches.

Some of the most significant roles in this work have been played by representatives of the Orthodox and the Roman Catholic communions. Thus it was entirely appropriate that the U.S. consultation should be held at Hellenic College/Holy Cross Greek Orthodox School of Theology. The Klingenthal document on the *filioque* was not the only impetus for the Holy Cross consultation however. In North America it was possible to bring together a range of Christian traditions whose voices have not been prominent in the historical faith and order discussions, most notably representatives of the Pentecostal and Holiness families. In addition it was possible to benefit from the participation of a significant number of women: scholars and theologians who brought their perspectives to bear on the trinitarian issues. Notable also was the conviction of some participants that the understanding of the Holy Spirit cannot proceed without reference to the work of the Spirit as it is manifest in the world beyond the Church. These would wish to call attention to the link which must exist between the Apostolic Faith study and the World Council study on "The Unity of the Church and the Renewal of Human Community."[6] Thus the consultation offered its own unique texture as a contribution to ecumenical reflection on the Holy Spirit.

---

[5]Lukas Vischer, ed., *Spirit of God, Spirit of Christ*, Faith and Order Paper No. 103 (London, 1981), pp. 3-18.

[6]Michael Kinnamon, ed., *Towards Visible Unity*, Vols. 1 and 2.

The papers which are published here reflect the diversity which enriched the consultation. We have arranged them in such a way that those dealing most directly with the *filioque* questions appear together, so the reader may have easy reference to them. Then we have grouped the papers which bring perspectives from traditions which have not participated in those particular historical conflicts but which are concerned with related issues. The summary statement which issued from our meeting is also published here. From it the reader may gain some indication of the nature of the discussion and dialogue which took place in the sessions of the consultation.

I cannot close this introduction without taking the opportunity to offer thanks to my co-editor, Father Theodore Stylianopoulos, for his care and energy in shepherding this volume into print. On behalf of the Faith and Order Commission I would also like to thank Father Nomikos Michael Vaporis, the editor of *The Greek Orthodox Theological Review,* for opening the pages of that journal to the work of the consultation. The special thanks of the Commission and the participants in the consultation go as well to His Eminence Archbishop Iakovos, under whose auspices we were able to meet in the gracious surroundings of Holy Cross and Hellenic College.

It is my prayer that our reflection together upon the Holy Spirit, "the giver of life," may be blessed by that same Spirit, to nurture and strengthen us on the journey to unity.

The Spirit, The Creed, and Christian Unity

LLOYD G. PATTERSON

THIS CONSULTATION HAS BEFORE IT not one but a whole congery of related issues, which ought to be acknowledged at the outset.

As part of the NCCC Apostolic Faith Study, the consultation is to take up "the issues in the creed which divide East and West" on the subject of the Spirit. But it does so in the light of the WCC consultations on the Holy Spirit and the Nicene Creed, and of the quite remarkable agreement on the present state of the subject reflected in the volume of essays from those consultations edited by Lukas Vischer, *Spirit of God, Spirit of Christ: Ecumenical Reflections on the Filioque Controversy.* At the same time, the set of questions which writers have been asked to address from the perspective of their various traditions includes, at least by implication, matters of a much broader sort, reflective of the fact that much modern thinking about the functioning of the Spirit beyond the structures of the Church and in social and political life has taken place without reference to the classic theological discussion of the Spirit, while differing assumptions among Western Christians about the nature and status of the ancient credal formulations have led to quite different views of their viability as unifying confessions of Christian faith in the contemporary world altogether.

To describe the agenda of the consultation in this way is not to suggest that these issues—and the combination of them—do not belong together. The "Nicene Creed" of the Council of Constantinople A.D. 381 is an obvious place to look for a basis of Christian unity, and indeed seems to me the only one immediately apparent to anyone

[5]

surveying the classic formulations of Christian faith from a fully ecumenical perspective. The doctrine of the Spirit is of renewed importance in ecumenical discussion, and a review of the *filioque* controversy immediately raises questions which are by no means of merely historical interest. But if account is not taken of the broader issues just mentioned, the consultation will have overlooked the concerns of a large part of its constituency. The task is thus a formidable one.

SPIRIT OF GOD, SPIRIT OF CHRIST

We have been asked to comment on the volume of essays edited by Lukas Vischer, and I do so with the agenda of the consultation chiefly in mind.

It is certainly not remarkable that the Western contributors to the volume generally reflect the growing body of informed Western opinion in support of the omission of filioque, the reference to the Spirit as "proceeding from the Father *and the Son*" from the Creed of A.D. 381, or that they recognize that such a step would simply remove a long-standing bone of contention rather than resolving basic theological issues between East and West. It must give us some pause to consider that Westerners can come to this position without investing the text of the Creed as such with the same importance as their Eastern counterparts, and that theological concern with the question is scarcely reflective of popular interest in it. But these are not matters for discussion here.

To return to the volume of essays, however, it certainly is remarkable that both Eastern and Western contributors have been able to come to the basic theological issues which have so long separated us. To have reached even modest agreement on the need to say something about the giving of the Spirit δι' υἱοῦ ("through the Son") while avoiding·the Western tendency to locate trinitarian thinking within a unitary concept of the Godhead is an achievement in itself. To have come to this point through such a careful study of the history of the controversy, as this is done in the essays of Dietrich Ritschl, Andre de Halleux, and Herwig Aldenhoven in particular, is a fine example of the effectiveness of historical study for understanding theological issues. It will be of interest to discover how the present consultation regards this beginning of an agenda for its own consideration of the theological issues dividing East and West on the subject of the Spirit.

But at least as important a feature of the essays, or many of them, seems to me to be their call to reconsider trinitarian theology today by reference to its emergence out of the life of the early Christian communities. As Ritschl writes, "One must not forget that . . . the doctrine of the trinity was intended to be a help for Christian believers, not an obstacle or an abstract intellectual superimposition upon the 'simple faith.' . . . [early Christians] did not deduce their theological conclusions from a preconceived trinitarian concept."[1] To put the matter in some such terms, as more than one of the authors of these essays do, is to go beyond the familiar point that even such a seemingly abstract subject as that of the procession of the Spirit has immediate ramifications for the doctrine of the Church. It is to call for an approach to trinitarian issues from a study of the character of the ancient credal formulations as such, and thus to the broader issues of the nature and status of those formulations and of contemporary questions about the functioning of the Spirit to which the present consultation is asked to address itself.

RECOMMENDATIONS

Since it is part of our task to make recommendations to the NCCC Apostolic Faith Study, it seems appropriate to suggest at just this point the desirability of focusing attention on the nature and character of the ancient credal formulations as such. Resurgent interest in baptism, baptismal catechesis, and indeed all aspects of Christian initiation, provides the obvious context for such a study. Its implications would clearly include but extend far beyond the particular aspects of the discussion of the Spirit which initially brought the consultation together.

My own interest in such a study will, in any case, become evident in the remarks which follow.

AN ANGLICAN APPROACH

We have been asked to devote the second part of our remarks to the series of questions, or some of them, set out for discussion, and to do so from the perspective of our several traditions. I suppose that this is an increasingly difficult task for most people just now, since critical historical issues and contemporary theological ideas are not respecters of clearly defined traditions. For Anglicans, such as myself, it has long been common to disclaim the possibility of speaking

---

[1] "Historical Development and Implications of the Filioque Controversy," *Spirit of God, Spirit of Christ,* ed. Lukas Vischer (London and Geneva, 1981), p. 65.

for our tradition, and such a disclaimer is intended in my reference to what follows as "an Anglican approach" to the series of questions before us. Anglicans have never embraced a particular theological system as authoritative, nor regarded the Articles of Religion of the Church of England as comparable to other sixteenth-century confessions of faith. We have taken acceptance of the scriptures, the Catholic creeds, our inheritance of the ancient orders of ministers, and our own liturgical formularies as sufficient indication of commitment to our communion. Perhaps by historical circumstance rather than profound insight, we have come to value this approach in a time when confessional conformity seems to have proved unproductive of Christian unity, and when discussion of theological differences has proved more fruitful for understanding Christian faith than otherwise.

In the present circumstances, of course, the questions before us require a review of the assumptions which have lain close to the heart of this "tradition" regarding the place and character of the creeds, their teaching about the Spirit, and its relation to the discernment of the work of the Spirit in the contemporary world. But I would still be remiss in proceeding without saying that, while I will be referring to Anglican history and writing along the way, I intend to say nothing that is peculiarly Anglican in character.

The Creeds, the Scriptures, and the Spirit

On the assumption that we can take the license to marshal in our own way the subjects set out for discussion, I begin by setting together three subjects which seem to me in extricably related.

Recent study of the confessional and catechetical formulae which underlie the Apostles' and Nicene Creeds, and of their relation to the practice of baptism, has done much to alter the way in which we look at the creeds in relation to the scriptures, and at their talk about the Spirit—and, indeed, many other things as well. Simply put, the creeds are not intelligible when taken as comprehensive theological statements or digests of the body of Christian teaching as a whole. Their particular language doubtless reflects the main themes which the emerging orthodoxy of the second century stressed in the face of Gnosticism, and in the case of the Creed of A.D. 381 positions hammered out in later phases of the Arian controversy regarding the ὁμοούσιον of the Son and the status of the Spirit. But at root the creeds have their origin in, and fundamentally retain the character of, catechetical explanations of the relationship with God, effected by the work of Christ, made effective through the Spirit, into which Christians are brought in baptism. Even the original statement of the "preaching" and "faith" of the Council of Nicea A.D. 325, while itself less a creed than a conciliar document devised to address the specific issue of the creation of the Son, retains this general character and, in so doing, shows much that is often overlooked about the sense of the council as to how to approach the issues before it.

Questions remain with respect to the relationship between such catechetical explanations and the underlying confession of "Jesus as Lord (or Christ)" also associated with baptism. But it at least seems obvious to me that no sharp distinction can be drawn between the catechetical and confessional materials which we have from the earliest Christian evidence at our disposal. When Paul speaks in Romans 6-8 about the Christian's baptismal relationship with God, in Christ, through the Spirit (or to Father, Son, and Spirit), he conflates references to the confession of Jesus as Lord with tripartite catechetical elaborations of its implications in what seems an entirely natural way. In any case, in the course of the second century the catechetical material was amalgamated with the confession of faith itself in such a way as to provide the basis for baptismal catechesis in the centuries which followed.[2]

Whatever else is said about them, the Roman or Apostolic and the "Nicene" Creeds which continue in use are of this general character. They do not offer comprehensive Christian teaching on all points of Christian doctrine, any more than they are adequate expression of trinitarian thinking. They are confessional-catechetical formulations about the work of God into which believers are brought through baptism. As such they are at once less and much more than they appeared to be when they were viewed, as they came to be viewed, as digests of doctrine—even trinitarian doctrine—in later times. Such a classic Anglican work as the *Exposition of the Creed* (1659) by John Pearson, bishop of Chester, follows the normal practice of using the text of the Creed as the basis for a rehearsal of orthodox trinitarian teaching, with the entirely understandable result of obscuring the confessional-catechetical character of the text. It has only been quite

---

[2] See R. A. Norris, Jr., "Creeds and Catechesis," XV International Conference on Patristic Studies (Oxford 1983), on current issues in the relation of confessional and catechetal formulae.

recently, through study of the background of the text to which Principal J. N. D. Kelly is doubtless the foremost Anglican contributor, but even more through growing ecumenical interest in the nature of early Christian confessional material and its baptismal setting, that a new approach to the subject has been forthcoming.[3]

To view the creeds in this way has, of course, an immediate bearing on the way they are seen in relation to the scriptures. The creeds do not stand over against the scriptures, as they have often been taken to stand when they have been regarded either as adequate digests of scriptural teaching devised by ecclesiastical authority or as inadequate to that same purpose—two views still current and based on precisely the same assumption regarding their nature and status. The creeds were formulated out of themes already present in the Christian communities to which we owe the writings which were set on par with the Jewish scriptures in the course of the second and third centuries. To watch these processes take place at the same time, as in the writings of Irenaios[4] and of Origen[5] is to see how difficult it is to compare and contrast credal and scriptural teaching in the fashion that seemed possible when the creeds came to be seen as digests of scriptural teaching.

This is not to deny that the creeds—as well as the developed body of Christian Scriptures, especially through the addition of the Pastoral Epistles—stress certain themes out of inherited Christian teaching to the exclusion of others developed by Gnostic teachers. Thus the God to whom Christians are related in Jesus Christ is the God of Israel and author of the whole creation ("Father, παντοκράτωρ, creator of heaven and earth"). Jesus Christ is an identifiable human being whose death and resurrection are central to the plan of redemption ("who . . . was crucified, died, and was buried, . . . rose again and is seated at the right hand of the Father"). The work of the Spirit is seen in the gathering of the Church, in baptism and forgiveness

---

[3] J. N. D. Kelly, *Early Christian Creeds* (New York, 1972). See also V. H. Neufeld, *Earliest Christian Confessions* (Grand Rapids, 1963), and the representative essays ed. J. H. Westerhoff III, *A Faithful Church: Issues in the History of Catechesis* (Wilton, CN., 1981), and A. Kavanaugh *et al.*, *Made Not Born: New Perspectives on Christian Initiation and the Catechumenate* (Notre Dame, 1976).

[4] *Against Heresies* 3.1-4.

[5] Cf. *De principiis* i, praef.

of sins, and in the hope of the resurrection. These themes are brought to the fore rather than those of Jesus as the bearer of a higher wisdom to elect souls destined for salvation beyond the confines of the physical creation. But it is possible to observe this selectivity, and even to debate its lasting significance, without being obliged to see it, as if often done these days, as an imposition of themes alien to the Scriptures by ecclesiastical authority. To do so is a common anachronism which obscures the nature of the creeds no less than the notion that they are digests of scriptural teaching.[6]

To turn specifically, then, to the question of the Spirit in the Creed, it will not now be supposed that the confessional-catechetical formulae reflect, or were intended to reflect, the "biblical witness" in an exhaustive manner. Even the central Christian affirmation of the outpouring of the Spirit through and in connection with the work of Christ as the fulfillment of the prophecy of the Jewish scriptures is assumed rather than stated explicitly. Rather, stress is laid, largely through Pauline allusions, on the operation of the Spirit in the assembling of the *ecclesia* (ἐκκλησία) through baptism, in forgiveness, and in the hope of the resurrection. The implication plainly is that exclusive limitation of the work of the Spirit to particular groups of Christians or insistence that salvation consists in something superadded to what is given through being gathered into the *ecclesia* is inconsistent with Christian teaching. No exclusive limitation of the work of the Spirit to the Christian community, and indeed no particular view of *ecclesia* is at issue here. That Irenaeos and Origen, for instance, could differ widely on such matters while using the same confessional annd catechetical language is instructive.

The Creed and Trinitarian Teaching about the Persons of the Godhead
In what has thus far been said, we have only had occasion to notice in passing that the "Nicene Creed" of the Council of A.D. 381 bears signs of its having been given its present form in the light of the orthodox trinitarianism which emerged in the later stages of the Arian controversy. The incorporation of the ὁμοούσιον of the Son from the original Nicene document of A.D. 325 reflects the agreement about the use of the term reached by Athanasios and the disciples of Basil of Ankyra in the face of the resurgent Arianism of Aitios

---

[6] E.g. H. Koester and J. M. Robinson, *Trajectories through Early Christianity* (Philadelphia, 1971), but also many other works.

and Eunomios and elaborated by the Cappadocians in the years preceding the council of A.D. 381. The language about the Spirit as "Lord, life-giver, proceeding from the Father" is, as we now know, the result of an attempt to head off disagreement with the Macedonians by using scriptural terms suggesting the independent and equal status of the Spirit. Innocuous as these additions to what was probably the confessional-catechetical formulae of the Church of Constantinople may now seem to the casual reader, they are reflections of the great controversy over the possibility of accomodating the Christian confession of Father, Son, and Spirit to the mediatorial cosmology of contemporary (Platonic) philosophy.[7]

It is important to put the matter of the indirect relation of the "Nicene Creed" to fourth-century trinitarian thinking in these terms. The idea still persists that the *Nicenum,* and perhaps creeds more generally, reflect and are even the products of orthodox trinitarianism. But the truth of the matter is almost the other way around. The teaching of the Arians about the relation of the Son to the Father as that of the created to the uncreated had from the outset to be squared with the Christian baptismal confession—as witness the Letter of Arius to Alexander of Alexandria[8] no less than the more familiar Letter of Eusebios of Caesarea to his congregation and its account of the formulation of the original Nicene document itself. Trinitarian teaching—and the trinitarianism of the Arians, for such indeed it was, no less than that of the orthodox—was, looked at from one point of view at least, an effort to find an interpretation of the baptismal confession consistent with the claims of contemporary thought about the relation of God and the cosmos. It is not the least of the contributions of the study of early Christian liturgy to our study that this fact is now clearer than it has been for some time.

Looked at from another point of view, however, the tripartite confessional-catechetical formulae played a far more significant role in the later Arian controversy than just mentioned. It is clear now that both Athanasios and Basil of Ankyra came to take the tripartite confession as the arbiter of opposed teachings, and as the spur to the effort to find a way of saying that Father, Son, and Spirit were equally and at once divine, since each had an equal role in establishing

---

[7] Cf. L. G. Patterson, "Nicaea to Constantinople: The Theological Issues," *The Greek Orthodox Theological Review* 27/4 (1982).

[8] Opitz, *Urkunde 6.*

the relationship into which Christians were introduced by baptism.[9] To be sure, neither Athanasios nor his contemporaries directly challenged the grounds of the Arian argument for the imperfection of the created Son in contrast to the uncreated Father. It remained for the Cappadocians to support the position of their predecessors with the sweeping argument that the nature of the Godhead is not knowable in the sense that the intelligible no less than the perceptible elements of the cosmos are knowable, and hence that talk about the Godhead was not susceptible of the same logical analysis as talk about them. But the function of the tripartite confession itself as a factor in the resolution of the controversy is not to be discounted. The rather slight accomodations of the Creed of A.D. 381 to what had become an acceptable trinitarian doctrine may be insignificant by comparison.

It is in the light of all this that we ought to look at the classic formulation of the Godhead as three "persons" (ὑποστάσεις), modes of being or separate realities, possessing the same "substance" (οὐσία), or perhaps more precisely possessing the οὐσία of the Father.[10] This formulation does not, of course, appear in the Creed of A.D. 381, except insofar as the ὁμοούσιον of the Son which appears there must be assumed to imply the formulation as it had become familiar to the participants of the council. In any case, the use of ὑπόστασις by the Arians no less than the orthodox[11] had long been a way of expressing the separate realities of the persons of the Godhead, however their relationship was otherwise understood.

As to what is to be made of this classic formulation today, Anglican writers differ from one another along the lines which divide their colleagues in other traditions. The influence of nineteenth-century German historians of doctrine, with their assumption that the terms of the formulation are merely reflective of contemporary philosophical thinking, suggests to some that the formulation is no longer relevant to present talk about the divine. Others, including myself, will insist that the formulation is scarcely philosophical in what it tries to say, and at the very least seeks to clarify points of the Christian confession of faith which must be preserved whatever language is used. The difficulty of saying that we encounter the divine in Father, Son, and

---

[9] Athanasios, *Serap.* 1.14, cf. 30; Basil of Ankyra in Epiphanios, *Haer.* 73.3.

[10] G. C. Stead, *Divine Substance* (Oxford, 1977).

[11] Cf. Opitz, *Urkunde* 6.

Spirit, but are not polytheists, remains a basic one. Efforts such as those of Cyril Richardson and Geoffrey Lampe, among Anglican writers, to expound a binitarian God-Son or a unitive God-Spirit view of what underlies the Christian confession rely for their cogency on the assumption that the triapartite formulae lack the primitive roots which we have insisted upon, and seem to me to concede too much to recent notions about those formulae.[12]

> I should note at this point that it is difficult for me to deal with the question put to us regarding "how 'our' tradition interprets the trinity as persons as well as powers," though some attention should be paid to it in this section. The English "person" badly translates both the Greek ὑπόστασις and the Latin *persona*, and its use may suggest a trinity of personalities foreign to the sort of thinking which lies behind classic trinitarian formulations. But surely the sense of Father, Son, and Spirit are denoting separate realities (and in this sense as "persons") is basic to trinitarian thinking, so that the question of whether we are dealing with a "trinity of persons *as well as* powers" is a rather peculiar one. Conversely, it is hard to see what could be meant by a trinity of powers in any strict sense. The reasons for the general rejection of monarchianism (even in its sophisticated Sabellian form) are still cogent, at least insofar as it sought to be an interpretation of the tripartite confession of faith. The Cappadocian insistence that we know the persons of the Godhead in their operations ἐνέργειαι rather than directly has nothing to do with the question of the separate existence of the ὑποστάσεις. The classic formulation of the trinity of persons is certainly in need of explanation, and its language may even be regarded as dated. But it is an effort to be faithful to the confession of the relationship with God, through Christ, in the Spirit into which Christians are brought in Baptism. Alternative language which does not do as well ought presumably not to be regarded as trinitarian language at all. It strikes me that this is the sort of consideration which Anglicans are not alone in pondering in our time. This is a matter which is well worth discussion, since it has to do with the fundamental character of trinitarian thinking.

---

[12]C. C. Richardson, *The Doctrine of the Trinity* (New York and Nashville, 1958); G. W. H. Lampe, *God as Spirit* (Oxford, 1981).

Christ, the Spirit, and the Church

We now bring together under one heading another selection from among the questions we have been asked to address, in this case having to do with the relation of Christ and the Spirit and with the work of the Spirit in the Church.

The WCC consultations, as reflected in the volume of essays edited by Vischer, have carried the discussion of the relation of Christ and the Spirit far beyond the confines of the controversy over the addition of the filioque to the Creed of A.D. 381, and even beyond the intensely reactive and often murky dispute over the Western commitment to the "double procession" of the Spirit altogether. As mentioned before, it is salutary for Westerners to have reached the point of being critical of their tendency to impose a unitary notion of the Godhead on their trinitarian thinking, while still insisting that account be taken of the giving of the Spirit "through the Son." For their part, Anglicans have long questioned the desirability of the addition of the *filioque,* at the same time that they have generally embraced Western teaching on the "double procession," albeit without having contributed much to the discussion of the subject.[13] It is time for them no less than for others to move beyond their inherited commitments.

At the moment, however, it is our intention to do no more than to comment on the bearing of the study of the classic confessional-catechetical formulae on this and several related subjects on the agenda of this consultation. Thus, whatever view is taken of the historical circumstances which led the Council of A.D. 381 to employ the language of John 15.26 in describing the Spirit as "proceeding" from the Father and the Son. The confessional-catechetical formulae of the sort from which the Creed takes its shape have to do with the relationship with God, in Christ, through the Spirit in which Christians stand through baptism. The credal definition of the separate and equal reality of the Spirit serves to clarify that relationship by saying that one's Christian identity cannot be adequately accounted for where any one of the elements of the confession is seen merely as an extension of the others. It will not really do to suppose that things will work "the other way around," so to speak, and that

---

[13]See Bishop Pearson, *On the Creed,* art. viii, with its running notes on the *filioque,* and Canon Allchin's remarks on Anglican views in Vischer, pp. 88ff.

theological definitions of the relation of the Spirit to the Father and the Son make any sense when treated in separation from the fundamental purpose of the confession as such. It has recently been common for Westerners, rightly or wrongly, to defend the "double procession" of the Spirit from the Father and the Son as an attempt to clarify or preserve the unity of the divine action confessed in the Creed, and then for Easterners to insist that such a defense compromises basic teaching about the equality of the persons, unless what their opponents have in view is merely the unity of the "operations" of the persons. But both "sides," if such they be, need to restart their thinking from the basic fact the Creed arises from confessional—even doxological—assertions about the source of Christian identity rather than from theological formulations in their right.

But it is just at this point that we can pass to the question of the work of the Spirit in the Church. As we have insisted earlier, it is the purpose of the classic confessional-catechetical formulae to assert that the gathering of the *ecclesia* into which Christians are introduced by baptism is a witness to the work of the Spirit, and to do so initially in the face of Montanist and Gnostic claims to the special possession of the Spirit or of unique saving knowledge not possessed by the Christian community at large. Its style and language—its confessional character—is not such that it can be said to limit the work of the Spirit to the Church or to guarantee the decisions of the ecclesiastic authority. The widely divergent views of the early centuries on both these subjects were impelled by very different considerations.

The creeds can, of course, be made to say any number of things, and it is now frequently said that they—and in particular the *filioque*—helped in the development of the notion that the structures of the Church are guaranteed in their functioning by the Spirit, and hence, negatively, in the apppearance of claims for the functioning of the Spirit beyond and even in opposition to the ecclesiastical authority which has been a recurrent phenomenon of the life of the Medieval western Church and its Reformation successors, including the Roman Catholic Church. It seems to me at best difficult to make such a sweeping generalization. The polarization to which we refer is real enough. But its theological and sociological roots in the life of western Christendom are such as to make it difficult to think that it has even a superficial relationship to western views of the "double procession" of the Spirit, which has been as common among western critics of the ecclesiastical authority as it has been among its supporters.

The English history of this polarization certainly shows a variety of features which recur elsewhere in one form or another. The Puritan critique of the structures of the Church of England was mounted on the ground that it did not conform to the biblical pattern from which alone a true church could take its existence, and the response of Richard Hooker[14] took shape around the central notion that the Church exists even where it is in need of reform rather than around any exclusive claim to the possession of the Spirit. The left wing sects of the Commonwealth period regarded both episcopal and presbyteral government as belonging to the powers of the present age which would be swept away at the judgment. The Wesleys and their associates differed within and among themselves a to whether baptism or personal conversion mark the beginning of the Christian life, and foreshadowed tensions which became evident in the later history of British and American Evangelicalism both within and beyond the Church of England. In all of these movements the assumption is made that the Spirit acts, rather exclusively than otherwise, in the formation of whatever is regarded as the true Church. The sources of the criticism of existing structures are to be sought elsewhere in the thought and circumstances of their critics and defenders.

At the present time, of course, the polarization to which we refer is enshrined in the background of the divided Christian communities which we represent, and is consequently an important matter for ecumenical discussion. But if the credal affirmation about the Spirit and the Church is to have any real significance in that discussion, as it surely ought to have, it will most likely be found where the creeds are read in the light of their character as classic confessional-catechetical formulae. If the gathering of the *ecclesia* is a witness to the work of the Spirit, then it is more rather than less incumbent upon us to see that its visible life is shaped in such a way as to proclaim and celebrate its spiritual origin. At the same time, whatever else is to be said about the work of the Spirit, its marks will be in the deepest and oldest sense "ecclesial" in character. To say this is not to resolve the differences which separate us, either with regard to the inherited structures of the Christian community or to what it means to be *ecclesia* in the midst of the contemporary world. It may be to provide a framework for a discussion of those differences

---

[14]*Laws* 3.

which arise out of the language and style—the confessional
character—of the credal affirmation as we can now understand
it.

The Sacraments, the Individual, and the Community

It is but a step further to comment on the questions of the work
of the Spirit in the sacraments, and in what is called in our agenda
"the individual believer and . . . the community." Moreover, it
is on these questions that I can say more than has thus far been
the case about "Anglican perspectives and writings," and should
add that, whatever the language of the questions I discuss may
be, I am not intending to suggest that there is any work or operation of the Spirit which is distinct from that of the Father and the
Son.

Definitions of sacraments and their effects belong to the Medieval
and Reformation west, as does the juxtaposing of the individual and
the community, and Anglican thinking in both areas has dealt with
these subjects in the terms dictated by the times. On the other hand,
Anglicans have come to think, not altogether wrongly, that their
patristic interests and their involvement in modern liturgical study
have made their contributions to the discussion of these subjects
valuable.

On the sacraments, then, Anglicans certainly debated the sixteenth-
century issues with which all were concerned, but very largely stood
in agreement with the views of Bucer and Calvin to the effect that
the water of baptism and the bread and wine of the Eucharist are
"effective signs" of our participation in the body of Christ through
rebirth in him in the baptismal washing and the receiving of his body
and blood in the eucharistic meal. In due course, however, patristic
study and knowledge of early liturgical materials helped bring to the
fore the conviction that is through invocation of the Spirit that the
elements are made vehicles of the divine action of incorporation into
the body of Christ. The interpretation and, where possible, revision
of Anglican liturgical formularies reflects this conviction on the part
of seventeenth- and eighteenth-century writers.

In any case, whether because of this conviction or not, it has been
easy to absorb and contribute to the present discussion of the continuity between Jewish and Christian forms of blessing and making
thanksgiving to God for what God has done and continues to do. For
us, as for others, the controversial subjects of offering, consecration,

and sacrifice, once debated in isolation from one another, fall together happily within the pattern of praising God, recalling the redemptive work of God over the water of baptism and the bread and wine of the Eucharist, and praying that the gifts presented be once again the means by which that work is effected according to God's promise. In this context, of course, the invocation of the Spirit assumes a significance far greater than seventeenth- and eighteenth-century Anglican writers ascribed to it—and, it should be added, a place in the whole pattern of Christian thinking about the work of the Spirit in the gathering together of the *ecclesia* similar to that given it in the creeds, for the good reason that the ancient prayer formulae which have come alive once again are of the same character as the ancient confessional-catechetical formulations. It is hard to exaggerate the significance of the fact that a new way of seeing the relation of the work of the Spirit in the sacraments and in the formation of the Church—new in the sense of rediscovered or reappropriated—is now open to us.

On the relation of the work of the Spirit in "the individual believer and . . . the community," it is perhaps possible to take a clearer line with respect to there being something of an Anglican position. The celebrated figures of seventeenth-century Anglican "spirituality," Andrewes, Herbert, Donne, and Taylor, among others, differed a good deal in the language which they used to talk about the development of the inner life of the Christian, whether treating it under the category of grace or celebrating it as the work of the Spirit. But a theme connecting them all, and arising out of their experience with and convictions about the "common prayer" of the Church, is that Christian worship is at once the celebration of the community and of the individuals which make it up. Each is the expression of the other, and each serves to direct the other towards its proper end. A colleague of mine echoes the tradition, which is also seen in Keble in the nineteenth century and in Martin Thornton in this, when he insists on saying that we have commonly adhered to a distinction between "public" and "personal" rather than between "public" and "private" prayer.[15]

I suppose that all this has some bearing on what Anglicans may want to say about the operation of the Spirit "in the individual believer

[15]David Siegenthaler, "The Oxford Movement," papers from Conference on Anglican Spirituality, Episcopal Divinity School, Cambridge, MA., 1984.

and . . . the community." At least in the discussions provoked by the Wesleys and the Anglican Evangelicals, who scarcely belong outside the "tradition" in its broader sense, it has been common to be wary about a distinction between the work of the Spirit in the individual and in the community, and to say that the authentic marks of the work of the Spirit are those which are conducive to the manifestation of the *ecclesia,* whatever tensions they may seem to create between the individual believer and the ecclesiastical authority, each of which needs to be open to the views of the other. Though it is too early to say what effect this general approach may have in the present circumstances of the appearance among of us of charismatic groups, it is already clear that it is according to some such definition of what is at stake that dialogue is now beginning to take place. Until it is proved otherwise, it seems to me that this is at least in line with the credal confession about the work of the Spirit as it has, however inconsistently, been perceived by us.

The Spirit Beyond the Confines of the Christian Community

Finally, I bring together two other questions we have been asked to address—one relating to the work of the Spirit beyond the Christian community and the other about the "politics of the Spirit" in the structures of the Church and the society—not because they naturally fall together but because they are often put together in a time when the church leadership is often seen as insufficiently aware of the relation of "systematic" social change to the betterment of the human condition.

On the subject of the work of the Spirit beyond the Christian community, then, we have already had more than one occasion to note that the confession of the work of the Spirit in the gathering of the *ecclesia* does not address the issue. It may indeed suggest ways in which Christians will seek to discern the work of the Spirit beyond the Christian community. But widely divergent views of the larger issue were held by people equally committed to the confessional language. Irenaios, a notable defender of the confession, was not entirely unsympathetic to the claims of the Montanists, while Origen limited the work of the Spirit to the perfection of souls returning to God through Christ but cast his view of that return in such cosmic terms as to embrace the whole plenitude of human souls. Latin African rigorists, including Cyprian, perhaps come closest in the early centuries to limiting the work of the Spirit to the community of conscious faith, but theirs was not by any means the common view of the time.

Among the Medieval and Reformation churches, the issue of the work of the Spirit beyond the Church may probably be described as largely speculative, except as it was transformed into the issue of the work of the Spirit beyond or in opposition to the ecclesiastical authority—the polarization mentioned earlier. But encounter with non-Christian cultures, and the rise of a new philosophical universalism have recreated the issue in new and pressing terms. To consider only Anglican writers, the nineteenth century saw claims to the limitation of the work of the Spirit to the Church, on the part of both Anglican Evangelicals and representatives of the Catholic Revival such as Canon Pusey, give way to various forms of "universalism," such as those seen in the authors of *Lux Mundi* and in the work of the now celebrated theologian F. D. Maurice. In fact, it has been Maurice's insistence that the Church is the visible witness to the universal sovereignty of God, the kingdom of Christ, and the operation of the Spirit which has, as much as anything else, provided Anglicans with a point of departure from which to address a wide range of contemporary issues, from the conflict of world religions, to the need for Christian unity, to the problems of human society.

We have no desire to exaggerate the importance of Maurice, who has in any case been more of a stimulus to thought than the founder of a "school" of his own. But it is certainly true that he was a major contributor to recent Anglican thinking about the work of the Spirit in and beyond the Christian community. While Maurice was outspoken against any claim to the exclusive possession of the Spirit, he took the confession of the Spirit as calling the Church into being as the clue to the universal purpose of God in the recreation and reconciliation of humanity.

Reference to Maurice can serve as a point of transition to the question of the "politics of the Spirit," at least as that question may refer to recent Christian attempts to take account of the way in which social and economic systems effect the character of human existence, for better or worse, and to assess calls for "systemic" social and economic change. Maurice himself, though he embraced the title "Christian socialist," belonged to a generation which was unaware of the significance of these issues. But it was Maurice's theology which inspired Anglican writers of the later nineteenth and early twentieth centuries to call for what we should now describe as "systemic" change in the interest of the betterment of the human condition. His influence is apparent, for instance, in the 1890 Church Congress address of B. F. Westcott, former student of Maurice and bishop of Durham, which spoke out of Westcott's experience with the coal miners of his diocese to the effect that the system of "wage labour . . . is as little fitted to represent . . . the connection of man with man in the production of wealth as in earlier times slavery or serfdom." And it is but a step from Westcott to the figure of William Temple, archbishop of Canterbury, whose concern for social change of a comprehensive sort extended beyond the Malvern Conference in an ecumenical direction, as well as into the policies of the British Labour Party.

Temple's work remains of real significance for Anglicans. It is true that his untimely death, in the midst of the absorbing events of World War II, came when he had only begun to appreciate Barth's comprehensive criticism of plans for social change which discount the human tendency to corrupt all social systems, however nicely constructed. He perhaps never grasped what his friend Reinhold Niebuhr was about in seeking practical ways in which the imperatives of the Gospel could lead to alliances with human self-interest in the creation of provisional plans for bettering the human condition. But he remained unshaken in this conviction that the involvement of the Church in social problems sprang from its existence as Church rather than from any secondary consideration.[16]

At the present, of course, Anglicans no less than others have to listen carefully to a rather different and differently originated concern to identify the impulse toward human liberation from oppressive social structures with the work of Christ or of the Spirit, and to do so in circumstances in which the structures of the Church are seen as themselves oppressive and at odds with the divine purpose. It is impossible to foresee what, if any, general consensus among Anglican writers will be forthcoming in response to this concern. But reports of the work of Inter-Anglican Theological and Doctrinal Commission, appointed by the present archbishop of Canterbury with these issues in mind among others, suggests an approach which has learned

---

[16]M. B. Reckitt, *Maurice to Temple:* A Century of the Social Movement in the Church of England (London, 1947), treats of Maurice's wide influence. A. G. Hebert, *Liturgy and Society:* The Function of the Church in the Modern World (London, 1935) is something of an Anglican classic which is consciously indebted to Maurice. I have tried to describe the trends of thought of the period in my "After the Oxford Movement," paper from the Conference on Anglican Spirituality aforementioned.

much positively and negatively from Temple. It is the task of the Church as Church to support the impulse toward human liberation from oppressive social structures, but to do so recognizing that the human spirit cannot easily be identified with the divine Spirit and that the most nobly conceived social structures are capable of corruption. The call to all Christians is for "repentance" or change of mind in the light of the imperatives of the Gospel. But this call is a call issued to people to understand their identity in terms of the Christian confession of faith, and its assertion that the gathering of the *ecclesia* is the work of the Spirit, rather than in some other terms.[17]

Conclusion

It is clear to me at this point that what I have written has much more to do than I had originally intended that it should with the notion that the study of the creeds against their background as ancient confessional-catechetical formulations shows that they have much more of a function as sources of unifying Christian thought and action than is often now assumed to be the case. But even if this is so—and if it seems a long way from consideration of the *filioque* to issues raised by "liberation" theology—it seems to me none the less that such a study may help to bring together the congery of issues with which the consultation has to deal, and to suggest a way in which its work may be carried forward.[18]

---

[17]The last of the present series of meetings of the Commission was held at Dublin in July 1985. Its report, thus far only available in a preliminary draft, will be forthcoming.

[18]This appended note must suffice to deal with the important question of "the problems of using languages and images that have been traditionally applied to the Spirit (wind, fire, and dove) in the contemporary context, and images which are emerging to enrich our understanding of the Spirit."

The question would seem to have in view the value of using inherited images at the present time, and the usability of unspecified images now said to be coming to the fore. But the general subject raised, that of expressing the experience of the divine in human imagery, is an extraordinarily large one, and even the most recent writing on the subject is virtually beyond commentary. Certainly all ways of imaging our experience of the divine are more or less adequate both to our experience and to the reality which they are intended to represent. Some images will be renewed in their usability by present experience, while others will doubtless be born, as has always been the case. It is hard to judge whether some images are more satisfactory than others. But it can at least be said that some images will commend themselves through use by congregations of Christians—in effect by liturgical use—while others may remain the property of particular individuals alone, and that without denying their significance themselves. This, too, has been the case in the past, and is likely to be the case in the future.

So far as images of the Spirit are concerned, it would seem that they are likely to be less "personal" in the modern sense of the word than is the case with the other persons of the Godhead. Thus the images of wind and fire are not surprising, since they suggest something beyond our control which scatters, purges, and recreates. But these images have commonly been used of the other persons of the Godhead as well, while the list of images "traditionally applied" to the Spirit omits those which have to do with sustaining, nurturing, and "mothering," which strike a more personal note. It would be hard to say what a study of the full range of imagery would show on this score.

With regard to new images of the Spirit, I would suppose that it would continue to be the case that some will prove capable of appropriation for general use and some remain the property of individuals. Recent Anglican experience with modern hymnody suggests that this will be the case.

The Filioque: Dogma, Theologoumenon or Error?

THEODORE STYLIANOPOULOS

THE THEOLOGICAL DEMANDS of the ecumenical movement are currently leading ecclesial-minded theologians to a fresh examination of the *filioque,* one of the long-standing doctrinal controversies dividing the Eastern and Western churches. The publication of *Spirit of God, Spirit of Christ,*[1] featuring a substantial memorandum of two consultations held at Schloss Klingenthal, France (1978 and 1979) and also excellent papers presented at those consultations by Orthodox, Protestant, and Roman Catholic theologians is a preeminent ecumenical expression of the new interest in the *filioque,* the Nicene Creed and related topics. Some of the key questions in the *filioque* discussion are the following: Is the *filioque* a dogma binding upon all Christians who seek unity on the basis of the one, catholic and apostolic faith? Is it a *theologoumenon,* that is, a valid but optional interpretation of Christian dogma? Or is it a doctrinal error that should be corrected? Moveover, how is the *filioque* related to the faith of the New Testament and to Christian life? In this paper I would like briefly to address some of these questions as pursued by the contributors to the above publication in the following three sections: (1) historical and theological presuppositions, (2) evaluating the *filioque,* and (3) the relevance of the *filioque* question.

HISTORICAL AND THEOLOGICAL PRESUPPOSITIONS

Any serious discussion of the *filioque* immediately raises a number

---

[1] Edited by Lukas Vischer (London and Geneva, 1981).

[25]

of related broader issues of considerable complexity. First, there is the whole question of the development of Christian doctrine[2] and the need to be extremely sensitive to context. If one is to appreciate the significance of the *filioque* question and not merely dismiss it as an exercise in sterile theologizing, as Dietrich Ritschl observes, "one must let one's thought sink into the classical trinitarian modes of argumentation,"[3] or, in the words of the Klingenthal Memorandum, "we should retrace and follow through the cognitive process of the early Church"[4] (meaning the ancient catholic Church and not only the early New Testament Church). In the instance of the *filioque* one must distinguish but not separate the following: (a) the history of the actual controversy beginning in the seventh century with Maximos the Confessor's attempt to provide, for Easterners, an acceptable interpretation of the *filioque* in the face of obvious anxieties about it (a dating earlier than that of Ritschl who points to the later refutations of the *filioque* by John of Damascus and Photios as the beginnings of the controversy); (b) the explicit teaching of the *filioque* developed by Augustine who is the intellectual father of the *filioque* and whether this teaching is consistent or inconsistent with the trinitarian dogma of the First and Second Ecumenical Synods, and (c) the earlier Christian teaching about the Holy Spirit not yet nuanced by the theological questions generated by the Arian heresy.

Because the *filioque* involves both historical and systematic aspects,[5] only the most careful attention to the intentionality, nuances, and terminology of various historical and theological contexts can assure proper sailing through these deep waters. Extreme care is needed to pursue analysis and synthesis, to trace continuity and discontinuity, and above all to discern consistency or inconsistency in the development of doctrine pertaining to the Holy Spirit during many

---

[2] For clarity's sake I may indicate that by "development of doctrine" I mean neither that the reality of the Holy Spirit changes from generation to generation nor that the experience of the Spirit is necessarily richer among later generations. Rather I mean that the conceptual formulations about the truth of the Spirit are modified and the relevant terminology is refined in the light of various factors, questions, and controversies over centuries.

[3] "Historical Development and the Implications of the Filioque Controversy," *Spirit of God, Spirit of Christ*, p. 46.

[4] Memorandum, "The Filioque Clause in Ecumenical Perspective," *Spirit of God, Spirit of Christ*, p. 7.

[5] See Ritschl, p. 48.

centuries of Christian theologizing. Ritschl importantly cautions that adequate grounding of the *filioque* could never rely on isolated passages in a few Greek Fathers but must be based on a wide examination of the trinitarian theologies of the Latin and Greek traditions.[6] Furthermore, if Ritschl is right that Tertullian is not, as is often supposed by Western theologians, a "crown witness" for later filioquism in its proper meaning, and that the originator of the *filioque* teaching is Augustine, whose more distinctly philosophical questions led him by necessity to develop the *filioque*,[7] then Augustine would seem to stand in isolated and questionable light as an interpreter of the Second Synod's article on the Holy Spirit, a point that John Romanides has been making for years.[8]

On the other hand, Jean-Miguel Garrigues' attempt to dissociate the *filioque* formula from its Augustinian or other later Western contexts in order to propose that only the dogmatic formula affirmed by the magisterium requires acceptance, not the interpretations, since interpretations can be further both clarified and modified until sufficient agreement is reached,[9] seems to be a superficial attempt at a resolution of the controversy. While doxological expressions of faith can and often do seek adequate interpretations, officially either to promulgate or to hold to a dogmatic formula which has no identifiable meaning received by the community of faith would be literally meaningless. The *filioque* can no more be divorced from its classic interpretations than the Nicene Creed can be divorced from the theology of the Greek Fathers, chiefly Athanasios and the Cappadocians, presupposed by the First and Second Ecumenical Synods. If the case were otherwise, the community of faith would have no criteria by which to receive dogmatic formulae except blind obedience to council or magisterium claiming inspiration without explanation.

No doubt the most crucial question is the systematic one, that is, the question pertaining to theological truth. Is the *filioque* consistent with the early Church's teaching about the Holy Spirit and

---

[6] Ibid., pp. 53-54.

[7] Ibid., pp. 59-61.

[8] See, for example, his article "The Filioque," *Kleronomia*, 7 (1975), especially pp. 295ff. John Romanides is an Orthodox member of the Anglican-Orthodox Joint Doctrinal Commission.

[9] "A Roman Catholic View of the Position now Reached in the Question of the *Filioque*," *Spirit of God, Spirit of Christ*, pp. 148-53.

consistent with the meaning of the Nicene Creed? Quite curious to this writer is Ritschl's comment that the *filioque* "controversy itself is more of church-historical than of theological significance,"[10] a comment which seems to run counter to the spirit of his whole essay concerned as it is with theological truth. Did not Photios' emphasis that the Spirit proceeds "from the Father *alone*" intend to preclude the Western position that the Son is also somehow a *cause* in the eternal procession of the Spirit from the Father? And did not the *filioque* controversy center on the question of the correct theological interpretation of the earlier patristic tradition and above all of the Nicene Creed? Similarly the Anglican consideration to remove the *filioque* from the Creed but at the same time to continue to affirm its theological value as a complementary Western understanding of the Holy Trinity,[11] while welcome, essentially depends on whether or not the *filioque* is at least consistent with dogmatic truth as officially promulgated by the ecumenical synods. Neither the *filioque* formula nor the interpretations in support of it or against it can be regarded as *theologoumena,* as some would have it, unless they can be clearly shown at least not to be opposed to early Christian doctrine and the Nicene Creed. *Theologoumena* cannot contradict promulgated dogmatic truth for otherwise, as Dumitru Staniloae pointedly observes, "it would be impossible to tell the difference between a *theologoumenon* and an error."[12]

Another broad issue presupposed by the *filioque* discussion is that of the nature of Christian theology and its relationship both to biblical revelation and to the experience of salvation. The Klingenthal Memorandum, following accents by contributors to *Spirit of God, Spirit of Christ,* especially by Ritschl,[13] stresses that early Christian theology is doxological rather than speculative; it is based on historical

---

[10]Ritschl, p. 61.

[11]Donald M. Allchin, "The Filioque Clause: An Anglican Approach," *Spirit of God, Spirit of Christ,* pp. 85-87. Allchin reports the official proposal to the Anglican Church by the Anglican membership of the Anglican-Orthodox Doctrinal Commission. He himself seems critical of the implications of the *filioque*. See pp. 95-96.

[12]"The Procession of the Holy Spirit from the Father and His Relation to the Son, as the Basis of our Deification and Adoption," *Spirit of God, Spirit of Christ,* p. 175.

[13]Ritschl, pp. 64-65.

revelation rather than abstract definitions.[14] According to this Memorandum ancient Christian thought concerning the Trinity does not derive from a preconceived trinitarian concept but reflects "the biblical and historical roots of Christian faith in the living God,"[15] personally revealed as Father and Creator, as unique Son and eternal Logos, and as sanctifying and renewing Spirit. If this presupposition regarding the nature of early Christian theology applies fundamentally to all trinitarian theology and is to be held consciously, as many would concur, then our efforts toward resolving the *filioque* controversy would have a far greater chance to bear fruit if they are concentrated on careful interpretation of the intentionalities of the biblical and patristic witness, and also on rigorous linking of our theologizing to Christian life, rather than seeking to provide additional speculative solutions to the *filioque* problem as if theologians had direct epistemological access to the ontology of the triune God.[16]

In the context of the fourth-century patristic theology it is fair to say that Augustine's trinitarian thought is more speculative, that is, more permeated by a spirit of philosophical inquiry, than that of Athanasios and the Cappadocians. Of course it is not a question of sharp contrasts, namely, that Augustine is philosophical whereas the Eastern Fathers are biblical, because all hold to Scripture as ultimate authority, employ discursive reason and feature philosophical terms and notions such as essence, hypostasis, immutability, time and eternity. The crucial difference seems to be that, despite his own repeated reservations, Augustine seems to try to explain the Trinity as a metaphysical problem; he thinks that he could possibly explain the matter of the generation of the Son and the manner of the procession of the Spirit in rational terms, and he presents his thought as a kind of tentative personal speculation about the Trinity anchored on the security of the Church's dogma which he unreservedly

---

[14]Memorandum, pp. 6-10.

[15]Ibid., p. 7.

[16]A brilliant suggestion and an example of this kind of speculative solution, it seems to me, is Jürgen Moltmann's proposal that "the Holy Spirit receives from the Father his own perfect divine *existence* (*hypostasis, hyparxis*), and obtains from the Son his relational *form* (*eidos, prosōpon*)," "Theological Proposals Toward the Resolution of the Filioque Controversy," *Spirit of God, Spirit of Christ,* p. 169.

accepts.[17] By appreciable contrast Athanasios and the Cappadocians write about the Trinity in terms of the immediate challenge of various forms of Arianism; they are concerned about defending the uncreated nature of the Son and the Spirit deriving from the very being of God, as they see these truths affirmed by the witness of the Bible and the worship of the Church, and they argue for both the unity and distinctiveness of the persons of the triune God on the basis of Scripture and liturgical tradition, while remaining extremely sensitive to the inability of reason to probe divine ontology.[18] These differences in theological approach signal, at least for many Orthodox theologians, tremendous implications regarding the way of Western theology and the way of Eastern theology, implications which are deeply involved in both the origins of the *filioque* in Augustine as well as the *filioque* controversy during subsequent centuries.

Through a short study of the article on the Holy Spirit in the Nicene Creed a few years ago this writer was amazed to confirm for himself the closeness between the biblical and Greek patristic witness regarding the Holy Spirit and his relationship to the Father and the Son.[19] In the writings of Athanasios, Basil, and Gregory the Theologian, not only the terminology but also the deep soteriological interests seeking to show *that the Spirit is what he does*[20] are thoroughly biblical. Once the authority of the biblical witness regarding

---

[17]*On the Trinity* 15.2.5, 22-24 and 28. See further Theodore Stylianopoulos, "The Orthodox Position," *Conflicts about the Holy Spirit,* ed. Hans Küng and Jürgen Moltmann (New York, 1979), pp. 26-27.

[18]Gregory the Theologian, for example, radicalizes Plato's famous dictum about the difficulty of knowing God (*Timaeus* 28E) by saying: "But in my opinion it is impossible to express him [God], and yet more impossible to conceive him" (*Theological Orations* 2.4). Gregory also writes that "the divine nature cannot be apprehended by human reason" (*Theological Orations* 2.11) and that "it is one thing to be persuaded of the existence of a thing, and quite another to know what it is" (*Theological Orations* 2.5). As far as seeking to explain the nature of the hypostatic attributes of unbegottenness, generation, and procession, Gregory comments this would be a matter of frenzy (*Theological Orations* 5.8).

[19]Theodore Stylianopoulos, "The Biblical Background of the Article on the Holy Spirit in the Constantinopolitan Creed," *Etudes théologiques 2: Le IIe Concile oecuménique* (Chambésy-Geneve: Centre orthodoxe du Patriarcat oecuménique, 1982), pp. 155-73.

[20]See Gregory the Theologian, *Theological Orations* 5.29.

the Trinity is accepted on a descriptive level, as presupposed by these Fathers (and not as that witness might be evaluated by biblical scholars today), then one could hardly ask for a more biblically cogent defense of the "evangelical faith."[21] Readers will suffer a citation from the conclusion of the above study:

> In the trinitarian debates at stake was not an abstract question but the truth of Christian salvation: the fundamental understanding of the living God in his relationship to creation, historical revelation, ecclesial life and daily Christian existence. The decisive criteria were biblical: (1) the radical difference between Creator and creatures and (2) the principle that God creates, redeems, and renews his creatures by his personal presence and action. The doctrine of the Trinity was formulated on soteriological rather than philosophical grounds.[22]

Thus, when Western theologians continue to talk in various ways and nuances about how biblical thought is "functional" and "developmental," whereas Greek patristic thought is "philosophical" and "substantialist," that the trinitarian and christological teaching of the great synods is determined by Greek philosophy rather than the Bible, and that therefore Greek patristic thought and the Nicene Creed can today more or less be dismissed as outdated,[23] they sound, at least to this writer, as tiresome as they are unconvincing. Would such theologians also dismiss the authority of the biblical witness? What theology was for the Greek Fathers, the ecumenical synods, and the way of Eastern Christianity is expressed by Jaroslav Pelikan's ringing statement: "Theology was not a science of divine ontology but

---

[21]To use the telling expression of the Synodal Letter of 382 which states that the Fathers of the Second Synod (381) endured persecutions, afflictions, and other pressures by heretics and kings for the sake of "the evangelical faith."

[22]Stylianopoulos, "Biblical Background of the Article on the Holy Spirit," p. 171.

[23]See, for example, the opinions both reviewed and expressed by Warren A. Quanbeck, "Developmental Perspective and the Doctrine of the Spirit," *The Holy Spirit in the Life of the Church*, ed. Paul D. Opsahl (Minneapolis, 1978), pp. 158-71 and also Olaf Hansen, "Spirit Christology: A Way out of Our Dilemma?" in the same volume, pp. 172-203.

of divine revelation.''[24] It should be noted that the contributors to *Spirit of God, Spirit of Christ,* as specialists, show great sensitivity to these matters. All would agree that the *filioque* and patristic trinitarian theology confront us not with the challenge of philosophical inquiry but rather, as Lukas Vischer puts it, with the crucial question of "how we are to speak of God on the basis of the revelation in Christ.''[25]

A final broad issue involved in the *filioque* discussion is ecclesiological, that is to say, having to do with the critical issue of the nature of authority and decision-making in the Church. Granted that all would hold to the authority of Scripture, what about the authority of the early Church which over several centuries gradually gathered and canonized Scripture? More specifically, what role should the authority of the First and Second Ecumenical Synods as expressions of univeral ecclesial decision-making play in the *filioque* discussion? After all, the *filioque* clause was added to the Nicene-Constantinopolitan Creed, an act which raises not only questions of canonical authority but also of theological consistency. One can not take lightly an addition to the Nicene Creed in which key words and expressions were forged on the anvil of decades of nuanced theological debate. Can a clause deriving from one theological tradition simply be inserted in a creed deriving from another theological tradition without council? I would like here to pursue a little further not the canonical but the theological aspect of this ecclesiological issue of authority.

The concern about continuity and discontinuity, consistency and inconsistency, pertaining to theological truth in the history of doctrine has already been mentioned. The thesis has also been asserted that Athanasios and the Cappadocians show intimate affinities with the biblical witness regarding the understanding of the Spirit and

---

[24]Jaroslav Pelikan, *The Christian Tradition 2: The Spirit of Eastern Christendom* (Chicago, 1974), p. 33. See, also, more recently, the emphases on John Zizioulas, "The Teaching of the Second Ecumenical Council on the Holy Spirit in Historical and Ecumenical Perspective," *Credo in Spiritum Sanctum: atti del Congresso teologico internazionale di pneumatologia, Roma, 22-26 marzo 1982* (Vatican, 1983), who writes that "the use of *homoousios* by Athanasios and Nicea was not intended to create a speculative or metaphysical theology," p. 32, and that the personal and relational understanding of the Trinity as *persons* by the Cappadocians was a "revolution" in Greek ontology, p. 36.

[25]Preface, *Spirit of God, Spirit of Christ,* p. vi.

the Spirit's relationship to the Father and the Son. But now I must, as well, firmly state that in at least two important ways these Greek Fathers differ from the biblical witness by reason of the new historical and theological context generated by Arianism: (1) they show a far more pronounced ontological interest pertaining to the nature of God because they had directly to face the ontological question of uncreated and created being sharply raised by Arianism, and (2) they developed the clear position that the Spirit is a distinct uncreated divine being, and not only the uncreated divine power or energy of God, with supportive *but not conclusive* evidence from the New Testament. Regarding the first difference I assume that the New Testament, especially the witness of John and Paul, surely testify to ontological interests respecting the Father and the Son, and I assume also that, as a matter of theological principle, an ontological question is not illegitimate simply because it is ontological,whatever the possibilities of dealing with such a question. Regarding the second difference I can only here say that this represents my own exegetical judgment in good faith and I can also cite the good company of Gregory the Theologian who honestly recognized that the eternal subsistence of the Spirit as a distinct divine being cannot, strictly speaking, be demonstrated by means of grammatical exegesis of the biblical texts.[26]

If there are, then, important differences between the biblical and patristic witness on such central matters, what authority is finally to judge whether these differences are legitimate or not in the development of doctrine, whether or not they are consistent with the biblical witness, and therefore whether a new position is true or false? Gregory the Theologian writes that in his days:

> of the wise men among ourselves, some have conceived of him [the Spirit] as an activity, some as a creature, some as God; and some have been uncertain which to call him, out of reverence of Scripture, they say, as though it did not make the matter clear either way.[27]

---

[26]See, further, Stylianopoulos, "Biblical Background," pp. 164-69, and also William G. Rusch, "The Doctrine of the Holy Spirit in the Patristic and Medieval Church," in *The Holy Spirit in the Life of the Church*, p. 77, who notes Gregory's "embarassment" by the lack of clarity of Scripture on this question and his consequent theory of progression in the revelation of the Father (OT), the Son (NT), and Spirit (Church).

[27]*Theological Orations* 5.5.

Unquestionably Gregory himself, along with Athanasios, Basil, and others, took a definite position on this theological issue based on what they considered the most cogent exegetical, soteriological, and ontological arguments and this position was upheld by the Second Synod as an authoritative expression of ecclesial experience of the Spirit. In other words, the hermeneutical issue unsolved in the debates of theologians about the nature and activities of the Spirit found official settlement by conciliar authority. This is to say that the new creative step taken by the Greek Fathers in opposition to Arianism, and approved by the Second Synod, represents no less than a new hermeneutical commitment by the historic Church regarding the Holy Spirit as a distinct uncreated being, the implications of which are of considerable magnitude. Thus the significance of the Nicene Creed lies not only in that it is a historic summary of the faith of the Bible but also in that it is an authoritative interpretation of the biblical witness by the universal Church.

With respect to the *filioque* clause the implications of the above paragraphs lead to two related affirmations. First, Eastern objections to the *filioque* which are based on the trinitarian dogma of the First and Second Synods, and the theology which is presupposed by them, cannot be conclusively answered by reference to the biblical witness because the biblical witness is not sufficiently nuanced to provide such answers. To be sure, Orthodox theologians would fully agree that the New Testament testifies to the intimate mutuality and reciprocity between Father, Son, and Spirit, and also that Christ is equally the bearer and the sender of the Spirit. Although agreement on these truths is of basic significance, the specific meaning of terminology such as "temporal mission," "eternal procession," "hypostatic properties," and "immanent" and "economic" Trinity cannot be fully elucidated, much less conclusively evaluated as the Klingenthal Memorandum seems somewhat to suppose,[28] by reference to the biblical witness. Thus, perhaps by an irony of history, while to Western theologians the *filioque* may well reflect biblical teaching about the intimacy of the Son and the Spirit, and also about the Son's prerogative both to possess and to send forth the Spirit—truths which Orthodox theologians themselves advocate—nevertheless the *filioque* as a doctrinal formula, from an Eastern perspective, runs counter to the nuances of fourth-century conciliar theology.

---

[28]Memorandum, pp. 8-9.

Secondly, the *filioque* clause, whatever its Western history and interpretations, if it is to be acceptable to Orthodox, must be modified or at least authoritatively interpreted in terms that are not in conflict with the intentionality of the Nicene Creed. Because the *filioque* was added to the Nicene Creed we must ask whether or not it sits well within it, whether or not its meaning is consistent with that of the Nicene Creed. But the meaning of the Nicene Creed itself cannot be ascertained apart from the trinitarian controversy of the fourth century and especially apart from the chief theological witnesses which stand behind it, namely, Athanasios, Basil, and Gregory the Theologian. We lack other decisive criteria by which to evaluate the Nicene Creed and, consequently, the *filioque* as an addition to that Creed. The Memorandum asks a rhetorical question which is incisive:

> Is it possible that the *filioque,* or certain understanding of it, may have been understandable and indeed helpful in their essential intention in the context of particular theological debates [in the West], and yet inadequate as articulations of a full or balanced doctrine of the Trinity?[29]

An Orthodox might easily answer yes if by "a full or balanced doctrine of the Trinity" is meant a doctrine anchored on the trinitarian commitments of the historic Church through its ecumenical synods. Thus the ecclesial authority of the ecumenical synods as well as the ecclesial authority of conciliar theology reflected in the writings of Athanasios and the Cappadocians are at the forefront of the *filioque* discussion.

EVALUATING THE *FILIOQUE*

The fourth and most substantive section of the Klingenthal Memorandum, entitled "Theological aspects of the *filioque*," evaluates in a fair and insightful manner the intrinsic issues involved in the *filioque* question. On the one hand it affirms the positive intent of the *filioque,* as interpreted by Western theologians, namely, to uphold the consubstantiality of the Trinity and to express the biblical teaching that the Spirit is also the Spirit of the Son. The Memorandum powerfully insists on the closest possible relations between Son and Spirit, and so between the generation of the Son and

---

[29]Ibid., p. 10.

the procession of the Spirit, on the unassailable grounds that the Holy Spirit "*only proceeds from the Father as the Father is also Father of the Son*" (emphasis is the Memorandum's).[30]

On the other hand the Memorandum equally affirms "the uniqueness of the Father, as the sole principle (ἀρχή), source (πηγή), and cause (αἰτία) of divinity,"[31] a trinitarian truth of decisive importance for the Eastern tradition. It perceptively points out that Photios' famous formula, "the Spirit proceeds from the Father *alone*," intends not to deny the intimate relations between the generation of the Son and the procession of the Spirit, but only to make utterly explicit that the Father *alone causes* the existence of both the Son and the Spirit, conferring upon them all his being, attributes, and powers, except his hypostatic property, i.e., that he is the Father, the unbegotten, the source, origin, and cause of divinity. The Memorandum recognizes that the persons of the triune God who is both unity and threefoldness must not be confused in a modalistic fashion. With regard to the origin of the Spirit the Memorandum therefore states: "The Spirit who is not a 'second Son,' proceeds in his own unique and absolutely originated way from the Father who, as Father, is in relation to the Son."[32]

On the basis of the above main points, then, the Memorandum sets down a truly revolutionary ecumenical proposal containing two parts, one negative and one positive:

> *First, it should not be said* that the Spirit proceeds "from the Father and the Son," for this would efface the difference in his relationship to the Father and to the Son. *Second, it should be said* that the procession of the Spirit from the Father presupposes the relationship existing within the Trinity between the Father and the Son, for the Son is eternally in and with the Father, and the Father is never without the Son (emphases are the Memorandum's).[33]

Having thus proposed the setting aside of the *filioque* ("it should not be said that the Spirit proceeds from the Father *and* the Son"),

---

[30]Ibid., p. 13.

[31]Ibid., p. 11.

[32]Ibid., p. 13.

[33]Ibid., p. 15.

just as in the end it clearly recommends the setting aside of the *filioque* clause by the churches, the Memorandum then completes its proposal by offering a choice of the following formulae in the place of the *filioque,* a list which is not necessarily closed:

—the Spirit proceeds from the Father of the Son;
—the Spirit proceeds from the Father through the Son;
—the Spirit proceeds from the Father and receives from the Son;
—the Spirit proceeds from the Father and rests on the Son;
—the Spirit proceeds from the Father and shines out through the Son.[34]

The amazing degree to which Orthodox theologians can accept the above proposal, as well as virtually all of the above alternate formulae, may be verified by Dumitru Staniloae's valuable contribution to *Spirit of God, Spirit of Christ.*[35] Engaging mainly Garrigues' conciliatory article in the same volume, Staniloae, who is one of the eminent Orthodox theologians of the twentieth century, not only accepts the correctness of Garrigues' own proposed formula of conciliation ("I believe in the Holy Spirit who goes forth from the one only Father insofar as he begets the only Son")[36] but also states that "the Father causes the Spirit to proceed from himself in order to communicate him to his Son, in order to be more united with the Son by the Spirit."[37] As if to relieve Western fears that Eastern triadology neglects the mutuality and reciprocity of the Son and the Spirit—including the sharing and participation of the Son in the eternal spiration of the Spirit from the Father—Staniloae speaks of "the active repose of the Holy Spirit in the Son" and an intimate "eternal relation of the Son to the Spirit [which] is the basis of the sending of the Spirit to us by the Son."[38] According to Staniloae, Eastern trinitarian theology as articulated by Gregory the Cypriot goes so far as

---

[34]Ibid., p. 16.

[35]"The Procession of the Holy Spirit," pp. 174-86.

[36]Garrigues, p. 153. However, it should be noted that Garrigues does not ask for the removal of the *filioque* from the Creed.

[37]Staniloae, p. 176. Here Staniloae also points to a statement by Gregory Palamas which is strikingly similar to that of Garrigues quoted above. According to Palamas "the Spirit has his existence from the Father of the Son, because he who causes the Spirit to proceed is also the Father."

[38]Ibid., pp. 180 and 182.

to posit an *active eternal projection or shining forth or manifestation* of the Spirit through the Son, a manifestaton which applies to the Spirit's eternal existence (ὑπόστασις) as well as to the temporal mission (οἰκονομία), a manifestation for which the presupposition "from" (ἐκ) as well as "through" (διά) may be used![39]

The positions of Staniloae and the Klingenthal Memorandum mark an unprecedented and astounding ecumenical convergence holding a startling promise for the resolution of the *filioque* controversy. It may be asked: what, then, is the burning objection to the *filioque* from an Eastern viewpoint? It is not that the *filioque* implies two sources in the Godhead because already Augustine himself taught that the Spirit proceeds from the Father and the Son as from a single source or principle.[40] Nor is it that the *filioque* subordinates the Spirit to the Son because the doctrine of consubstantiality clearly implies the full unity and equality of the three persons of the Trinity. Rather it is the objection that the *filioque* as a doctrinal formula and as articulated by Augustine and all his later interpreters posits that not only the Father but also the Son is a source or origin or cause of the Spirit. In view of Staniloae's position this objection may be refined in a crucial way as follows. It can be said that the Son even causes the eternal *manifestation* of the existence of the Spirit, but it cannot be said that the Son causes the Spirit's *coming into existence* or *hypostasis* itself. The Father fully gives the Spirit to the Son so that, according to a striking patristic image, the Spirit is the treasure while the Son is the treasurer. In other words, the Son in every way receives and manifests the Spirit but does not *cause its existence as such* because only the Father is the source or origin or cause of both the Son and the Spirit through ineffably different but united acts (i.e., generation and procession).

If explored more fully in future discussions the above fine distinction may well be the key to an authentic resolution of the *filioque* controversy because it would seem to completely satisfy the deeper

---

[39]Ibid., pp. 182-84. But Garrigues speaks about "a dominant trend in the Eastern tradition to regard the mediation of the Son merely as a passive and quite non-causal condition of the procession of the Spirit from the Father alone" (p. 153). Obviously for Garrigues "passive" and "non-causal" are identical, whereas Staniloae shows that the Eastern tradition holds to an active, yet non-causal, participation of the Son in the Spirit's procession from the Father.

[40]*On the Trinity* 5.14; 15.27.

theological concerns of both sides. On the Western side theologians have seen the *filioque* as affirming the intimate relation between Son and Spirit, that is to say that the Spirit of God is also in every way the Spirit of Christ over against any Arian subordinationist tendencies. In terms of trinitarian theology this would mean affirmation of the truth that the Son participates in both the eternal and the temporal going forth of the Spirit from the Father. Although the Nicene Creed does not explicitly speak about the relation of the Son and the Spirit, a silence which Moltmann[41] and others have seen as a weakness in the Creed, this silence in the words of Moltmann himself, "cannot be interpreted as a dogmatic decision of the conciliar Fathers against any participation of the Son in the going forth of the Spirit from the Father."[42]

Orthodox theologians would not only fully agree with Moltmann's above words, but they would also point out that the Cappadocian teaching of the περιχώρησις (mutual containing or indwelling) of the three persons of the Trinity, a touchstone in Eastern triadology, is a crowning affirmation of the close relations of the Son and the Spirit as frequently affirmed by both the pre-Nicene and the post-Nicene Fathers. According to Gregory of Nyssa, the Son in some sense even "mediates" in the procession of the Spirit.[43] Moreover, the Nicene Creed is not totally silent about these matters because its formulation that the Spirit is, in Basilian doxological language, "co-worshiped and co-glorified with the Father and the Son" clearly suggests the teaching of the περιχώρησις. Basil's doxology, "Glory be to the Father with (σύν) the Son, [and] with (σύν) the Holy Spirit," so Gregory the Theologian explains, signifies the co-presence and co-existence of all three persons at once.[44] Finally, according to Staniloae's interpretation of the later patristic tradition, as we have seen, Eastern trinitarian theology explicitly affirms the participation of the Son in the Spirit's eternal procession from the Father not only in terms of an intimate eternal *accompaniment* (so Gregory Palamas) but also *manifested* accompaniment, i.e., an active eternal manifestation

---

[41]Moltmann, pp. 165-66.

[42]Ibid., p. 166. Zizioulas puts it more strongly: the Creed's phraseology "does not exclude a mediating role of the Son in the procession of the Spirit" (p. 44).

[43]So Zizioulas, "Interpreting the Greek Fathers," p. 43.

[44]Ibid., pp. 38 and 40.

of the existence or ὑπόστασις of the Spirit "through" and even "from" the existence or ὑπόστασις of the Son (so Gregory of Cyprus)! Thus the deeper theological concerns of those who value the positive intentionality of the *filioque* would be fully satisfied by Eastern trinitarian teaching.

On the Eastern side, since the days of Maximos the Confessor Eastern theologians have on the basis of conciliar theology expressed strong anxieties about the *filioque* as compromising the principle of the "monarchy" of the Father and confusing the hypostatic properties of the Father and the Son, as if one could have (perish the blasphemous thought!) a hybrid Father-Son person. According to Cappadocian teaching, faithfully followed by later Eastern interpreters, the Father confers *all that he is* upon the Son and the Spirit, *except for his personal or hypostatic distinctiveness as Father* (his eternal Fatherhood or unbegottenness or personal mode of existence as unoriginate and uncaused source within the Trinity) which he passes on neither to the Son nor to the Spirit. So, too, the Son is *all that the Father and the Spirit are, except for his personal or hypostatic distinctiveness as Son* (his eternal Sonship or begottenness or personal mode of existence by generation from the Father) which he communicates neither to the Father nor to the Spirit. Likewise the Spirit is *all that the Father and the Son are, except for his personal or hypostatic distinctiveness as Spirit* (his Spirithood or eternal spiration or personal mode of existence by procession from the Father) which he communicates neither to the Father nor to the Son. Thus, all three persons of the Trinity are one God by hypostatic περιχώρησις and consubstantial unity but never to be confused in their personal distinctiveness, as they were by the modalistic heresy, because the Father is forever the Father, the Son is forever the Son, and the Spirit is forever the Spirit—one triune God revealed as the living God of the Bible. Thus, also, according to the Cappadocian doctrine of the Trinity, the "monarchy" of the Father means that, as Moltmann correctly states, "the first person [the Father] must guarantee *both* the unity of the godhead *and* the threefoldness of the persons" (emphasis is Moltmann's),[45] that is to say, insofar as the Father is the only personal source or origin or cause of both the Son and the Spirit.

But does the *filioque* teaching intend to diminish the Father's

---

[45]Moltmann, p. 172.

"monarchy"? On this decisive question the Klingenthal Memorandum, interpreting a Western perspective which is sensitive to the Eastern tradition, states:

> It may be said that neither the early Latin Fathers, such as Ambrose and Augustine, nor the subsequent medieval tradition ever believed that they were damaging the principle of the Father's "monarchy" by affirming the *filioque*. The West declared itself to be as much attached to this principle as were the Eastern Fathers (emphasis is the writer's).[46]

Similarly Moltmann observes that "the filioque was never directed against the 'monarchy' of the Father" and that the principle of the "monarchy" has "never been contested by the theologians of the Western Church."[47] If these statements can be accepted by the Western theologians today in their full import of doing justice to the principle of the Father's "monarchy," which is so important to Eastern triadology, then the theological fears of Easterners about the *filioque* would seem to be fully relieved. Consequently, Eastern theologians could accept virtually any of the Memorandum's alternate formulae in the place of the *filioque* on the basis of the above positive evaluation of the *filioque* which is in harmony with Maximos the Confessor's interpretation of it. As Zizioulas incisively concludes:

> The "golden rule" must be Saint Maximos the Confessor's explanation concerning Western pneumatology: by professing the *filioque* our Western brethren do not wish to introduce another αἴτιον in God's being except the Father, and a mediating role of the Son in the origination of the Spirit is not to be limited to the divine Economy, but relates also to the divine οὐσία. If East and West can repeat these two points *together* in our time, this would provide sufficient basis for a rapprochement between the two traditions.[48]

However, can Western and Eastern theologians repeat these truths together today? Some additional comments will disclose the need of

---

[46]Memorandum, p. 13.

[47]Moltmann, p. 166.

[48]Zizioulas, p. 54.

further clarifications toward an integrated theological solution to the controversy. First, Western theologians who perceive Eastern sensitivities cannot continue to state, as does André de Halleux, that the specific difference between East and West pertaining to the *filioque* is a "peripheral difference."[49] Halleux recommends that the *filioque* be removed from the Creed, but only as a token of reconciliation and without repudiation of any of its undesirable implications.[50] But his solution cannot be accepted by the Orthodox because it avoids the problem. Helleux seems to defend an optional *filioque* as a *theologoumenon* on the basis of the Cappadocian teaching of the περι-χώρησις and consubstantiality of the Trinity, but he neglects to take full account of the Cappadocian teaching of the "monarchy" (not "monopatrism" as used by Halleux). Neither does he consider that the Synodal Letter of 382, written by Fathers who were at the Second Synod (381) and who interpret this Synod with surprisingly analytical terminology, specifically warns that "neither the *hypostaseis* are confused, nor the individual properties abolished" by an adequate trinitarian theology.[51] This writer could agree with Halleux that the difference over the *filioque* is not "the nodal point of contradiction between two irreconcilable pneumatologies"[52] because of what East and West share as a common teaching about the Spirit quite apart from the unacceptable aspects of the *filioque*. But there are other options in assessing this difference than Halleux's two extremes of either "irreconcilable pneumatologies" or "peripheral difference."

Secondly, there is the delicate but crucial question of the Western ascription of "secondary cause" to the Son in the procession of the Spirit. Garrigues' solution fails because, despite all of his erudite explanations, Garrigues nonetheless wants not only to maintain the *filioque* as a doctrinal formula approved by the magisterium, but finally also to uphold the principle of the double cause of the Spirit's origin: "The Holy Spirit . . . proceeds in origin from the two [the Father and the Son]."[53] The problem is precisely the *que* ("and")

---

[49]"Toward an Ecumenical Agreement on the Procession of the Holy Spirit and the Addition of the Filioque to the Creed," *Spirit of God, Spirit of Christ,* p. 75.

[50]Ibid., pp. 81-84.

[51]See Stylianopoulos, "Biblical Background," p. 161.

[52]Halleux, p. 75.

[53]Garrigues, pp. 162-63.

in the *filioque* which posits the Son, along with the Father, as the source or cause of the Spirit. Gregory of Nyssa does not say in the quote cited by Garrigues[54] that the Son "causes" the Spirit. Although Gregory, in the context of his discussion of causality in the final paragraphs of his *An Answer to Ablabius* refers to the Father as the "first cause," almost begging the question of the Son as "second cause," nevertheless he meticulously avoids this easy inference. He grants a "mediation" of the Son in the Spirit's eternal procession from the Father, but this is a mediation which does not compromise the phrase "from the Father," that is, it "does not allow for the Son to acquire the role of αἴτιον ('cause') by being a mediator."[55]

The Cappadocians, and most certainly the two Gregories, could never have used the creedal ἐκπορευόμενον with the conjunction καὶ ("and") to describe the Spirit's relation to the Son in the manner of the *filioque*. Gregory the Theologian himself coined the noun ἐκπόρευσις ("procession") in order to affirm the opposite, to *distinguish* between the three persons of the Trinity, and in particular to differentiate the Son's generation and the Spirit's procession, both originating from the Father but each in their own ineffably unique ways, so that the Spirit might be confessed not as a "second Son" but in his own personal distinctiveness as Spirit.

Nor will it do to appeal, as Garrigues does, to the etymological meaning of *procession*.[56] The context of the Creed, in which the

---

[54]Ibid., p. 156.

[55]So Ziziloulas, pp. 43-44.

[56]Garrigues correctly gives the different etymological meanings of the parallel verbs used in the Greek and Latin versions of the Creed, the first (ἐκπορεύεσθαι) meaning "to go forth out of" or "to issue from" and the second (*procedere*) meaning "to go forward" or "to progress forward." It follows that *procedere* is not exactly equivalent to ἐκπορεύεσθαι but to another Greek verb προχωρεῖν ("to go forward"), just as ἐκπορεύεσθαι may more precisely be rendered with the Latin *exportare*. Thus the participle ἐκπορευόμενον ("who goes forth out of") used in the Creed for the Spirit's origin from the Father should have been translated in Latin as *qui ex Patre se exportat* ("who goes forth out of the Father" or "who issues from the Father"), so Garrigues correctly explains, and not *qui ex Patre procedit* because the *pro* in *procedere* gives us the meaning "who goes forward from the Father." But then, in a startling turn of reasoning, Garrigues suggests to English-speaking Orthodox in the West, when they recite the Creed, not to use "proceeds" which can imply a *filioque* but a more precise alternative for ἐκπορευόμενον! He fails inexplicably to see that the opposite is the

Greek ἐκ τοῦ Πατρὸς ἐκπορευόμενον ("who proceeds from the Father") parallels the earlier confessional formula ἐκ τοῦ Πατρὸς γεννηθέντα ("begotten from the Father"), has clearly in view the Son's and the Spirit's eternal origin from the Father and only the Father. In other words, the acquired technical meaning of procession, accurately based on the ἐκ ("out of") of the creedal term ἐκπορευόμενον ("who proceeds out of"), renders the *filioque* a doctrinal error because *in the context of the Creed the filioque formula inescapably confesses a joint cause (Father "and" Son) in the Spirit's origin.* But any ascription of joint cause to the Son in the Spirit's *coming into existence* or ὑπόστασις as such cannot avoid blurring the persons of the Father and the Son, according to Cappadocian presuppositions, into a single, unthinkable Father-Son person, which was Mark of Ephesos' sharp criticism of the *filioque* at the Council of Florence.[57] This is the reason why Staniloae, in his response to Garrigues, observes that Garrigues' conciliatory proposal is not exactly the same as the *filioque*.[58] This is also the reason why the Klingenthal Memorandum, if I interpret its intent correctly, mentions but does not support the teaching of the Son as a "secondary cause" and consequently recommends the removal of the *filioque* formula from the Creed.[59]

Thirdly, Moltmann's view of the "monarchy" of the Father needs to be addressed as well. Although he advocates the withdrawal of the *filioque* as an "interpretative interpolation" into a common creed, and also speaks of a "justified rejection" of an unqualified *filioque*, Moltmann grounds this rejection not on the principle of the "monarchy" of the Father but rather on a new proposal of his own.[60] I regard this proposal as speculative because I do not know exactly how to relate it to the historico-theological discussion of the *filioque*. I would

---

case. The Orthodox can accept the use of "proceeds" in its etymological meaning (thus literally, "the Holy Spirit . . . who goes forward from the Father and the Son") because such use implies no *filioquism*, but they cannot by any means accept a precise alternative based on *exportare* or another such verb because that would heighten *filioquism* by emphasizing the Spirit's eternal origin from the Father and the Son as from a joint cause.

[57]See Markos A. Orphanos, "The Procession of the Holy Spirit according to Certain Later Greek Fathers," *Spirit of God, Spirit of Christ*, p. 35.

[58]Staniloae, pp. 174-77.

[59]Memorandum, p. 13.

[60]See above, note 16.

only ask, as Photios might have asked,[61] how can the Spirit receive a "perfect" existence from the Father and still need to obtain a "personal" form by relation to the Son? Is not the Spirit's origin from and relation to the Father already both perfect and personal?[62]

Despite Moltmann's emphasis on "concrete thinking," i.e. thinking about the Trinity emphatically as concrete, different persons rather than as three abstract homogeneous equivalents, he paradoxically misinterprets the Eastern teaching of "monarchy" of the Father as "monopatrism" ("the concept [sic] of the sole causality of the Father") which allegedly subverts the Cappadocian balance between the unity and the threefoldness of the Trinity.[63] But this approach misses the point that, among the Cappadocians and their later Eastern interpreters, terms such as "unbegotten," "unoriginate," "source," and "first cause," which were used to describe the Father's uniqueness, were always intended not as philosophical definitions of the divine being (so Eunomios!) but rather as confessional descriptions of the distinctiveness of the person of the Father. Precisely because of the biblical and Cappadocian identification of God with the *Father*, i.e., the person of the Father who safeguards both the unity and the threefoldness of the Trinity, we must describe the Father as the only "cause" in the Trinity.[64] To quote Zizioulas: "The ultimate ontological category cannot be other than the Person, the hypostasis of the Father *alone*, since two hypostases being such an ultimate category would result into two gods"[65] (or an impossible double person). This would also completely vindicate Photios whose emphasis on the "alone" was a defense of the Cappadocian balance over against

---

[61]See Orphanos, p. 23.

[62]Nonetheless one can discern that Moltmann's proposal is somewhat related to a significant point that Staniloae, p. 184, makes about Gregory of Cyprus' view of the relation between the Son and the Spirit: "The Son marks a progress (πρόοδος) in the existence which the Spirit receives from the Father, one might say a fulfillment, the achievement of the end of which he came into existence." This Gregorian teaching is described as "very bold" by Staniloae because it obviously suggests that the Spirit receives less than perfect existence from the Father. Yet, cautions Staniloae, according to Gregory, the eternal "shining out of the Spirit from the Son is, in the last analysis, due to the Father" and so Gregory does not relinquish "the patristic teaching about the monarchy of the Father" (ibid).

[63]Moltmann, p. 172.

[64]So Zizioulas, p. 46. See his relevant statement above in note 24.

[65]Ibid.

the misguided "and" of the *filioque* positing a joint cause. Photios neither taught a "monopatrism" in the sense of isolating the Father from the Son and the Spirit (indeed, he well knew the teachings of the περιχώρησις and ὁμοούσιον or consubstantiality of the Trinity) nor did he think of the sole causality of the Father, in Moltmann's erroneous interpretation of "monopatrism," as a "concept." Rather, while upholding the unity of the divine persons in all common things (τὰ κοινά), Photios also differentiated their uncommunicable personal properties (τὰ ἀκοινώνητα), that is to say, he viewed the triune God as concretely different persons—the Father, the Son, and the Holy Spirit, both united and differentiated—and thus strongly objected to the *filioque's* implication of a joint Son-Father *hypostasis* (υἱοπατρία), which he regarded as the teaching of Sabbelios or some other half-Sabellian monster.[66]

A final note of clarification is necessary concerning the *filioque* and its relationship to the Eastern distinction between "immanent" and "economic" Trinity which, according to Ritschl,[67] lies behind "the difference between East and West" on the *filioque*. Ritschl's is an important observation but it has to be qualified in two ways. First, as this paper has stressed, the Eastern tradition teaches a "mediation" of the Son in the "eternal procession" as well as the "temporal mission" of the Spirit. To quote Staniloae: "The eternal relation of the Son to the Spirit is the basis of the sending of the Spirit to us by the Son."[68] This teaching is a touchstone for the ecumenical resolution of the *filioque* problem today. Secondly, although the above distinction properly differentiates between, on the one hand, God's relations to himself and, on the other hand, God's relations to creation, it by no means intends to suggest two Trinities. In speaking about "immanent" and "economic" Trinity we are speaking about one God, united yet differentiated both within the Trinity and over against creation. As many of the contributors to *Spirit of God, Spirit of Christ*, including Ritschl himself, and the Klingenthal Memorandum, emphasize: we must confess *one* Trinity, "the living God [who] from eternity to eternity was, is, and will be none other ('immanent Trinity') than he has shown himself to be in history ('economic

---

[66]See Orphanos, p. 22.

[67]Ritschl, p. 78.

[68]Staniloae, p. 182.

Trinity').[69] The Eastern teaching about the "monarchy" of the Father not only presupposes this biblical principle that the "economic" Trinity is the only basis for all reflection about the "immanent" Trinity, but also affirms the biblical truth that the one, living God, who is the Father, reveals himself in his Son, and through his Son in the power of the Spirit, three uncreated persons who are united but not confused.

Thus Ritschl's above point may more accurately be expressed by saying that the distinction between "immanent" and "economic" Trinity, as well as the parallel distinction between the "essence" and "energies" of God, are *additional* background differences in the Eastern and Western doctrinal traditions which need systematic attention but which do not necessarily have to be resolved prior to arriving at a solution of the *filioque* problem. These additional differences are related to the *filioque* question but did not necessarily produce the *filioque*.[70] The *filioque* clause by reason of its placement in the Creed has to do with the "immanent" Trinity. Augustine himself was chiefly concerned with explaining the "immanent" Trinity, i.e., the inner trinitarian relations, when he formulated the *filioque* teaching. Had Augustine converged on the preposition "through," instead of the conjunction "and," to describe the Spirit's relation to the Son, he would have saved Christendom a lot of headaches. For the doctrinal formula "who proceeds from the Father *through* the Son" expresses correct teaching by Eastern criteria according to the twofold "golden rule" of Maximos the Confessor, i.e., negatively not to introduce another cause or principle or source in the Trinity except

---

[69]Memorandum, p. 10.

[70]I do not quite agree with Ritschl (p. 61) and Romanides (p. 297) who state that Augustine on account of his own presuppositions *had* to teach the *filioque*. According to Romanides, Augustine's whole reasoning about the differentiation of the Trinity may be reduced to this: the Father is from no one, the Son is from One, and the Spirit is from Two (ibid). But Augustine, without violating his own presuppositions, could have speculated, theoretically speaking, that the Spirit "is" from the Father and is "eternally breathed" by the Father "through" the Son, i.e., he could have speculated that the Spirit is from Two not by means of the conjunctive "and" but by the prepositional "through," had he been sensitive to the Cappadocian teaching of the "monarchy" of the Father and the intent of the Second Synod's use of ἐκπορευόμενον. Of course this is not to say that Augustine's philosophico-theological approach, and especially his teaching about created grace, would be acceptable to Eastern theology.

the Father and positively to affirm a mediating role of the Son in the Spirit's eternal origin from the Father. The same golden rule, which is the sound theological foundation for an ecumenical resolution of the *filioque* controversy today as proposed by the Klingenthal Memorandum, is also found in John Damascene who writes: "The Spirit is the Spirit of the Father as proceeding from the Father ..., but he is also the Spirit of the Son, not as proceeding from him, but as proceeding through him from the Father, for the Father alone is the cause."[71] Augustine *intended* to affirm nearly the same truths, namely, the intimacy between the Son and the Spirit, as well as the Father's primacy in the Trinity. But familiar neither with the Cappadocian presuppositions nor the intentionality of conciliar terminology, Augustine's great mind followed another direction and settled on what proved to be the critical *que* ("and") of the *filioque* teaching and he did so in order to stress the unity between Father and Son as a single principle or joint cause. However, he thus committed an unsuspecting but fateful error by Cappadocian criteria, i.e., confusing in a modalistic way the persons of the Father and the Son, an error which stands in its specificity in irreducible conflict with the conciliar principle of the "monarchy" of the Father and therefore should be removed from the Nicene Creed on theological as well as canonical grounds.

THE RELEVANCE OF THE *FILIOQUE* QUESTION

The Klingenthal Memorandum presents to the churches a remarkable theological opening for the resolution of the *filioque* controversy which has troubled the Eastern and Western churches for over a millenium. The Klingenthal proposal, to use Staniloae's words about Gregory the Cypriot's teaching, "opens to us a door of understanding" by emphasizing the relation of the Spirit to the Son and yet not abandoning the patristic teaching of the "monarchy" of the Father.[72] The solution of the *filioque* problem would be a profound testimony to the value of the modern ecumenical movement which renounces polemics and fosters deep mutual understanding of different

---

[71]"Πνεῦμα τοῦ Πατρὸς ὡς ἐκ Πατρὸς ἐκπορευόμενον . . . καὶ Υἱοῦ δὲ Πνεῦμα, οὐχ ὡς ἐξ αὐτοῦ, ἀλλ᾽ ὡς δι᾽ αὐτοῦ ἐκ τοῦ Πατρὸς ἐκπορευόμενον· μόνος γὰρ αἴτιος ὁ Πατήρ," *Exposition of the Orthodox Faith* 1.12.

[72]Staniloae, p. 184.

positions in the sincere hope of achieving authentic resolution of conflicts. In addition it would be a dramatic crowning of the "ecumenism of love" with a specific great victory in the realm of the "ecumenism of truth," a tremendous step toward Christian unity especially significant to the Orthodox who value the Nicene Creed to the highest degree and who are not always certain about the seriousness with which Westerners regard classic Christian doctrines.

However, what is the intrinsic value of resolving the *filioque* problem apart from its contemporary ecumenical significance? What real difference, one way or the other, would settlement of the *filioque* question signify, and what is the degree of magnitude of that difference? In the process of making decisions and introducing liturgical changes according to the Klingenthal recommendations the churches should by all means seriously consider the intrinsic value of these steps based on the wider relevance of the *filioque* pertaining to the theology, spirituality, and practical life of the churches. I would like to offer comments on these matters with the view to sketching a wider context for evaluating the importanc of the *filioque* question.

On a doctrinal level the specific impact of the *filioque* is on the confession of the faith of the universal Church as attested in the Bible and summed up by the Nicene Creed. The reexamination of the *filioque* question raises the possibility of a universal confession of faith by Christians today and the appropriation of the Nicene Creed as the normative Creed of Christianity. As a confession of faith, forged by momentous debates and expressing the universal Church's affirmation of basic Christian truths pertaining to God and salvation, the Nicene Creed is not merely an "ancient historical" confession, as some would seem to refer to it, but rather a living confession of the universal faith of the Church constantly proclaimed in worship and always offered as a celebration of Christian truth. It is reasonable to expect that such a confession of faith, being the doctrinal anchor of a united Church, should be in every way accurate, consistent with itself, and truly universal. On this doctrinal level the *filioque* is an "interpretative interpolation" which at minimum stands in doubtful consistency with the theology of the Creed, as we have shown.

But, if we grant that the *filioque* is a doctrinal error, how serious an error is it? The *filioque* does not question the trinitarian dogma but only seeks to interpret it. It is not a difference in dogma but in the interpretation of dogma. On the positive side the *filioque* intends to affirm the closeness of the Son and the Spirit, as well as the unity of the Son and the Father, so that the Spirit may be confessed as the mutual eternal bond of love of the Father and the Son and as their common gift to human beings.[73] Augustine himself who provides the classic reasoning behind the *filioque* in no way doubts the dogma of the Trinity but rather powerfully defends it through philosophico-theological explanations based on Scripture and Christian tradition. On the negative side the theological charge that the *filioque* implies a subordination and a consequent "depersonalizing" of the Spirit[74] cannot be sustained because the Creed, Augustine, and all later Augustinian interpreters of the dogma of the Trinity firmly uphold the teaching of both the threefoldness and consubstantial unity (ὁμοούσιον) of the Trinity. *The only legitimate theological objection to the filioque is that it compromises the "monarchy" of the Father as the only first principle or source or cause within the Trinity*, a compromise which was wholly unintended by Augustine and later Western thinkers.

The specific theological difference may be reduced to this: the *que* ("and") of the *filioque* does not seem to relinquish the "monarchy" of the Father in the Augustinian context but unintentionally does relinquish it in the Cappadocian context. But does this difference in the interpretation of dogma justify the divisive centrality which the *filioque* has been given in history by force of human stubbornness and polemics? Probably not. Could one suggest that the *filioque*'s unwitting blurring of the Father and the Son into a single, unthinkable person does actually blur the Father and the Son in their eternal existence? Absolutely not.

The real problem, then, is the uncanonical inclusion of the *filioque* in the Creed which automatically attributes to it dogmatic authority, an issue of the greatest magnitude on both counts. That an unintended error in the interpretation of dogma should not itself be given dogmatic status is a truth so evident as to need no defense. It is on this canonical and dogmatic level that the *filioque* became,

---

[73]See Boris Bobrinskoy, "The Filioque Yesterday and Today," *Spirit of God, Spirit of Christ*, pp. 141-42, for a rare case of an Orthodox theologian seeking to discern some "positive values" in the *filioque*.

[74]An unfair charge often repeated by Orthodox. The same charge is made by some Western theologians, for example see Alasdair Heron, "The Filioque in Recent Reformed Theology," *Spirit of God, Spirit of Christ*, p. 113, and Herwig Aldenhoren, "The Question of the Procession of the Holy Spirit and its Connection with the Life of the Church," ibid., p. 130.

according to Vladimir Lossky's words, "the one dogmatic reason for the separation between East and West" and "the primordial point" of linkage of all other divergencies "to the extent that they have any doctrinal content."[75] In this perspective the *filioque* is a dogmatic clue or doctrinal pointer to a theology which tilts the Cappadocian balance between the threefoldness and the unity of the Trinity toward the Sabellian side. To quote Moltmann: "The teaching on the Trinity in the Western Church right down to Karl Barth and Karl Rahner has a tendency to modalism."[76] This is not to say that East and West are locked into "two irrenconciliable pneumatologies" because, quite apart from the specific theological difference on the *filioque,* and most often in total oblivion of questionable Augustinian presuppositions, Christians of the East and the West have enjoyed a common biblical and liturgical heritage pertaining to both the divine person and "economy" of the Holy Spirit. But it is to say that the raising of the *filioque* to the level of dogmatic authority not only created a doctrinal crisis in the consciousness of the Church but also gave Augustinian trinitarian theology with which the *filioque* is associated a role which it would not otherwise have had. Should the *filioque* be withdrawn from the Creed by the Western churches and consequently deprived of dogmatic significance, then the discussion about theological backgrounds could also be more relaxed.

On a general theological level, then, the relevance of the *filioque* question involves a fresh appropriation of classic biblical and patristic modes of thought. Discussion of the *filioque* problem raises many questions about differences in theological approaches and differences in the understanding of the nature of theology itself, especially a theology rooted in the Church as a community of faith. On this level we must be careful not unnecessarily to abstract or absolutize mutually exclusive "Western" and "Eastern" approaches, or mutually exclusive Augustinian and Cappadocian "presuppositions." There are substantial similarities of faith, work, and thought between Eastern and Western Fathers. Broad sources and truths are shared by the Eastern and Western traditions. There are also differences in approaches and teachings *within* major strands of Christian tradition from New Testament times. Augustine's greatness as an interpreter of the Bible and the Christian tradition cannot be fairly questioned by Orthodox on

---

[75]See Brobinskoy, p. 137.

[76]Moltmann, p. 173. See also Heron, p. 113.

the grounds that he held certain unconscious presuppositions which were faulty. Let the specific faulty presuppositions be pointed out but not used as a base for a general rejection of a major theological witness. Above all salvation comes to us from Christ and by way of the Gospel and the central Christian truths, not by way of "approaches" and "presuppositions." Variety in approach and teaching is not necessarily divisive, and if it is occasionally conflicting, the conflicts of theological opinions do not necessarily have to be raised to the level of the division of the churches unless they are absolutely and demonstrably damaging to the heart of the Christian life and witness.

Having laid down that caveat, we may indicate certain questions which can analytically be examined in future ecumenical discussions pertaining to the *filioque* and related background issues. Is Lossky's unrelieved criticism of the *filioque* as a doctrine which brings an "alien light" of fallen reason into mystical theology really justified?[77] What are the features and dimensions of this "alien light" as defined by reasonable scholarly discourse? Allchin finds that the theology which produced the *filioque* led to an "understanding of the nature of man and his relationship to God" in terms of isolation and opposition, rather than the "theocentric humanism" of the Eastern tradition.[78] Romanides states that "as a heresy the *filioque* is as bad as Arianism" because of the questionable Augustinian presuppositions about created grace, the nature of scriptural revelation, and view of God as substance.[79] Staniloae, too, is concerned about a theology of created grace which would seem to deny the biblical witnes to Spirit-bearing humanity.[80]

All these questions seem to revolve around the issue of the distinction of immanent and economic Trinity which the Orthodox view as implied by biblical revelation and explicitly taught as early as Athanasios in the context of his struggle with Arianism. But Western theologians seem to hold a different view on this matter. According to Ritschl "*the* basic theological-epistemological thesis in Karl Barth's dogmatics" is "the ultimate abolition" of that distinction, which abolition is "dear to Western theology."[81] Is the West, then,

---

[77]Bobrinskoy, p. 137.

[78]Allchin, p. 95.

[79]Romanides, pp. 308-11.

[80]Staniloae, pp. 178-79.

[81]Ritschl, p. 56.

"substantialist" on account of a deep philosophical view of God and the East "personalist" on account of a deep biblical view of God as the living God who truly reveals himself yet remains transcendent? To quote Zizioulas: "It is in the light of this absence of an ontology of the Person in the West that we must place the entire history of East-West relations in theology."[82] This writer is not comfortable with the generalizations made or implied by the above comments. Analytic studies on specific problems are in order. Such studies would be on considerable help to future ecumenical discussions on the *filioque.* They would also provide the groundwork for a more balanced comparison of the methods, nature, and accents of Western and Eastern theology.

The above remarks have addressed the question of the relevance of the *filioque* to theology in general. But what of the practical life of the Church? The relevance of the *filioque* question to the concrete life of the Church deserves serious reflection, too. The ancient doctrinal controversies centered on issues of immediate relevance for Christian life. For example, Gregory the Theologian in his *Theological Orations* reasons that the adoration of the Holy Spirit in Christian worship proves that he is God. "If he is not to be worshiped, how can he deify me in baptism? . . . And indeed from the Spirit comes our new birth, and from the new birth our new creation, and from the new creation our deeper knowledge of the dignity of him from whom it is derived."[83] Likewise the contemporary ecumenical discussion on the *filioque* offers to the churches the opportunity of reflecting on the Spirit's presence in the life of the Church and of encouraging a deeper awareness of the renewing action of the Spirit in the personal life of Christians. As Harold Ditmantson writes:

> A great deal of the church's weakness and lack of effective leadership in society spring from a failure to invigorate the thought, work, and worship of the Church by recovering a deeper and wider vision of the workings of the Spirit.[84]

In what way does the *filioque* question impact on similar concerns?

---

[82]Zizioulas, p. 48.

[83]*Theological Orations* 5.28.

[84]Harold H. Ditmanson, "The Significance of the Doctrine of the Holy Spirit for Contemporary Theology," *The Holy Spirit in the Life of the Church,* p. 208.

It is clear that the dogma of the uncreated nature of the Holy Spirit has direct impact on Christian worship and our confession of faith that we are saved by the Spirit's activity. But how does the filioquist interpretation of this dogma make any clear difference with regard to ecclesial life, spirituality, and witness? This writer must confess his perplexity about answering this question because on this practical level the theological debates on the *filioque* have all too often seemed to him, in Sergius Bulgakov's words, "a sterile war of words." The following quote from Bulgakov perfectly expresses my thoughts:

> For many years, as far as I have been able, I have been looking for the traces of this influence, and I have tried to understand the issues at stake, what was the *living* significance of this divergence, *where* and *how* it was revealed *in practice*. I confess that I have not succeeded in finding it; rather I should go further and simply deny its existence. This divergence exists at no point in patristic teaching on the activities of the Holy Spirit in the world, on his "mission," his gifts, on the mysteries, on grace . . . we end up with a strange dogma, deprived of dogmatic power.[85]

In view of the complexities and divergent phenomena of history the charges that the *filioque* doctrine has led to ecclesiasticism, authoritarianism, clericalism, and even the dogma of Pope[86] are wholly unconvincing. When strains of clericalism and ecclesiasticism develop in any Christian tradition the work of the Spirit, to be sure, is often restrained and impeded whether in the East or the West. But it does not at all follow that the specific doctrine of the *filioque* itself has caused such developments in the West. The West offers such a diverse picture of both authoritarian and renewal movements, and yet the whole Western world has presupposed the *filioque*. Roman Catholicism itself, despite the *filioque,* testifies to a tradition of rich spirituality and deep renewal currents. Where and how can one begin to connect this plethora of Western phenomena with the *filioque* and its "presuppositions" of which most people are hardly aware?

---

[85]Cited by Bobrinskoy, p. 136. Curiously, Bulgakov later vitiated his statement by linking, as Bobrinskoy points out, "the *filioque* with the Western Christocentricism which culminates in the dogma of the Pope as Vicar of Christ," ibid.

[86]See Heron, p. 113; Aldenhoven, p. 130; and Bulgakov cited by Bobrinskoy, p. 136.

The practical implications of Staniloae's magisterial contribution to *Spirit of God, Spirit of Christ* are also difficult to grasp. He writes that "the filioque is opposed to our adoption as sons by the Spirit of the Son."[87] His reasoning is that "if the Spirit also comes [sic][88] from the Son, he would no more be the Spirit of the Son, but would be exclusively the Spirit of the Father"[89] and thus "would rather make us fathers."[90] Does Staniloae intend to say "exclusively the Spirit of the Father" by reason of the Father being the principle cause according to the Augustinian interpretation of the *filioque*? Why would that be opposed to our adoption as sons by the Spirit of the Son? Is not the Spirit, according to the Augustinian filioquist interpretation, also the Spirit of the Son? Furthermore, does not Staniloae's thinking suggest a qualitative similarity between the hypostatic sonship of the Logos (immanent Trinity) with our adopted sonship by grace (economic Trinity) which is impossible by Eastern criteria since our adopted sonship is a common adoption by the Trinity? Finally, do we not have in Staniloae's exposition a confused use of the terminology of "sons" and "fathers" suggesting that earthly daughters, fathers, and mothers are adopted literally as "sons" and only "sons" by God?

On the practical level it seems impossible to show how such subtle theological interpretations actually impact on the life of a Christian because the Holy Spirit can act or cease to act in a person whether or not he or she is informed about such subtleties. Western Christians have not depended on the *filioque* to appropriate the gracious actions of the Spirit. Their language and thinking about the Spirit are far more directly dependent on the Bible and also the liturgical traditions based on the language of the Bible. Even if a specific undesirable practical influence could immediately be connected to the *filioque*, which seems hardly possible, this doctrine certainly has not impacted on the life of Western Christians as widely as some generalizations would have it. Allchin gives an isolated example of Ann Griffiths, a keen theological mind of the eighteenth century, who confessed that she had thought of the Father and the Son as co-equal,

---

[87]Staniloae, p. 177.

[88]Read "originates" for "comes." Of course the Spirit comes also from the Son! Some problem of translation is probably involved here.

[89]Ibid,. p. 177.

[90]Ibid., p. 176.

and the Spirit "as a functionary subordinate to them," and that this error of her mind struct at the root of Christian life.[91] But how? Griffith's point is not practically illustrated. Besides, her intellectual error was not an accurate interpretation of the *filioque* in its context of classic trinitarian doctrine. There may also be a well-meaning Orthodox theologian or two somewhere who intellectually do not exactly maintain the Cappadocian balance but rather tend to think of the Trinity as separate persons. How does such an intellectual error impact on his or her practical life? How would one go about demonstrating it?

An example having to do with the relation of the teaching about the Spirit to personal and corporate Christian life can be offered in the reverse direction. One of the greatest witnesses to the living presence of the Spirit in the Orthodox tradition has been Symeon, the eleventh-century monastic who was later given the honorific title of New Theologian. His writings[92] indicate with what holy passion he proclaimed to his contemporaries that the same life that the apostles lived by the power of the Spirit was possible for them in their days, too, and that to think otherwise was a denial of Christ's saving work. Based on his reading of John and Paul, and his own deep experience of renewal, he powerfully called his generation to true repentance and to a new birth "from above" (Jn 3.3). He emphasized a "baptism of the Holy Spirit," juxtaposing but not opposing it to sacramental baptism. For Symeon the Holy Spirit marks the soul's resurrection. The Spirit brings sinful Christians to life "as from the dead" (Rom 6.13). Symeon advocated an uncompromising and wide renewal for all, bishops, monks, and lay people alike, through repentance and through the real (οὐσιωδῶς) and conscious (αἰσθητῶς) presence of the fire of the Spirit in their hearts, for otherwise titles, positions, and theological learning meant, so he declared, nothing for them but divine judgment. Symeon proved to be a prophetic voice in a Christian society inundated by formalism and ecclesiasticism. The incessant response to him was: But that's impossible! No one can live the apostolic life today! Pride is deluding you! Symeon was also persecuted by monks

---

[91]Allchin, p. 95.

[92]See, for example, *Symeon the New Theologian: Discourses*, trans. C. J. de Catanzaro in the series *The Classics of Western Spirituality* (New York, 1980). See also George A. Maloney, S.J., *The Mystic of Fire and Light: St. Symeon the New Theologian* (Denville, NJ, 1975).

and hierarchs. He was finally driven to exile. I cannot think of a more telling example of a Christian tradition which, despite its rejection of the *filioque* and its correct teaching about the Holy Spirit, nevertheless was marked by such clericalism and formalism that actual readiness to welcome the presence of the Spirit in the practical life of the Church was the exception rather than the rule.

CONCLUSION

By way of conclusion it may be helpful to summarize the main points of this paper. Two key factors are crucial to the ecumenical settlement of the *filioque* question. The first is the recognition that the theological use of the *filioque* in the West against Arian subordinationism is fully valid according to the theological criteria of the Eastern tradition. In the West the *filioque* has been used to stress: (1) the consubstantial unity of the Trinity, (2) the divine status of the Son, and (3) the intimacy between the Son and the Spirit. All these points are also integral elements of Eastern trinitarian theology anchored on the Cappadocian teaching of περιχώρησις ("mutual indwelling") of the persons of the Trinity, a teaching reflected by the Nicene Creed which professes an equal worship and glorification of the Holy Trinity. Thus a fundamental and wide agreement exists between Eastern and Western trinitarian doctrine affirming the complete reciprocity and mutuality of the Son and the Spirit in their eternal relations (immanent Trinity) as well as their manifested action in creation, Church and society (economic Trinity). Christ is both the bearer and the sender of the Spirit. The Spirit of God is in every way also the Spirit of the Son.

The second key factor in the resolution of the *filioque* question is the recognition that biblical and patristic theology commonlly affirm the teaching of the "monarchy" of the Father, i.e., that the Father is "the sole principle (ἀρχή), source (πηγή), and cause (αἰτία) of divinity" (Klingenthal Memorandum). This teaching is of decisive importance to Eastern trinitarian theology and a teaching which the *filioque* clause in the West, according to contemporary Western interpretations, has never intended to deny. However, the Augustinian interpretation of the *filioque,* i.e., that the Father and the Son are the *common cause* of the eternal being of the Spirit, unintentionally compromises the "monarchy" of the Father according to Cappadocian trinitarian theology presupposed and reflected by the Nicene Creed in which the verb "proceeds" (ἐκπορευόμενον) refers to the eternal origin of the Spirit from the Father. Eastern trinitarian thought as expressed by Gregory of Nyssa, Gregory the Cypriot and Gregory Palamas conceives of the Son as *mediating,* but not *causing,* the Spirit's procession from the Father. On this nuanced difference in doctrinal interpretation hangs the whole weight of centuries of controversy between the Eastern and Western churches. The formula "who proceeds from the Father *through* the Son" is a sound theological resolution of this problem in the conciliatory spirit of Maximos the Confessor laying aside the above specific Augustinian interpretation as an erroneous theological opinion but at the same time affirming the active participation of the Son in the eternal procession of the Spirit from the Father.

Finally, the *filioque* question does not signal a "great divide" between the Eastern and Western churches because these churches commonly confess the dogma of the Holy Trinity and share broad agreement regarding the work ("economy") of the Spirit according to Scripture, tradition, and liturgy. The *filioque* marks not a decisive difference in dogma but an important difference in the interpretation of dogma due to the differing Cappadocian and Augustinian approaches to the mystery of the Trinity. The theological implications of this difference are a more consistently biblical and personal understanding of the Trinity as concrete persons and careful avoidance of any modalistic tendencies confusing the uniqueness of each of the divine persons. The well-known critique that the *filioque* subordinates the Spirit to the Son and thereby "depersonalizes" the Spirit seems to express theological polemic rather than theological truth. As far as the practical implications of this difference is concerned, i.e., the often repeated charges that the *filioque* leads to authoritarianism, institutionalism, clericalism and other similar tendencies, one is hard pressed to demonstrate these historically and theologically because such tendencies, as well as their opposites, have existed in most churches with or without the *filioque.* More fruitful for further study are the specific implications of the Augustinian and Cappadocian approaches to the Trinity and theology in general, especially the implications for life, spirituality and practice. This kind of direction in ecumenical theology would be welcome because, next to and after a resolution of the specific *filioque* question, which is a highly nuanced question of trinitarian theology, such a direction would help focus attention on the wider role of the Spirit in the churches, society and creation today.

The Holy Spirit and the Apostolic Faith, A Roman Catholic Response

FRANCINE CARDMAN

TAKEN ON THE TERMS WHICH IT SETS FOR ITSELF, the *Spirit of God, Spirit of Christ* volume makes it unnecessary to repeat or revise the work of the consultations which it represents.[1] Numerous other recent studies, which need not occupy us here, corroborate its conclusions, expand on its main themes, and provide more extensive documentation of its historical and theological arguments.[2] What I intend to do, then, is to comment on some of the themes summarized in the Klingenthal memorandum, raise questions on some specific points, and evaluate its recommendations.

(1). The question of *use*—actual, experienced, Sunday to Sunday use—of the Nicene Creed is a fundamental question to be addressed to the work on the *filioque* controversy and, indeed, to the Apostolic

---

[1] *Spirit of God, Spirit of Christ: Ecumenical Reflections on the Filioque Controversy,* ed. L. Vischer, Faith and Order Paper No. 103 (Geneva, 1981). References to the Klingenthal memorandum and the essays in this volume will be given by page number in parentheses in the text.

[2] Yves Congar, *I Believe in the Holy Spirit,* 3 vols., trans. D. Smith (New York, 1983); *Credo in Spiritum Sanctum,* Atti del Congresso Theologico Internazionale di Pneumatologia, 2 vols. (Rome, 1983); see also the essays in *Conflicts About the Holy Spirit,* eds. H. Küng and J. Moltmann, Concilium 128 (New York, 1979).

Faith Study as a whole. In order to evaluate the significance of efforts to resolve the ancient and acrimonious controversy over the *filioque,* it is necessary to assess the importance that the Creed and the question of the Spirit's procession have for the life of the churches today. Is the question largely an academic matter, the concern of theologians, ecumenists and bureaucrats? As far as it is a live question for ordinary churchgoers, is work done on the level of Faith and Order likely to affect either experience or attitudes? If so, how? In a sense, this is simply the question again of *reception*—of any ecumenical work, convergence or text. But it is reception with a poignant twist, as the churches are being asked, in effect, to receive for a second time the deliberations of an ecumenical council (accepting the Symbol of Nicaea and Constantinople as the ecumenical expression of the apostolic faith) and, by so doing, simultaneously to resolve a long-standing conflict.

The introductory remarks to the memorandum (p. 3) recognize the question of use, as does recommendation C (p. 16), though not as much significance is given to it as I find necessary. On the one hand, this is, I think, at least a *Roman Catholic* concern that I am presenting, insofar as it touches on the continuing authority of tradition in the life of the Church. But it is also an *ecumenical* concern, insofar as it pertains to the eventual fruitfulness of the present work of Faith and Order. It can be argued that the three current projects (the reception of the *Baptism, Eucharist, Ministry* document, the study Toward a Common Confession of the Apostolic Faith, and the Unity of the Church/Renewal of Human Community study) represent a summing up of this century's efforts at visible unity via the pathway of Faith and Order. Indeed, many would hope that this summing up would be widely received by the turn of the century/millenium, as a prelude to more concrete steps and structures to manifest the unity of the Church. For this to happen, the question of use and the process of reception must be attended to most carefully in each of these three areas.

(2) In regard to the *filioque* controversy, the Klingenthal memorandum and its supporting papers clearly acknowledge the importance as well as the limitations of historical understanding of the theological and controversial development of the question. Deepened understandings of our divisive history on this matter must, moreover, be viewed in the context of a much broader shared faith in the Holy

Spirit[3] and a renewed interest in pneumatology in almost all the churches. Placed in this context, the work on the *filioque* represents a significant advance, for once the historical circumstances and theological intentions of the clause and its insertion into the Creed are understood and generally agreed on, it then becomes possible to consider a return to the original wording of the Creed.

(3) Likewise, locating the *filioque* discussion in the context of trinitarian faith and theology as it has developed in the Church's experience makes it possible to appreciate the degree of shared faith as well as to measure the extent of genuine difference realistically. Thus, it would help to alleviate over-emphasis on Jesus in some kinds of Christian spirituality if the "full and constant reciprocity of the incarnate Word and the Holy Spirit" (p. 9) were more carefully and consistently attended to, especially in catechesis and preaching. The warning not to carry too far the conceptual distinctions between the economic and immanent Trinity, or the temporal mission and eternal procession is well taken. If anything, this point needs to be made even more strongly and observed more consistently, particularly in regard to some of the theological reflections in the fourth section of the memorandum.

(4) In its treatment of the place of the Son in relation to the procession of the Holy Spirit, the memorandum appears to have taken to heart its own admonition that our reflections on the immanent Trinity must be guided by the revelation of the economic Trinity. By failing to heed its own advice when considering the Spirit's role in the generation of the Son, however, the Klingenthal statement seems to have violated this principle. One is left with the impression that it is only in the earthly begetting of the Son that the Spirit plays a role, but not in the eternal generation. Two tantalizing phrases from the memorandum's list (p. 16) of possible alternative formulations for the relationship of Spirit and Son therefore deserve further reflection and development: "the Spirit proceeds from the Father and rests on the Son"; and "the Spirit proceeds from the Father and shines out through the Son."

A second problem arises in the way in which the Klingenthal

---

[3] As Andre de Halleux points out in "Towards an Ecumenical Agreement on the Procession of the Holy Spirit and the Addition of the *Filioque* to the Creed," *Spirit of God, Spirit of Christ*, pp. 74-75. See also Michael Fahey, "Son and Spirit: Divergent Theologies between Constantinople and the West," *Conflicts About the Holy Spirit*, pp. 15-16.

statement appears to give temporal priority to the generation of the Son in the inner-trinitarian life, despite disclaimers in this regard and acknowledgment of eastern difficulties with any suggestion of temporal priority (p. 15). By emphasizing that it is "the Father of the *Son*" from whom the Spirit proceeds (pp. 13-15), the memorandum appears to reinforce a position it claims to want to exclude. The statement asserts that "*it should be said* that the procession of the Spirit from the Father *presupposes* [emphasis mine] the relationship existing within the Trinity between the Father and the Son, for the Son is eternally in and with the Father, and the Father is never without the Son" (p. 15). Should it not, then, also be said that the generation of the Son presupposes the relationship existing within the Trinity between the Father and the Spirit, since the Spirit is eternally in and with the Father (is the Spirit of God as well as the Spirit of Christ),[4] and the Father is never without the breath and love of the Spirit?

(5) Finally, the Klingenthal memorandum rightly concludes that the *filioque* question must be placed in the even broader context of the revitalization and reappropriation of trinitarian theology in the life of the churches, and not only among theologians and ecumenists. Only then will Faith and Order work on the question begin to bear lasting fruit.

Recommendations to the NCCC

A. That the process of education for reception be recognized as twofold: as flowing from Faith and Order and its participants to their churches; and, perhaps more importantly, from the churches to Faith and Order. By acting on this recognition in its own response to the Apostolic Faith study, the NCCC can model for the WCC the far-more contextual, grassroots or listening approach that this study and the *filioque* project still require.

B. That the NCCC develop materials for use in parishes and local churches to evoke and foster the understanding and expression of trinitarian faith in worship, in communal structures and patterns of

---

[4]This despite Moltmann's assertion that "God the Father is always the Father of the Son. He is never simply 'universal Father'. . . He is not called 'Father' merely because he is the unique cause on whom all things depend" (p. 167). Similarly, "the Father is in eternity solely the Father of the Son. He is not the Father of the Spirit" (ibid).

relationship within the Church, in spirituality, and in mission. Particular though not exclusive attention should be given to the person and work of the Holy Spirit in the life of the Church and the individual believer.

C. That the NCCC recommend to its member churches that the original text of the Creed of Nicaea-Constantinople (i.e., without the *filioque*) be accepted as the common form of this historical confession of the apostolic faith. Further, that churches that do not (or only rarely) use the Creed in their worship be encouraged to include it on suitable occasions and with some regularity. At the same time it follows that churches that use the Creed exclusively in their liturgical celebrations should be encouraged to find opportunities in their common prayer for more contemporary confessions of the apostolic faith as well.

D. That the NCCC, in its dealings with its member churches, and especially in its response to Faith and Order, urge that the Apostolic Faith study give more serious and sustained attention to the recommendations addressed to it from the Community of Women and Men in the Church study. In particular, emphasis should be placed on the Community study's restatement of the question of acceptance of the Creed: "Are the language, thought and imagery of the Nicene Creed sufficiently inclusive to keep together the community of women and men . . .?" In other words, "Is it possible for the *community of women and men* [emphasis mine], the earthly form of the body of Christ, to accept the Nicene Creed?"[5]

As its recommendations suggest, the Community study has implications for every article of the Creed. In regard to this consultation on the Holy Spirit, two points are of particular importance. The first is the Community study's recommendation that "the trinitarian language of the Creed needs particularly careful investigation," especially in regard to the adequacy of what many perceive as the exclusive terminology of Father, Son and Holy Spirit, and the possibility of "new terms for confessing our belief in the Holy Trinity."[6] In its own work on the Apostolic Faith study, then, the NCCC should

---

[5]"The Community Study and Apostolic Faith: Memorandum from the Working Group on the Community of Women and Men in the Church," in *Towards Visible Unity,* Commission on Faith and Order, Lima 1982, Faith and Order Paper No. 112 (Geneva, 1982), vol. 2, pp. 47, 48.

[6]Ibid.

continue to make it a priority to address the question of language and imagery with all the care and resources at its disposal. The second is a point that I would add: that the role of the Holy Spirit in the inspiration and empowerment of women and other powerless persons and groups within the churches should be explored in its historical manifestations and its contemporary ramifications. This would involve considering questions of authority and community, as well as structures of ministry and decision-making in relation to the work of Spirit.

E. That the NCCC take an active role, not only in the United States but at the World Council level as well, in the development and implementation of the second phase of the Apostolic Faith study, "towards the common explication of this apostolic faith in the contemporary situation of the churches." In particular, it should seek to ensure that this phase of the study employs a contextual and grassroots methodology modeled after the Community of Women and Men and the Giving an Account of Hope studies.

F. That the NCCC recognize that the most important contribution that the churches of the United States can make to the Apostolic Faith project is to help keep it firmly grounded in the real world of faith today and related to the pressing concerns of persons and groups who had no part in the process of creedmaking in the early Church. Indeed, if the experience of the Church in the sociopolitical context of the fourth century teaches us anything, it is that creeds by themselves do not suffice to safeguard either the unity of the Church or the inclusiveness of its community.

Roman Catholic Recommendations and Concerns

All the above recommendations to the NCCC should be taken to apply to the member churches and to the Roman Catholic Church as well. Here I want to raise some concerns and make some recommendations that apply specifically to the Roman Catholic Church.

A. That the Roman Catholic Church, through the appropriate bodies, restore the original text of the Creed of Nicaea-Constantinople in its liturgical books and other usages.

By returning to the original text, without the *filioque*, one important step toward healing the divisions between the churches of the West and those of the East will have been taken. In addition to expressing good faith and humility, such action would also reflect and encourage the mutual renewal of trinitarian theology throughout the churches. Advances in both historical and theological understanding now make such a move possible. The historical evidence about the manner in which the *filioque* came to be incorporated into the Creed in the West suggests that, while there may have been theological motivations for the regional use of the phrase, it was largely a matter of historical accident that this text of the Creed spread throughout the Carolingian empire in the early ninth century and was adopted into Roman usage several centuries later. Similarly, contemporary theological developments and convergences have made it possible to recognize the shortcomings of both controverted positions as customarily expounded, and to argue strongly for returning to the original text of the Creed as formulated at Constantinople in 381 and affirmed and acknowledged as the standard confession of faith at Ephesos in 381 and Chalcedon in 451.

In 1981 John Paul II demonstrated graphically his desire to restore the original text by twice quoting the article on the Holy Spirit without the *filioque.* In his letter to the Roman Catholic bishops' conferences asking them to send representatives to Rome for Pentecost ceremonies that year, the Pope announced his intention of commemorating the 1600th anniversary of the Council of Constantinople and, in particular, its heritage of doctrine on the Holy Spirit. He then quoted the text of 381: "I believe in the Holy Spirit, the Lord, the giver of life, who proceeds from the Father. With the Father and the Son he is worshiped and glorified. He has spoken through the prophets." John Paul's remarks for the Pentecost celebration, which he was unable to attend due to his injuries in the assassination attempt, repeated the point made in the letter:

> We wish to confess with a loud cry of our voices and our hearts the truth that sixteen centuries ago the First Council of Constantinople formulated and expressed in the words we know so well. We wish to express that truth as it was then expressed: "We believe in the Holy Spirit, the Lord, the giver of life, who proceeds from the Father. With the Father and the Son he is worshiped and glorified. He has spoken through the prophets."

The quotation from the Creed was given first in Greek and then in Latin—not the familiar text of medieval and later liturgies, but the

Latin formula from the fifth session of the Council of Chalcedon.[7]

In both these documents John Paul repeatedly punctuated his text with the phrase "Credo in Spiritum Sanctum, dominum et vivificantem." And except for the explicit reference to returning to the ancient formula, no direct mention is made of the *filioque* as a point of contention between the Roman Catholic and Orthodox Churches. Indeed, the very downplaying of the *filioque* in the Pope's remarks argues that he, at least, does not consider it an obstacle to unity.

Additional support for returning to the ancient formula follows from the treatment of the Creed in the modern Greek version of the Roman rite today. There, the Byzantine text of the Creed is used, in which the *filioque* does not appear, and the Sacred Congregation for the Doctrine of the Faith expressly prohibits the use of the *filioque* in the vernacular Greek Mass. The International Orthodox/ Roman Catholic Commission likewise lends support for restoring the original text. In its discussions in Crete in 1984, the Commission recommended that the text of 381/451 be understood as the "Ecumenical Creed," to be used for occasions of worship between Eastern and Western churches. As a corollary to this recommendation, it was suggested that individual churches might also make use of this text if they wished.[8]

Given the Pope's example, the implications of current liturgical practice, and the recommendations of the International Commission, Roman Catholic theologians and even curial officials should have no hesitation in moving promptly and purposefully to restoring the integrity of the original text of the Creed.

---

[7] ". . .et in Spiritum Sanctum dominum and vivificatorem, ex Patre procedentem, cum Patre et Filio adorandum et conglorificandum, qui locutus est per prophetas." For the letter of March 25, 1981 see *Acta Apostolica Sedis* 78/8 (1 Oct. 1981) 515. The French text of the letter appears in *Irenikon* 54/2 (1981) 250, along with a report and comment on the Pentecost observances in the same issue, particularly pp. 223-28. In this regard it is amusing to note that the English translation of the letter in *Origins* 10/44 (Apr. 16, 1981) has the Pope quoting the current English text of the Roman rite: (the Holy Spirit) "who proceeds from the Father *and the Son*" (p. 698). Whether this is due to a slip of the typewriter or a lapse in credulity, I do not know.

[8] The Byzantine text of the Our Father is also used in the modern Greek version of the Roman rite. Documentation of the Crete meeting is not due to be published until the summer of 1986. For information on both these points I am indebted to John Long, SJ, in conversation.

B. That as a step to the full restoration of the original text of the Creed, and in order to familiarize both pastors and faithful with the forthcoming change, the Greek and Latin texts of Constantinople and Chalcedon be authorized as *alternative* texts (in translation) for occasional liturgical use in the interim. Appropriate educational and pastoral efforts should accompany this change in practice.

C. That more careful consideration be given to the *operative* theology of orders and church structure that popular understandings of the *filioque* seem to encourage. (I include here the opinions of bishops and priests, not simply those of the presumedly theologically uneducated.)

It is a prerequisite to ecumenical discourse to reject caricature and polemical misrepresentation of controverted theological positions. Little, however, is gained by overlooking problems that such ecumenical etiquette can mask. Thus, for instance, in rejecting as exaggerated and uncritical the oftentimes polemical claim that, in subordinating the Spirit to the Son, the *filioque* leads to a subordination of Church to Pope as vicar of Christ, or of charism/Spirit to office, it is all too easy to overlook the way in which such assumptions do in fact function in the Roman Church.[9] Even without explicit appeal to the *filioque* for justification, a common understanding of orders seems to attribute to Christ the gift of the Spirit in the sacramental act of ordination, so that the Spirit is seen as originating from him, rather than as being given by Christ as the Spirit he always receives from another (the Father). A similar effect can be observed in the treatment of the epiclesis in the renewed Roman rite following Vatican II. While it cannot be denied that the invocation of the Spirit has been restored to prominence in the eucharistic prayer, nevertheless the placement and the division of the epiclesis in that prayer deserve attention. In attempting to reconcile a traditional theological understanding of the consecratory significance of the words of institution with the renewed emphasis on the work of the Spirit, the Roman rite resorts to placing part of the epiclesis— the prayer to the Father to "send your Spirit upon these gifts to make them holy, that they might become for us the body and blood of our Lord, Jesus Christ"—*before* the words of institution and part *after*—

---

[9]Thus, ironically, I find myself in disagreement with Theodore Stylianopoulos' sincere admonition to his Orthodox colleagues in his essay on "The Orthodox Position," in *Conflicts About the Holy Spirit,* p. 30.

"May all of us who share in the body and blood of Christ be brought together in unity by the Holy Spirit." Thus the epiclesis is weakened and stands in uneasy relationship to a theology which identifies the consecration of the bread and wine with the priest's repetition of the words of Jesus.[10]

Turning from the *Spirit of God, Spirit of Christ* work and recommendations for the Apostolic Faith Study, I want now to take up several current issues in regard to the Holy Spirit and the naming of God.

---

[10]Despite scholarly and theological opinions to the contrary, I have long felt—ever since first trying to understand the controversy—that the *filioque* functioned in a particular fashion to legitimate the kind of Western understanding of Spirit, order and orders that I have been describing here. The example of the epiclesis, and the particular way of putting the question of the Spirit in orders, I owe to Peter Fink, SJ, in conversation. Hermann Haring, in "The Role of the Spirit in the Legitimation of Ecclesial Office," illustrates the opposite point of view (in *Conflicts About the Holy Spirit,* 74). He argues (rightly) that the linking of office and Spirit is also and perhaps especially an *Eastern legacy,* and not simply a Western or Roman question. He goes on to note that the link between Spirit and ecclesial office is a real question for the churches of the Reformation as well. Although I concur with his arguments, I nevertheless find that they tend to mask the reality of the rhetoric and experience of orders that has been commonplace in the Roman Church. For this reason it is interesting to see how Jürgen Moltmann handles the question in his dialogue with Elisabeth Moltmann Wendel at the Sheffield Conference ("Becoming Human in New Community," in *The Community of Women and Men in the Church,* ed. C. Parvey, [Philadelphia, 1983], pp. 29-42). There, in responding to Elisabeth's comment that "the Holy Spirit was chained to official ministries and robbed of the renewing power," Jürgen frankly acknowledges that "the Church quite early in its history tied the Holy Spirit to successive holders of the episcopal office." Further, he points out that:

> The Western Church also tied the Spirit to the chain of Christology by means of the *Filioque* clause in the Nicene Creed. The Spirit then becomes simply the internal subjective reality of Christ, of the Word and sacraments of the Church. No room is left for the creatively new or for the surprises of the Holy Spirit, not even room to expect them (p. 14).

This is, I think, a more accurate representation of the actual reality of the effects of the *filioque* on the practical understanding of office and orders in the Roman Church.

CONTEMPORARY ISSUES: NAMING GOD

Confident that traditional aspects of the doctrine of the Holy Spirit and of the Trinity will receive sufficient coverage in this consultation, I want to address here the issue of trinitarian language and imagery as it arises in the context of questions about the inclusivity and wholeness of theological vision. I do so not only out of my Roman Catholic tradition, but also out of the feminist community within and beyond that tradition, with whom I also stand.

The question of language has been raised extensively enough both in feminist theory and feminist theology not to need documentation here.[11] It is sufficient to note that exclusively (or predominantly) masculine imagery, the assumption that masculine grammatical forms are generic, and the language of domination and alienation are commonly thought to be inadequate representations of the fullness of human reality and experience. Rather than being exempt from charges of exlusivity or sexism, theological language is particularly susceptible to them, seeking as it does to speak truly not only of humankind but also of God. Measured against standards of inclusivity, the language of faith is found to be inadequate to the realities it attempts to describe, thereby leaving itself open to the liabilities of both idolatry and mystification.

Perhaps the most obvious place in which the language of faith reveals its limitations and exclusivity is in the Christian doctrine of the Trinity: Father, Son and Holy Spirit. In a church which makes constant use of the sign of the cross and rather frequent reference to the blessed Trinity, one is struck again and again by the overwhelmingly masculine nature of the image conveyed by this naming of God. When Christian tradition then goes on to speak of humankind as

---

[11]For the general case about sexist language, see Dale Splender, *Man = Made Language* (London and Boston, 1980); for more detailed and technical studies see the essays in *Sexist Language: A Modern Philosophical Analysis,* ed. Mary Vetterling Braggin, (Totowa, NJ, 1981), and *Language, Gender and Society,* eds. Barrie Thorne, Cheris Kramarae, and Nancy Henley, (Rowley, MA, 1983). For language in theology and religious education, see Marianne Sawicki, *Faith and Sexism: Guidelines for Religious Educators* (New York, 1979). And for analysis of the effects of sexism in language on a theological discipline, see Beverly Harrison, "Sexism and the Language of Christian Ethics," in her *Making the Connections: Essays in Feminist Social Ethics,* ed. C. Robb, (Boston, 1985), pp. 22-41.

created in the *imago Dei,* it is no wonder that our social and inter-personal relationships are characterized by gender-stratification and patterns of domination and subordination.

Concerns about language and its social and ecclesial implications are not new to members of this consultation or to the NCCC. Nevertheless, our reflections on the Holy Spirit and on a particular linguistic problem—the *filioque*—have helped focus for me the problem of the naming of God and the role of the Spirit in that naming. In the remainder of this paper, therefore, I propose to consider some particular questions about speaking of the Spirit in the framework of traditional trinitarian language, as well as to present some of the alternative ways of naming and imaging the Trinity currently being explored in feminist theology.

The Holy Spirit and the Language of the Trinity

In a dialogue presentation at the Sheffield Conference which concluded the Community of Women and Men in the Church study, Elisabeth Moltmann-Wendel and Jürgen Moltmann spoke together about "Becoming Human in New Community."[12] Both commented on the masculine nature of trinitarian language and sought more adequate expressions. It is perhaps typical of many women and men in the Church today that Jürgen looked for alternatives or corrective possibilities within the tradition, while Elisabeth spoke enthusiastically about the powers of women's imagination and "theo-fantasy" as partner with "theo-logy." For Elisabeth, new images of God will emerge especially from women's experience; for Jürgen, newly rediscovered images will arise from within the tradition. Neither approach is sufficient in itself for the reconstruction of our language about God, but both are necessary. In order to honor both approaches, I will begin here from Jürgen's remarks and relate to them to his work for the *filioque* consultation; and in the following section I will consider some of the possibilities opened up by Elisabeth's comments.

In his part of the Sheffield presentation, Moltmann suggested that the "maternal office of the Holy Spirit, the divine motherhood" is a suppressed tradition that has surfaced from time to time in Christian

---

[12]In *The Community of Women and Men in the Church,* ed. Constance Parvey, (Philadelphia, 1983), pp. 29-42.

history and ought to be reclaimed today.[13] He found it helpful "not only because it discovers the female principle in the Godhead but also because it picks up an element of the truth in pan[en]theism," since, with the Spirit as our mother we can experience ourselves as "in God" and not just "under God." A similar line of thought is pursued by Yves Congar in his work on the Holy Spirit, in which he promotes the "femininity of the Holy Spirit" and propounds the Spirit's "maternal function" as the expression of "motherhood in God."[14] Significant difficulties, however, arise out of efforts to speak of only one person of the Trinity as feminine while the other two persons remain masculine. Rather than advancing either the linguistic problem or trinitarian conceptuality, such efforts serve simply to reinforce a practical subordinationism within the Trinity (so that the one female figure appears of lesser significance than the two male figures) and a social subordinationism (of women to men) within the human community.[15]

Other reasons for speaking of the Spirit as feminine are commonly adduced: in most Semitic languages "spirit" is feminine in gender; Wisdom, often associated with the Spirit, is a female personification of God's presence with humanity. Although Moltmann does not employ these arguments, Congar and many others do. In any case, they are subject to the same difficulty raised above. Further, because in Christian tradition Wisdom is early identified with Christ and her attributes taken on by the Logos, the proper role and reality of the Spirit tend to be overshadowed by the christological appropriation of Wisdom, despite the use of a fuller range of masculine and feminine images in this naming of God.[16]

Taking a somewhat different approach to the question of how to

---

[13]Ibid., p. 36. Cf. *The Trinity and the Kingdom* (San Francisco, 1981) pp. 164-65.

[14]*I Believe in the Holy Spirit*, 3, pp. 155-62.

[15]See, for instance, Margaret Farley, "New Patterns of Relationship: Beginnings of a Moral Revolution," *Theological Studies* 36/4 (1975) 643; and Mary Rose D'Angelo, "Beyond Father and Son," in *Justice as Mission: An Agenda for the Church*," eds. T. Brown and C. Lind, (Burlington, Ontario, Canada, 1985), pp. 107-18.

[16]For the limitations of this approach, see Elizabeth Johnson, "The Incomprehensibility of God and the Image of God Male and Female," *Theological Studies* 45 (1984) 457-60; and D'Angelo, pp. 112-13.

incorporate the feminine into the Godhead, Moltmann argued, in another article from the same year as the Sheffield dialogue, that an understanding of the "motherly Father" and "a trinitarian patripassianism" seem to be in the process of replacing "theological patriarchalism." In that argument, the trinitarian lopsidedness remains but is weighted toward the Father, who now takes on maternal as well as paternal characteristics, not only begetting (fathering) the Son, but giving birth to (mothering) him as well.[17] Here the attribution of female qualities to one of the persons of the Trinity does not reduce that person in stature, but, because he retains the masculine "Father" qualities at the same time, the valence of this persona is instead increased.

There are several difficulties to this approach to trinitarian imagery and language. The first is the imbalance that results from all efforts to "incorporate the feminine" into what remains a predominantly and, presumably, normatively masculine God. The second is the literal meaning that Moltmann attaches to the fatherhood of God. Moltmann understands the begetting of the Son, as well as the generative relationship by which we become daughters and sons of the Father, to be the *literal* sense of the way in which God is Father. This stands in sharp contrast, for instance, to the metaphorical sense which he gives to the affirmation that the Father is "almighty creator and lord of all things."[18] One is led to ask what is at stake in Moltmann's insistence on a literal meaning of fatherhood.

The *filioque* discussions provide a clue to Moltmann's motivations. In both his essay in the *Spirit of God, Spirit of Christ* volume and in the Klingenthal memorandum there is a marked christological skewing of the Trinity. Moltmann argues that it is only through Christ that the true—the "literal"—meaning of God as Father can be known: "It is only in relationship with his Son that God can literally be called Father." Indeed, his trinitarian theology rests on a christological presupposition: "The doctrine of the Trinity does not deify Christ but 'christifies' God, because it pulls the Father into the life-story of the Son."[19] Moltmann therefore asserts that, "God the

---

[17]"The Motherly Father," in *God as a Father?* eds. J. Metz and E. Schillebeeckx, Concilium 143 (New York, 1981) 53.

[18]Ibid. p. 51.

[19]Ibid. p. 53.

Father is always the Father of the Son. . . . It is solely and exclusively in the eternal begetting of the eternal Son that God shows himself as the 'Father'."[20] In its insistence that the Father from whom the Spirit proceeds is the Father *of the Son,* the Klingenthal memorandum bears the imprint of Moltmann's thought. The Spirit is understood as the Spirit of the Son, by whose inspiration we are able to call God "Father" (Rom 8.15; 2 Cor 3.17). Thus, in an odd sort of way, it is the *Son* who becomes the *arche* of the Trinity on his view.

A christologically skewed Trinity is as unbalanced as a Trinity in which only one of the persons is feminine, or in which only one person is both masculine and feminine. What is lacking in each case is the radical equality, even in the differentiation of persons, that must be the basis for trinitarian conceptualization. It is simply not adequate to consider only *one* person of the Trinity to be feminine; *all* must be. Or, better, all must be both masculine and feminine. It may be possible to get a hint of why Moltmann shies away from naming each person as feminine when he remarks that, "The Christian doctrine of the Trinity, with its affirmations about the motherly Father, represents a first step towards limiting the use of masculine terminology to express the idea of God, *"without, however, changing over to matriarchal conceptions"* (emphasis mine).[21]

Fear of matriarchy, or, perhaps more accurately, fear of the full emergence of the repressed feminine/female, both symbolically and socially, is no more conducive to a true naming of God than is exclusively masculine language. In any case, false naming of God flirts with idolatry, all the more so when that naming is raised to unchallenged norm and taken to be the expression of unalterable truth. While not wishing to claim that Moltmann holds such a view, I do find a serious inconsistency to his proposals. On the one hand, he recognizes the limitations of masculine terminology and the need to overcome its exclusivity. On the other hand, he is extremely hesitant to go beyond the approach of simply looking for a less patriarchal and more Christian meaning of "Father." Others tread more perilous ground than he when they contend that the *only* legitimate naming of the triune God is as Father, Son and Holy Spirit.

---

[20]"Theological Proposals Towards the Resolution of the Filioque Controversy," in *Spirit of God, Spirit of Christ,* p. 167.

[21]"The Motherly Father," p. 53.

For the Christian tradition demonstrates that alternative namings were possible and acceptable (e.g., Augustine's "psychological analogies" for the Trinity, culminating in the familiar "memory, understanding and will"), just as, it can be argued, the tradition itself demands more adequate namings in our own times in order to make known the saving mystery of this God.[22] I turn, then, to the efforts of feminist theology to name God in the power of the Holy Spirit and in the light of women's experience.

New Namings of God

Language both reflects and gives form to reality. In Christian experience this can be seen most graphically in Paul's reflections on the gracious effects of the Spirit within us, enabling us to call God "Abba," bearing witness with us to our relationship to God, and interceding for us with sighs too deep for words (Rom 8.15-16,26). On the one hand, it is because we are sons and daughters that God has sent the Spirit into our hearts, crying "Abba" (Gal 4.6); on the other, it is because we cry "Abba" that we are children and heirs of God (Rom 8.15-16). Language, then, the gift of the Spirit, both reflects a reality that already exists and at the same time continues to call that reality into being. It conveys a sense both of the structure of human community and a sense, as Beverly Harrison puts it, of "power-in-relationship."[23] That is what makes false naming so constricting and damaging, and true naming so freeing and empowering. This final section, therefore, examines some of the current feminist efforts to reimage and name God more inclusively, and concludes with the suggestion that such undertakings are themselves manifestations of the same reflective and creative power of the Spirit that Paul saw at work in the early Christian community.

The feminist revisioning of God begins from a critique of God = language that by now has become common currency. In addition to stressing the world-shaping function of language, this critique analyzes the significance of gender relations in establishing and distorting

---

[22]See Catherine M. LaCugna's reconceptualization of the Trinity in soteriological terms, which argues for new models and imagery as well as for a closer connection between pneumatology and Christology: "Re-conceiving the Trinity as the Mystery of Salvation," in *Scottish Journal of Theology* 38 (1985) 1-23.

[23]Harrison, p. 24.

patterns of social relationship, which then in turn inform the structures of language in ways that reinforce the social reality of inequality and domination in human relationships.[24] Ethical questions of fundamental importance arise from this analysis: how to account morally for the nearly universal patterns of social subjugation; how to overcome the consequences of our tolerance for such subjugation at the interpersonal level and its translation into tolerance for sociocommunal forms of subjugation; how to reconstruct the foundations of equality from the theoretical sources of inequality.[25] Newly emerging patterns of male-female relationship, the increasing value that women are placing on their own experience, and the pressure exerted by these and other ethical questions all argue for the necessity of new namings of both divine and human reality. The challenge of feminist theology is forcefully described by Elizabeth Johnson: "Is the God of the Judeo-Christian tradition so true as to be able to take account of, illumine, and integrate the currently accessible experience of women?"[26]

Efforts to answer that question affirmatively have taken three basic forms: 1) incorporating "feminine traits" into the patriarchal image of God the Father; 2) developing an understanding of the "feminine dimension" of the divine, particularly but not exclusively in terms of the feminity of the Holy Spirit: and 3) beginning to image God equivalently as male and female.[27] The first and second approaches have largely been the province of male theologians (e.g., Visser't Hooft, Congar, Moltmann), the third more usually the approach of women (e.g., Farley, Harrison, Ruether). The first two approaches founder on the rock of gender stereotyping, and the second is subject to the additional liability of a skewed trinitarian formulation. The third, however, offers considerable hope for the future of both God-language and human community.

In a germinal essay from 1975 on "New Patterns of Relationship: Beginnings of a Moral Revolution," Margaret Farley examines the

---

[24]E.g., Harrison, pp. 24-25; Farley, "New Patterns of Relationship," p. 629 and "Sources of Sexual Inequality in the History of Christian Thought," *Journal of Religion* 56 (1976) 167; Johnson, p. 442; D'Angelo, pp. 107-08.

[25]Harrison, pp. 26-27; Farley, "Sources," p. 169.

[26]Johnson, p. 445.

[27]The threefold typology is Johnson's, p. 454 ff.

ethical significance of changing social roles and interpersonal relationships between women and men. In analyzing the challenges these
changes present to our understanding of the norms of Christian agape
(equal regard, self-sacrifice and mutuality), she makes several important suggestions about the reconstruction of trinitarian doctrine as
a model of mutuality.[28]

She argues that "Christian theology has failed to grant equality to women precisely in so far as it has failed to attribute to women
the fulness of the image of God," and she asks "whether sexual
identity does indeed give graded shares in the *Imago Dei*" and
whether God's self-revelation as Trinity includes "revelation of a
model of interpersonal love which is based upon equality and infinite mutuality."[29] Farley concludes that there are solid grounds
for "naming each of the persons in the Trinity feminine as well
as masculine," though her major example is restricted to Father/
Son or Mother/Daughter, and is justified by the changed understandings of human generativity, on the one hand, and the changed
social position of women and of male/female relationships on the
other.

By appealing to Augustine, she is able to make the argument
more nearly trinitarian: "With Augustine new images were introduced . . . which described a triune life in which all that the Father
is communicated to the Son, and all that the Son receives is returned to the Father, and the life of utter mutuality, communion,
which they share, is the Spirit."[30] At this point her argument suffers from the same problem that all Western trinitarian thought has
so far experienced: the difficulty of conceiving a truly personal and
"life-size" role for the Spirit, along the lines of the much fuller and
more integral portraits of Father and Son that Western theology has
traditionally drawn. Even in the truncated two-person form
characteristic of Western trinitarian theology, Farley's argument
comes to very different conclusions than do the classical expositions in regard to what this model of Trinity reveals, both for
our understanding of God and our understanding of human relationships. I quote part of her rhetorical summing-up of this
point:

---

[28]Pp. 640-43.

[29]Ibid. p. 640. LaCugna makes a similar point, pp. 13-14.

[30]Ibid. p. 642.

Is it not possible on this account to describe the First Person as masculine and the Second Person as feminine and the bond which is the infinite communion between them (the Spirit of both) as necessarily both masculine and feminine? Do we not have here revealed a relationship in which both the First Person and the Second Person are infinitely active and infinitely receptive, infinitely giving and infinitely receiving, holding in infinite mutuality and reciprocity a totally shared life? Do we not have here, in any case, a model of relationship which is not hierarchical, which is marked by total equality, and which is offered to us in Christian revelation as the model for relationship with Christ and for our relationships in the Church with one another?[31]

Many would respond that we do—or at least that we have the lineaments of such a model. Farley's suggestions are affirmed in the statement on "Authority-in-Community" offered by a study group of the NCCC's Commission on Faith and Order as part of the Community of Women and Men in the Church study.[32] Arguing that "the absence of subordination or inequality in the Trinity ought to be reflected in the community of women and men," the statement concludes that adequate imaging of God in the structures of language and of human community requires deeper reflection on and greater appreciation of the mutual relatedness of the Trinity, as well as common use of a wider range of language and the imagery of many "trinities."[33] Similar conclusions are reached by Elizabeth Johnson and Catherine LaCugna in their reflections on language and the doctrine of God.[34]

A very helpful contribution to expanding the range of trinitarian language is offered by Mary Rose D'Angelo in an essay entitled "Beyond Father and Son."[35] There she demonstrates that exclusively male language for the Trinity "evokes a theological context that has been abusive of women," and she argues that biblical and theological

---

[31]Ibid. pp. 643.

[32]The paper produced by the study group was drafted by Madeleine Boucher, "Authority-in-Community," *Mid-Stream* 21 (1982) 402-17; see particularly pp. 406-11.

[33]Ibid. pp. 408, 410.

[34]Johnson, pp. 460, 463; LaCugna, pp. 17, 19.

[35]See reference in n. 15 above.

tradition not only permits but requires the use of alternative trinitarian formulations. She then makes two critical methodological observations. The first is that substitution of a single formula for "Father,
Son and Spirit" will not be sufficient either to overcome the inherent
subordinationism of most traditional trinitarian language or to exor-
cize the damaging effects on women of language that separates and
alienates the female from God. Rather, what is needed is "to reduce
drastically our use of these terms, especially in the liturgy, and to
juxtapose and overwhelm them with a flood of alternative language
and imagery."[36]

Her second methodological point has to do with the supposed
uniqueness, hence normativity, of Jesus' naming of God as "Father."
Arguments that "Jesus' use of 'Father' was radically different from
contemporary Jewish and Greek theology are," she asserts, "extremely
weak, and frequently tinged with anti-Judaism." Instead, she con-
tends that:

> Historical and moral responsibility are better served if we assume
> that this name for God came to Jesus and the Church with the
> heritage of Judaism and spoke profoundly to Jew and Greek alike
> of God's being as author and sustainer of life and of our being
> as God's kin. Our obligation to the New Testament witness is
> not to repeat the title for its sacredness, but to sanctify God's
> name in words that ever more fully disclose its call upon our be-
> ing and its challenge to human dominions.[37]

A multiplicity of names for God is therefore needed. It is not only
Son and Spirit that need to be reconceptualized—whether along the
lines of Wisdom christology or feminine imagery of the Spirit (with
their attendant limitations)—but also the Father. D'Angelo considers
Phyllis Trible's recovery of the vivid Old Testament metaphor of God
as womb (from the root *rhm*, womb/mercy/have compassion) an

---

[36]Ibid. p. 111.

[37]D'Angelo points out (n. 27) that the customary arguments for the
uniqueness of Jesus' use of "Father" all depend on an argument by J. Jere-
mias, "Abba," in *The Prayers of Jesus* (London, 1967), pp. 11-65, and she
suggests instead that "a more sophisticated and sympathetic reading of the
same evidence would conclude that Jesus and the New Testament were part
of the evidence for first-century Jewish use of 'Father' in prayer."

important contribution to the revisioning of the Father, as is Elisabeth Schüssler Fiorenza's suggestion that "Wisdom" was as central to Jesus' understanding of God as was "Father."

At the conclusion of her essay, D'Angelo presents a number of alternative trinitarian formulas, fashioned from the rich biblical imagery of light, water, wisdom, yearning, and compassionate mother-love:

Creator, Redeemer, Sanctifier
Creator, Liberator, Advocate
Wise God, Wisdom of God, Spirit of Wisdom
God, Source of Being; Christ, Channel of Life; Spirit, Living Water

And she offers as well some brief trinitarian invocations:

Mothering God, make us drink the spirit that flows from the breast
of Christ
From the womb of your compassion, O God, bring forth in us
a new order of justice and equality, that the Spirit may breathe
freely in all who share Christ's humanity.[38]

If it was in the power and freedom of the Spirit that Paul and other early Christians were able to call God "Father," it is equally possible—indeed, likely—that it is also in the power and freedom of the Spirit that women today are calling on that same God by names that move us "beyond Father and Son." At Sheffield Elisabeth Moltmann-Wendel commented on a fact that scholars in biblical and historical-theological fields have begun to notice once again: the way in which, as she puts it, "in the long history of the patriarchal Church women were able again and again to breach the dominant structures in the power of the Holy Spirit. But the Church constantly distrusted both women and the Spirit, condemning their works as extremism, heresy, paganism."[39] The communities created by these periodic

---

[38]Ibid. p. 113.

[39]"Becoming Human in New Community," p. 41. For historical analysis see Elisabeth Schüssler Fiorenza, *In Memory of Her: A Feminist Theological Reconstruction of Christian Origins* (New York, 1983), pp. 130-51, and her essay "Word, Spirit and Power: Women in Early Christian Communities," in *Women of Spirit: Female Leadership in the Jewish and Christian Traditions*, ed. R. Ruether and E. McLaughlin (New York, 1979), pp. 30-70. Also,

outpourings of the Spirit were egalitarian in character and stood in sharp contrast to the increasingly patriarchialized institution that claimed the name "Church" exclusively for itself. Today that Church is again being offered, through the unexpected and even at times unwanted gifts of the Spirit, a chance to turn from patriarchal modes of being and to become instead the new community of women and men, a community joined together in the memory and expectation of Jesus, empowered by the radiant love of the Spirit to live in the presence of the inclusive reign of God. And the urgent question that faces us is this: will we be able, this time, to receive the "hint half guessed, the gift half understood,"[40] and make incarnate among us that new community?

Elaine C. Huber, *Women and the Authority of Inspiration: A Reexamination of Two Prophetic Movements from a Contemporary Feminist Perspective* (Lanham, MD., 1985), pp. 20-64.

[40]T. S. Eliot, "The Dry Salvages," from *Four Quartets,* in *Collected Poems 1909-1962* (N.Y, 1970), p. 199.

Let the Spirit Come: Lutheran Interpretation of the Holy Spirit

MARTHA ELLEN STORTZ

INTRODUCTION

But the Holy Spirit has called me through the Gospel, enlightened me with his gifts, and sanctified and preserved me in true faith, just as he calls, gathers, enlightens and sanctifies the whole Christian church on earth and preserves it in union with Jesus Christ in the one true faith. Martin Luther, *Small Catechism,* Explanation to the Third Article.[1]

CALLS, GATHERS, ENLIGHTENS, SANCTIFIES, PRESERVES: these five verbs elaborate Luther's thinking on the work of the Spirit. The work of the Spirit was at the heart of Luther's debate with Rome, on the one hand, and with the radical reformers, on the other. The work of the Spirit was the subject of this *inter*-ecclesial Reformation controversy.

The work of the Spirit was also the subject of a more recent and *intra*-ecclesial controversy: discussion between charismatic and non-charismatic Lutherans. The work of the Spirit was the subject of much theological rumination during the 1970's, as Lutherans struggled to understand the Holy Spirit in the life of the church.

Both the Reformation and the contemporary controversies have similar issues: the role of the word of God in Scripture and the definition of the work of the Spirit. Both controversies have relatively little to say about the person of the Spirit. Who the Spirit is must be defined by extrapolation.

The paper proposes to examine both controversies in turn: first,

---

[1] Theodore G. Tappert (ed.), *The Book of Concord* (Philadelphia, 1959), p. 345.

the inter-ecclesial debate: the debate between Luther and his contemporaries; then, the intra-ecclesial debate: the debate between
charismatic and non-charismatic Lutherans. In this way we hope to
present how Lutherans have understood confessing the apostolic faith
with reference to the Holy Spirit.

THE INTER-ECCLESIAL CONTROVERSY: LUTHER AND HIS CONTEMPORARIES

The occasion for Luther's thinking on the Holy Spirit is explication of the creeds of Christendom. The audience for his thought is
the community of the faithful. The context for his thought is controversy with the Roman Catholic Church, on the one hand, and with
the radical reformers, on the other.

This section proposes to examine occasion, audience, and context in the course of explicating Luther's thinking on the work and
person of the Holy Spirit. The operative presupposition is that one
best understands Luther's thinking on the Holy Spirit when one understands both (1) how Luther intends for the Triune God *to be presented* within the community of the faithful and (2) how he believes
that the Triune God *is present* within the community of the faithful.

Catechetical instruction is the context for Luther's thinking. In
the Large and Small Catechisms he states what he wants the congregations within his care to know about the Holy Spirit. Lutherans today may well want to say more and less than did Luther, but they
must first be advised of the context in which Luther wrote. They must
then examine the context in which they write today, as they struggle
to confess the apostolic faith in a dangerous world.

The Book of Concord lists three symbols of the faith, or "creeds
of the Christian faith which are commonly used in the church." These
symbols are the Apostle's Creed, the Nicene Creed, and the Athanasian Creed. The Large and Small Catechisms explicate the creed most
commonly used in the churches: the Apostle's Creed. Because the
catechisms state explicitly the relationships between God and the creatures and between commandments and creeds, as well as the relationships between the three persons of the Trinity, these catechetical sections on the Apostle's Creed are helpful in understanding Luther on
the apostolic faith.

Commandments and creeds are locked together. Commandments
promulgate the imperative; creeds proclaim the indicative: "This is
what we are to do, because this is what God does." Although the

Decalogue precedes the creed in each catechism, there is a soterio-logical priority of indicative over imperative. The statement of what God does grounds the commandment. The Small Catechism, for example, has a formulaic explanation for both the prescriptive ("thou shalt") and the proscriptive ("thou shalt not") commandments: "We should so fear and love God, that . . . " Then follows the commandment, which Luther characteristically states prescriptively and dispositionally. For example, the fifth commandment, the proscriptive "thou shalt not kill," becomes a prescriptive injunction for neighbor-regard: "We should . . . help and befriend him in every necessity of life."[2]

The commandments set forth everything that God expects of the creatures; the creeds set forth everything that the creatures can expect of God. The Large Catechism is adamant:

> Thus far we have heard the first part of Christian doctrine. In it [the Decalogue] we have seen all that God wishes us to do or not to do. The creed properly follows, setting forth all that we must expect and receive from God; in brief, it teaches us to know him perfectly. M. Luther, *Large Catechism,* Second Part: the Creed.[3]

The presumption is that, were the creatures to know God perfectly, they would have the strength to keep the commandments. But the creatures do not know God perfectly, and they do not have the strength to keep God's commandments.

> If we could by our own strength keep the Ten Commandments as they ought to be kept, we would need neither the Creed nor the Lord's Prayer. M. Luther, *Large Catechism,* Second Part: the Creed.[4]

Knowledge of God is three-fold: knowledge of God the creator, knowledge of God the redeemer, knowledge of God the sanctifier. Of the sanctifier the Large Catechism states:

> But God's Spirit alone is called Holy Spirit, that is, he who has sanctified and still sanctifies us. As the Father is called Creator

---

[2] Ibid. p. 343.
[3] Ibid. p. 411.
[4] Ibid.

and the Son is called Redeemer, so on account of his work the Holy Spirit must be called Sanctifier, the One who makes us holy. M. Luther, *Large Catechism,* Third Article.[5]

Here the distinction between person and work of the Spirit is made, but the text focuses on the work of the Spirit. Of the person of the Spirit little is said, other than that the Spirit is God's spirit. Other passages in the Book of Concord mention the procession of the Spirit from the Father and the Son, but there is little elaboration.

These passages addressing the *filioque* clauses are of note. In the first part of the Smalcald Articles, which treat "the sublime articles of the divine majesty," it is stated "that the Father was begotten by no one, the Son was begotten by the Father, and the Holy Spirit proceeded from the Father and the Son."[6] In the Solid Declaration we see the procession of the Spirit stated in relationship to Christ.

But we believe, teach, and confess that God the Father gave his Spirit to Christ, his beloved Son, according to the assumed human nature (whence he is called Messiah, or the Anointed) in such a way that he received the Spirit's gifts not by measure, like other saints. The "Spirit of wisdom and understanding, of counsel and might and knowledge" (Is 11.2, 61.1) does not rest upon Christ the Lord according to his assumed human nature (according to the deity he is of one essence with the Holy Spirit) in such a manner that as a man he therefore knows and can do only certain things in the way in which other saints know and can do things through the Holy Spirit who endows them only with created gifts. Rather, since Christ according to the Godhead is the second person in the holy Trinity and the Holy Spirit proceeds from him as well as from the Father (and therefore he is and remains to all eternity his and the Father's own Spirit, who is never separated from the Son), it follows that through personal union the entire fullness of the Spirit (as the ancient Fathers say) is communicated to Christ according to the flesh that is personally united with the Son of God.[7]

---

[5] Ibid. p. 415.

[6] "The Smalcald Articles," Part 1, in Tappert, p. 291.

[7] "Solid Declaration," Article 8. Person of Christ, in Tappert, p. 605.

The status of the *filioque* is here not in question. Perhaps Lukas Vischer's observation is pertinent: "While the Reformers were very critical of many of the developments in medieval theology, the question of the *filioque* was not seriously raised in the sixteenth century."[8] Vischer's remark may be pertinent, but it is not altogether correct. The status of the *filioque* was seriously raised in another sixteenth-century context: the context of discussion between Tübingen and Constantinople.

That discussion is beyond the scope of a paper limited to Luther's controversies with Rome and the radical reformers.[9] It is, however, a critical chapter in ecumenical relations in the sixteenth century. As the Lutheran movement consolidated, its leaders made attempts to establish cordial relations with the Orthodox Church. A first attempt occurred when Philip Melanchthon wrote to the Orthodox Patriarch of Constantinople, Ioasaph II, in 1559. The patriarch responded immediately and sent Deacon Demetrios Mysos to meet with leaders of the Lutheran movement. Melanchthon and Mysos spent time together studying the Augsburg Confession, and a translation of the Confession in Greek was prepared. Mysos, however, failed to return to Constantinople and this ecumenical attempt was aborted. Contact with the Orthodox Church was reestablished in 1578. Lutheran Tübingen theologians under the leadership of Professor of Theology and University Chancellor Jacob Andreae initiated dialogue with Patriarch of Constantinople Jeremiah II. This correspondence resulted in an exchange of letters between Tübingen and Constantinople in which points of agreement and disagreement between the churches surfaced. One of the key points of disagreement was the *filioque* clause.

Jeremiah II argues from "true philosophy" and contrasts the nature of binity and trinity. The Tübingen theologians counter with scriptural arguments addressing the work of the Spirit in the forgiveness of sins (Jn 14.26, 15.26). They appeal to Christ's sending of the Spirit to justify the *filioque* clause. No consensus was reached on the point, perhaps because the arguments were incommensurable. From Tübingen the arguments move from the work of the Spirit as delineated in scripture to the necessity of the *filioque* clause. From

---

[8] Lukas Vischer (ed.), *Spirit of God, Spirit of Christ: Faith and Order Paper No. 103* (London, 1981), p. 6.

[9] This analysis is indebted to Regin Prenter's masterful study, *Spiritus Creator* (Philadelphia, 1953), especially pp. 3-202.

Constantinople the arguments move from the person of the Spirit as illuminated by "true philosophy" and buttressed by synodical and conciliar judgments to rejection of the clause.

The Tübingen theologians of 1578 merely echo sentiments of earlier theologians. During the Reformation controversies themselves, questions concerning the *person* of the Spirit were not seriously raised. Questions concerning the *work* of the Holy Spirit, however, were at the core of the controversies between the Roman Catholic Church and the magisterial reformers and between the magisterial reformers and the radical reformers.

Luther's debates with "the papists," as he called them, on the one hand, and with "the enthusiasts," on the other, are debates about the *work* of the Spirit. It is critical to examine these debates. Only then can we assess Luther's thinking on the *person* of the Spirit and the status of the *filioque* clause.

Against the Papists

Luther's break with late medieval scholasticism can be construed as an extended debate over the work of the Holy Spirit. Indeed, Luther's arguments with Rome *must* be seen as debates over the work of the Holy Spirit in order more fully to understand the significance of his thinking on the Spirit. He charges the papists with abandoning the word of God in scripture and ignoring the Spirit.

As Luther assesses it, an Aristotelian metaphysics undergirds scholastic thinking. God was both first cause and final end of all creation. A strong natural law tradition stipulates complementarity between creaturely nature and divine supernature. The anthropological counterpart of divine causality is creaturely cooperation. Thus, creaturely nature is fitted to divine nature. The creatures are inexorably returning to the creator. The *exitus-reditus* schema of Saint Thomas' *Summa Theologica* reflects this causality of divine nature and its complementarity with creaturely nature. God is the fixed point from which the creatures proceed and toward which the creatures return. The work of the Holy Spirit is to guide the procession of the creatures from God and to effect the creatures' return to God. The work of the Holy Spirit is to operate on and to cooperate with the creatures in their return to God.

Scholasticism sums up the work of the Holy Spirit with two words: *gratia* and *caritas*. The work of the Spirit is defined almost exclusively in terms of grace and charity. The Spirit infuses charity (*caritas*) into the heart of the believer. *Caritas* raises nature to the supernatural level toward which it is tending and equips the believer for supernatural works. The Spirit's infusion of charity enables the creature to journey back to God. The path of this journey presupposes a congruity between self-love, love of friend and neighbor, and eventually a love of God in God's self.

Luther breaks with this tradition. He judges the Aristotelian metaphysics undergirding scholasticism too sterile and too dispassionate for his experience of God. He replaces the Aristotelian metaphysics with biblical revelation. Thus, the image of a metaphysical God, first cause and final end of all creation, recedes quickly behind a biblical God, whose divine wrath is as powerful as his love. There is only christological reconciliation. Both wrath and love, judgment and mercy are brought together in Christ. God is neither transcendent cause nor final end; God is the biblical God: real, personal, and anthropomorphic. Again, Luther elaborated christologically. Christ was the Word of God. All of Scripture was about Christ: *was Christum treibet.*

Rejecting the natural law tradition and its complementarity between creaturely and divine natures, Luther posited a radical discontinuity between creaturely and divine natures. Nature is vitiated by sin. No effort on the part of the creature can repair the break. Only Christ can repair it.

The creature is the fixed point in this soteriological drama. God is the moving, dynamic, personal God, reaching out in mercy and judgment. The crucifixion and resurrection of Christ chronicle the journey that God made to redeem a fallen humanity. The Holy Spirit is the continuing presence of God within the believer's life. The work of the Spirit, in short, is to present God; the Spirit is the presence of God. Luther sums up the whole of his thinking of the work of the Spirit in Romans 8.26 (RSV).

> Likewise the Spirit helps us in our weakness; for we do not know how to pray as we ought, but the Spirit himself intercedes for us with sighs too deep for words.

For Luther, then, the work of the Spirit could be contained n the single biblical word *emanuel*: God with us. Christ is the God with us in redemption. The Spirit is the God with us in sanctificaton.

Luther rejects the *caritas* causality of scholastic metaphysics. Self-love, neighbor-love, and love of God in God's self are discontinuous.

So far from leading to love of God, self-love could lead only to self-hatred (*odium sui*), as the creature concurs with God's judgment of it as a sinner. It is in the midst of this anguish and hatred—Luther calls it *Anfechtung*—that the creature experiences God's mercy. Because of sin there is no analogy between self-love and divine love. Sin destroys any complementarity between human and divine natures; sin vitiates the natural law. Because of self-love's inexorable progression to self-hatred, love recedes in Luther's theology. It is replaced by faith, the greatest of the triad faith, hope, and love. Faith is believing in a God who was crucified and resurrected for the sins of the creature. Faith is believing in a God who is present daily through the work of the Spirit.

In sum, then, Luther charges scholasticism with having abandoned the word of God in Scripture and ignoring the Spirit. Luther discards the Aristotelian metaphysics with its divine-human complementarity and *caritas* causality. In its place he puts the biblical God: a personal, anthropomorphic deity whose judgment and mercy form the dialectic in which the believer wages the life of faith. Through the crucifixion and resurrection God establishes a presence with the creatures. Through the Holy Spirit God proclaims an ongoing presence within creation.

Against the Enthusiasts

Luther's arguments with the enthusiasts are surprisingly similar to his arguments against Rome.[11] "The heavenly prophets," as he called them, have also abandoned the word of God in Scripture and ignored the Spirit. Theirs is the error of Rome: presuming that the creature could of its own actions come to the creator. Worse in Luther's eyes is that the enthusiasts have inverted God's order of sanctification by placing the internal work of the Spirit before the external word of Scripture.

Now when God sends forth his holy gospel he deals with us in a twofold manner, first outwardly, then inwardly. Outwardly he deals with us through the oral word of the gospel and through material signs, that is, baptism and the sacrament of the altar. Inwardly he deals with us through the Holy Spirit, faith, and other gifts. But whatever their measure or order the outward factors should and must precede. The inward experience follows and is effected by the outward. God has determined to give the inward to no one except through the outward.[12]

The enthusiasts, he says, have utterly "spiritualized" the interpretation of Scripture. But the human spirit is their hermeneutic for Scripture, not the Holy Spirit. The enthusiasts, he says, made the Holy Spirit the goal of human action. Luther criticizes Andreas Karlstadt: " . . . he wants to teach you, not how the Spirit comes to you, but how you come to the Spirit."[13]

At the outset, it must be admitted that the theological issues at stake are clouded by invective. Luther's intense animosity towards Thomas Muentzer and Andreas Karlstadt is barely above personal attack. Luther's revealing comparison of the reformers Melanchthon, Erasmus, Karlstadt, and himself is scathing:

> Philip has substance and eloquence [*res et verba*]; Erasmus eloquence without substance [*verba sine re*]; Luther substance without eloquence [*res sine verbis*]: and Karlstadt neither substance nor eloquence [*nec res nec verba*].[14]

Thomas Muentzer is regarded as a full-scale representative of Satan.

> Fortune would have it that whenever the holy Word of God blossoms forth Satan opposes it with all his might by employing, first of all, the fist and outrageous force. When this method proves unsuccessful, he attacks it with evil tongues and false spirits and teachings.[15]

Those who were slandered responded in kind. The title of Muentzer's treatise, "Highly provoked defense and answer against the spiritless, soft-living flesh at Wittenberg, which has befouled pitiable Christianity in perverted fashion by its theft of Holy Spirit," speaks for

---

[12]M. Luther, "Against the Heavenly Prophets," in Conrad Bergendoff (ed.), *Luther's Works: 40* (Philadelphia, 1958), p. 146.

[13]Ibid. p. 147.

[14]Cited in Steven Ozment, *The Age of Reform: 1250-1550* (New Haven, 1980), p. 342, n. 7.

[15]M. Luther, "Letter to the Princes of Saxony Concerning the Rebellious Spirit," in *Luther's Works: 40,* p. 49.

itself.[16] Throughout the treatise Muentzer refers to Luther as Doctor Liar, Cousin Steplightly, the poor Flatterer. Beneath all of this invective, however, are tough theological issues concerning the interpretation of Scripture and the work of the Spirit.

The enemies even agree on what these issues are. The most problematic issue is the relationship between Scripture and Spirit. Luther accuses the enthusiasts of inverting the order of sanctification and placing the Spirit before the word contained in Scripture. Luther argues that God deals with the creatures first outwardly, then inwardly; outwardly through word and sacrament, inwardly through the Holy Spirit, faith, and other gifts.[17] For Luther external word, i.e., the word of God in Scripture, precedes internal calling. Karlstadt, however, "has as his purpose to reverse the order."[18] Yet it is precisely Luther's order that Muentzer challenges in "The Prague Manifesto":

> Yet all the days of my life (God knows, I lie not) I have never been able to get out of any monk or parson the true use of faith, about the profitableness of temptation [*Anfechtung*] which prepares for faith in the Spirit of the Fear of the Lord, together with the condition that each elect must have the Sevenfold Holy Ghost. I have not learned from any scholar the true Order of God which he has set in all creatures, not the least word . . . [19]

Citing Paul in 1 Corinthians 14.6 as his witness, Muentzer holds that the preacher must have a revelation before preaching the word. The Spirit enlightens the elect; the elect interprets the word of God in Scripture. For Muentzer this is the order of sanctification. Internal enlightenment precedes the external word.

A second issue between the enthusiasts and Luther is the matter of works. Throughout the various strains of radical Christian testimonies, there is a strong perfectionist ethic. Although the precise distinctions vary from community to community, the lives of the elect are distinctive. Muentzer is one of the most revolutionary. Suffering and death mark the lives of the elect, and he swears in "The Prague

---

[16]Thomas Muentzer, "A Highly Provoked Defense," in Lowell H. Zuck (ed.), *Christianity and Revolution* (Philadelphia, 1975), pp. 38-44.

[17]M. Luther, "Against the Heavenly Prophets," p. 146.

[18]Ibid. p. 147.

[19]T. Muentzer, "Prague Manifesto," in Zuck, p. 32.

Manifesto": "In order to bring this truth to the light of day, I am ready to offer my life, if it be God's will."[20] Another radical reformer, Conrad Grebel, admonishes Muentzer. Grebel advocates withdrawal from the world instead of revolution and martyrdom. "Moreover, the gospel and its adherents are not to be protected by the sword, nor are they thus to protect themselves, which, as learn from our brother, is thy opinion and practice."[21] Within Grebel's radical Christian communities the ban accomplishes internal discipline.

To Luther this all sounds like the works righteousness he had attacked in Rome. Attention to visible marks of election he attacks as a "new monkery."[22] For Luther the passion for a distinctive lifestyle constitutes an attempt to come to the Spirit, rather than letting the Spirit come to the believer. The enthusiasts' appropriation of the Spirit enslaves the work of the Spirit to the works of a perfectionist ethic.

In response to the enthusiasts Luther gives the Spirit both more authority and less. In his order of sanctification the external word of God in Scripture precedes the Spirit. This move is to curb what he perceives to be the Spirit's subjective appropriation by the enthusiasts. It could be seen to be a gesture of subordination; a more appropriate interpretation is that Luther filters everything through the word of God in Scripture. The Father presents the word from the Decalogue: "I am the Lord your God"; Christ is the incarnate Word; the Spirit is the word present and active in the individual believer and in the community of believers. Scripture presents the work of the Trinity; Scripture is the hermeneutical key to the Trinity. Luther grounds his thinking scripturally.

Luther charges the enthusiasts with abandoning the word of God in Scripture and ignoring the Spirit. He locates the work of the Spirit in Scripture, citing Romans 8.26. The Spirit activates, enlivens, and sustains the life of faith. His interpretative verbs in the Small Catechism are more precise: calls, gathers, enlightens, sanctifies, and preserves.

> I believe that by my own reason or strength I cannot believe in Jesus Christ, my Lord, or come to him. But the Holy Spirit has called me through the Gospel, enlightened me with his gifts, and sanctified and preserved me in true faith, just as he calls, gathers,

---

[20]Ibid. p. 34.

[21]Conrad Grebel, "A Letter to Thomas Muentzer," in Zuck, p. 60.

[22]M. Luther, "Against the Heavenly Prophets," p. 81.

enlightens, and sanctifies the whole Christian church on earth and preserves it in union with Jesus Christ in the one true faith. In this Christian church he daily and abundantly forgives all my sins, and the sins of all believers, and on the last day he will raise me and all the dead and will grant eternal life to me and to all who believe in Christ. This is most certainly true.[23]

The initial confession is witness to the work of the Spirit: "I believe ... that I cannot believe." Impetus for belief comes from the Holy Spirit. Eliminated entirely is any action on the part of the believer. The proper relationship between Scripture and Spirit follows the statement of creaturely capacity and spiritual empowerment: "the Holy Spirit has called me through the Gospel." The gifts of the Spirit are given place but not priority within the spectrum of the Spirit's work: "enlightened me with his gifts." Sanctification is the task of making one holy; preservation, the task of keeping one holy.

But the believer is part of a community of faith, and the work of the Holy Spirit in the individual believer is set firmly within the context of that community. The Holy Spirit works in the individual Christian "just as he calls, gathers, enlightens, and sanctifies the whole Christian church on earth and preserves it in union with Jesus Christ in the one true faith." The critical dialectic between individual and community is set: the Spirit works with individuals within the context of a community.

Conclusion

Luther levels the same charge against both papists and enthusiasts: each has abandoned the word of God in Scripture and ignored the work of the Spirit. For Luther the error has serious consequences. First, each has truncated the work of the Spirit. Second, each has fallen into legalism and works righteousness. Finally, each has ignored the proper relationship between Spirit and Scripture.

The Work of the Spirit

As Luther sees it, the papists absolutize *gratia*; the enthusiasts absolutize the wrong spirit—the human spirit. Scholasticism restricts the Spirit to the operation of grace. The operation of divine grace,

---

[23]M. Luther, "Small Catechism," Explanation to the Third Article, in Tappert, p. 345.

in turn, requires creaturely cooperation. A whole causal schema leading to works righteousness is erected. Thus, the Spirit's working is
confined to sanctification. The enthusiasts, on the other hand, restrict
the working of the Spirit to inspiring the elect. This strikes Luther
as dangerously subjective and internal. The Spirit's working is confined to enlightenment. Luther prefers to anchor the interpretation
of the Spirit's working on the external word. Against both sides Luther
asserts that the Holy Spirit calls, gathers, enlightens, sanctifies, and
preserves both the individual believer and the community of believers.

Legalism

Luther accuses both papists and enthusiasts of overestimating the
efficacy of human actions. Both the *caritas* causality of the scholastics
and the perfectionist ethic of the enthusiasts lead to works righteousness. Against both sides Luther asserts that the Spirit invades every
aspect of the believer's life; the Spirit precedes every action, intention, and disposition. The Spirit is God's presence in the life of faith.

Scripture and Spirit

As Luther sees it, the papists ignore the relationship between Scripture and Spirit, substituting Aristotelian metaphysics for biblical
revelation. The enthusiasts display equal ignorance, subordinating
the Holy Spirit to the human spirit and subordinating the word of
God in Scripture to both. Against his opponents Luther claims the
primacy of the word of God in Scripture.

We would want to quarrel with Luther regarding his assessment
of his opponents' opinions, the blatant name-calling he employs
against them, and his *ad hominem* attack. But when we strip away
the polemic, Luther's thinking on the work of the Holy Spirit emerges.
Luther tried to ground his thinking scripturally. He surrounded all
of creaturely being and doing with the working of the Spirit. The
Holy Spirit was not God's efficient causality among the creatures,
nor God's gift to the elect. Rather, the Spirit was nothing more,
nothing less than God's presence among the believers.

Commandments state what the creatures can expect from God.
The Third Article of the Apostle's Creed reassures the creature *that*
it can expect God to be present. The Third Article further elaborates
how it can expect God to be present: through the Holy Spirit who
calls, gathers, enlightens, sanctifies, and preserves.

After elaborating Luther's thinking on the work of the Spirit, it is critical to reexamine what he says and does not say about the person of the Spirit. As we have noted, Luther repeats traditional Western church phrases on the procession of the Spirit. When he does elaborate, however, he elaborates biblically, not philosophically. From his discussion it is clear that Luther understood *filioque* as the Son's sending of the Spirit, described in John 15.26: "When the Comforter comes, whom I shall send to you, the Spirit of truth, who proceeds from the Father, he will testify of me." Luther explains this:

> There we hear that the Holy Spirit proceeds from the Father and is sent by the Son. One who is sent, however, is also said to "proceed from." Just as the Son is born of the Father and yet does not depart from the Godhead, but on the contrary remains in the same Godhead with the Father and is one God with him, so also the Holy Spirit proceeds from the Father and is sent by the Son, and does not depart from the Godhead either, but remains with the Father and the Son in the same Godhead, and is one God with both.[24]

Consistent with his polemic against the papists and enthusiasts, Luther understands the *filioque* biblically. The Spirit proceeds from the Father and is sent by the Son. Luther does not quarrel with the procession of the Spirit from the Father and the Son, because he understands "to proceed from" as synonymous with "to be sent by." "To be sent by" describes the Spirit's relationship to Jesus the Son of the Father.

Thus, Luther presents a heavily christological interpretation of both the work and the person of the Spirit. The Spirit is sent by the Son. This is how Luther understands the person of the Spirit; this is how he speaks of the *filioque* clause. Then, Luther locks the word of the Spirit into the word of God in Scripture. The word of God is christologically conceived; all of Scripture bears witness to Christ. The Holy Spirit calls, gathers, enlightens, sanctifies, and preserves both the individual believer and the community of believers. This is how Luther understands the work of the Spirit. Both person and work of the Holy Spirit are elaborated christologically.

---

[24]M. Luther, "The Three Symbols or Creeds of the Christian Faith," in *Luther's Works 34,* p. 217.

THE INTRA-ECCLESIAL CONTROVERSY: THE CHARISMATIC
MOVEMENT AND CONTEMPORARY LUTHERANISM

Questions concerning the person and work of the Spirit confront contemporary Lutherans in this country much the way they confronted Luther and his contemporaries. The charismatic renewal or the charismatic movement forces American Lutherans to reframe these questions; it forces American Lutherans to rethink Reformation solutions in view of new contexts. American Lutherans find themselves saying both more and less than did Luther on the person and work of the Spirit. It is critical to examine both the points of silence and the points of expansion.

Four study conferences between 1970 and 1975 addressed the Holy Spirit.[25] Participants included a broad spectrum of American Lutherans: those heavily involved in the charismatic movement, the tolerant but uninvolved, those disaffected by the movement, and those opposed entirely to the movement. The thematic underlying all the conferences, however, was not how American Lutherans are to regard the charismatic movement, but a question: how are Christians to regard the Holy Spirit in the life of the Church? Specific reference was made to the charismatic movement, but investigation broadly included biblical, historical, and ecumenical thinking on the Spirit.

The charismatic movement poses problems to a Church that sees itself as being always undergoing reformation (*semper reformanda*). A superficial problem is only apparently so: what to call the movement? "Charismatic renewal" seems to render a value judgment, while "movement" is more descriptive. Moreover, "renewal" seems to apply broadly to all forms of renewal in the Church. All participants in the study conferences could consent to the designation "charismatic movement."

Lutheran charismatics regard themselves as a movement. Their aim is "to see a separate 'movement' fade out as its message is integrated into the ongoing life of the Church."[26] The language echoes that of other Lutherans, who have seen their confession as a movement within the church catholic. Dr. Timothy Lull put this quite bluntly in a conference for Lutheran leaders in August, 1985. The subject of the conference was the Holy Spirit. In speaking of the Spirit and ecumenism Lull said:

---

[25]The conferences resulted in a study volume: Paul D. Opsahl (ed.), *The Holy Spirit in the Life of the Church* (Minneapolis, 1978). Hereafter, Opsahl.

[26]Appendix A: Section 4, Pastoral Concerns, in Opsahl, p. 243.

We cannot be God's faithful people in the Lutheran Church as long as our pride is in that church, its glorious traditions, its theology, its people, its willingness to fight for truth . . . We are at best a movement for the gospel in the church, a stage along the way to eternal life where there are, we assume, no Lutherans dressed as Lutherans.[27]

If this is the message of the Holy Spirit to Lutherans churches in 1985, it is startlingly similar to the message charismatic Lutherans made within the church in the 1970s. What was the message of this "movement," self-designated as an interim measure in a pilgrim church, within the church of the 1970s? "The charismatic movement wants to tell the church that the third article of the Creed—the person, works, and gifts of the Holy Spirit—has been neglected."[28] The charismatic movement within the Lutheran Church of the 1970s wanted to recall the church to certain neglected facets of the Christian tradition.

Some of these facets had diminished during the course of confessional development. Personal prayer and personal devotional reading of Scripture, gifts of the Spirit, the reality of the faith relationship, the validity of a ministry of healing, the existence of home churches (*ecclesiolae*)—which even Luther had permitted in certain circumstances: all had taken back seat in contemporary practice. The charismatic movement sought to move these pieces of Christian life into their rightful place.

It is important to compare this contemporary controversy over the work of the Spirit to the Reformation controversy. It is startling to see the similarities and differences between this discussion and that one. The chief similarity is that both Lutheran charismatics and Lutheran non-charismatics charge each other with abandoning Scripture and ignoring the work of the Spirit. The ironic difference, however, is that these differences have now arisen *within* the very church that started as a protest for many of the same reasons against both the "papists" and the "enthusiasts."

---

[27]Timothy Lull, "The Holy Spirit and Ecumenism," Lecture for Lutheran Bishops and Presidents, Keystone, Colorado, 19 July 1985.

[28]Appendix A: Section 4, Pastoral Concerns, in Opsahl, p. 243.

The Charismatic Position

Charismatic Lutherans challenge the church to pay closer attention to the Bible and to reexamine the work of the Spirit. Under the rubric of "expectancy," these Lutherans identify five expectations they have for communities that experience the working of the Spirit.

1. experience and exercise of the charismata described by Paul in 1 Corinthians 12.4-10;
2. a deepened appreciation and use of prayer;
3. the possibility of an experience of God which makes one's Christian heritage come alive in new modalities of Christian growth;
4. a greater love of the Bible and its message;
5. an awareness of a dimension described biblically as "principalities and powers."[29]

Chief among these expectations is a renewed and deepened appreciation for the Bible. It is interesting to see the term "Bible" surface in comparison and contrast with "Scripture." Usage suggests that "Bible" is the descriptive term for the canonical books of the Old and New Testaments. "Scripture" refers to the normative content of these books. Charismatic Lutherans suggest two ways in which the "Bible" nurtures a sense of expectancy. In a general sense, charismatic Lutherans recognize that the Bible is authoritative for Christian faith and life. In a second and more specific sense, charismatic Lutherans seek to define explicitly how the Bible is authoritative for Christian faith and life. "Scripture" appears here to interpret and even circumscribe the appropriate ways in which biblical texts can be authoritative for Christian community.

On the one hand charismatics find the Bible the source of their expectations; they expect the gifts and power of the Spirit to be operative in their lives because these things are promised in Scripture. On the other hand, charismatic experience is very much subjected to the tests and norms of Scripture; it is not spiritual experiences and phenomena as such which gain a standing in the charismatic movement but rather that which is understood, on the basis of Scripture, to be a manifestation of the Holy Spirit.[30]

---

[29]Appendix A: Section 2, Concerns the Charismatic Movement among Lutherans Addresses to the Lutheran Church, in Opsahl, p. 232.
[30]Ibid. p. 234.

Charismatic Lutherans maintain that this renewed appreciation
for the Bible does not lead to new ways of interpreting Scripture;
rather, it offers new insights into biblical stories of miracles, healings, visions, exorcisms, etc. The charismatic position on the relationship between Bible, Scripture, and Spirit could be summarized
as follows: the Holy Spirit interprets the Bible; Scripture is the inspired and normative interpretation of the biblical texts.

In sum, then, and although it was not so precisely stated by
Lutheran charismatics, one could conclude that charismatic Lutherans
nuance the traditional interpretation of the relationship between Bible, Scripture, and Spirit. The Holy Spirit interprets the Bible. Scripture is that inspired and normative interpretation. Scripture describes
the Spirit's working in the community of faith. Rather than a logical
or soteriological ordering of Bible, Scripture, and Spirit, charismatic
Lutherans relate these three statements dialectically. The Holy Spirit
is constantly interpreting the Bible; Scripture, that normative interpretation, is constantly interpreting the work of the Spirit within the
community of faith. This dialectic between Spirit and Bible, on the
one hand, and between Scripture and Spirit, on the other, affords
more subtlety than Luther either needed or stated.

The Non-charismatic Position

Non-charismatic Lutherans agree with charismatic Lutherans that
the Spirit has been neglected. They differ, however, on what has been
neglected and how that deficit should be addressed. In short, their
charge is that charismatic Lutherans have abandoned the word of
God in Scripture and misunderstood the work of the Spirit.

The use of Scripture is a critical issue between Lutheran charismatics and non-charismatics. The non-charismatic contingent uses
the word "Scripture" exclusively: the "Bible" is the collection of
books in the Old Testament and the New Testament; "Scripture"
is the "Bible's" normative content. That normative content is
christological.

Lutherans cherish the fullness of Scripture as the manifold witness of God's covenant with humanity. The Bible, especially in
its prophetic and apostolic witness to Christ, is the rule, norm,
and touchstone of the Lutheran confessional movement.[31]

---

[31]Appendix A: Section 3, Concerns Addressed to Lutheran Charismatics,
in Opsahl, p. 239.

Specific passages in Scripture must be interpreted in view of the whole. In contrast to the charismatics' assertion that the Holy Spirit interprets the Bible, these non-charismatic Christians contend that Scripture interprets Scripture.

Non-charismatic Lutherans further note specific problems with letting the Holy Spirit—or one group's interpretation of the Holy Spirit—interpret Scripture.

1. Certain biblical phrases—baptized by the Spirit, "gifts of the Spirit," *charismata*, speaking in tongues—are sometimes used in ways which are not supported by the broader context, parallels elsewhere, or Scripture as a whole.

2. Certain early Christian practices are sometimes interpreted as preferable, or even normative, for the charismatic movement. This manner of interpretation is in danger of making normative what Scripture regards as descriptive.

3. The tendency is to highlight specific *"charismata"* (1 Cor 12.8-10) as normative for the renewal of the church. Why not also emphasize other *charismata* (Rom 12.6-21)?

4. The descriptive material in Acts and the writings of Paul are seen as more important for understanding the work of the Holy Spirit and his gifts than the clearly didactic sections of the New Testament.[32]

In this view, non-charismatic Lutherans maintain that charismatic Christians have returned to the Bible but abandoned Scripture. They have lost the sense of what is normative in Scripture and substituted their own ideas about what is normative onto the biblical materials, ignoring all evidence to the contrary.

The work of the Spirit is also at issue. Non-charismatic Lutherans argue that word and sacrament are appointed means for the church's constant renewal. These are the ordinary, but effective means of God's work to draw the church closer to its Lord. "Gifts of the Spirit" are tacitly dubbed "extraordinary" means through which the Spirit works. Thus, while it seems both Lutheran groups could agree with confessional language that the Holy Spirit calls, gathers, enlightens, sanctifies, and preserves, the charismatic Lutherans would see the work of the Spirit happening in a variety of ways; non-charismatic Lutherans would locate this work within the ministry of word and sacrament.

---

[32]1 Cor 12.8-10; Rom 12.6-21.

Conclusion

The contemporary debate among charismatic and non-charismatic Lutherans runs along Reformation lines: it is a debate over the word of God in Scripture and the work of the Spirit. Charismatic Lutherans accuse the non-charismatic contingent of abandoning the word of God in Scripture and ignoring the work of the Spirit. Non-charismatic Lutherans make the same charges against the charismatic contingent. The two issues are interpretation of Scripture and understanding of the work of the Spirit.

Interpretation of Scripture

Charismatic Lutherans significantly distinguish between "Bible" and "Scripture." "Bible" refers to the books of the Old and New Testaments. Informed by the Spirit the believing community reads the Bible. "Scripture" is the inspired and normative interpretation of the biblical texts. This is a pneumatological interpretation of Scripture. Non-charismatic Lutherans do not make such a distinction between "Bible" and "Scripture." Scripture interprets Scripture, and all of Scripture bears witness to Christ. The normative content of Scripture is Christ. This is a christological interpretation of Scripture.

The Work of the Spirit

Charismatic Lutherans extend the work of the Spirit to include "gifts of the Spirit," as elaborated in 1 Corinthians 12. In the eyes of the opposition this is a needless expansion. Non-charismatic Lutherans speak of the chief gifts of the Spirit as being word and sacrament. What more does one need? they argue. In the eyes of the opposition this is an unjustified truncation.

Resolution of these differences may well come only in time and in the faith life of the church. Interestingly, the debate between charismatic and non-charismatic Lutherans revolves around the Reformation issues of Scripture and the work of the Spirit. Ironically, each group charges the other with faulty interpretation of Scripture and incomplete understanding of the work of the Spirit—the same charges Luther leveled against both Rome and the radical reformers. And yet, both charismatic and non-charismatic Lutherans have a common concern: how is the work of the Spirit within the life of the church to be understood? The question still directs the church today. In a very real sense what the charismatic movement hoped to accomplish is being accomplished. Concerns of charismatic Christians are being integrated into mainstream thinking in the church.

A conference in August, 1985 for synodical bishops and presidents in the Lutheran Church Missouri Synod, the Lutheran Church in America, the American Lutheran Church, and the Association of Evangelical Lutheran Churches pressed questions surrounding the work of the Spirit still further. Papers addressed the Spirit's working in intra-confessional and extra-confessional settings: how are we to understand the work of the Spirit in the whole arena of Christian experience? how are we to understand the work of the Spirit in the ecumenical movement?

A northern California coalition of churches hopes to set as its task healing and wholeness. Their mission has both personal and social goals. The rationale is the conviction that personal healing can only occur when people are actively working for healing of the neighbor, the community, and the world. The Spirit asserts its presence more and more forcefully within the church's faith and practice.

And yet, in another sense, the charismatic movement's challenge has not been met. The question—how do we understand the Holy Spirit in the life of the church?—has not been adequately answered. Part of the reason the question is still pending is that adequate answer forces two additional questions: how do we understand the relationship between christology and pneumatology, between the second and third persons of the Trinity, between Son and Spirit? how do we understand the Trinity itself?

CONFESSING THE APOSTOLIC FAITH TODAY: THE WORK AND PERSON OF THE HOLY SPIRIT

"We are at best a movement for the gospel in the church . . . " Dr. Lull's comment indicates that we are still in transit. We are still reframing questions and rethinking solutions. We are a church that is always undergoing reformation.

Luther's attack on works righteousness persists throughout the tradition that bears his name. Lutherans maintain that how the creatures present themselves to God is a false concern. All creatures are totally sinful in themselves, totally saved through Christ. Of solitary and paramount importance is how God is present within creation. Christ is the embodiment of God's presence among the creatures. The creeds elaborate this: God is present as creator, redeemer, and sanctifier. Christ has revealed this to be truth.

Two observations are in order. First, Luther's presentation is heavily christological. Second, the presentation is more concerned with the work of each member of the Trinity, less concerned with the person. Each of these observations warrants further elaboration.

Christology and pneumatology. Christ is the lens through which Christians view the working of deity. All of Luther's thinking bears this heavily christological stamp. His thinking on the Spirit is no exception: both the person and work of the Spirit are christologically conceived. On this point, at least, Lutheranism has followed his lead.

The problems of such a perspective are acknowledged. An American Lutheran Church document offering counsel to pastors dealing with the charismatic movement noted: "There is truth in the contention that 'we sometimes divide Christ from God,' and that 'Lutherans are dominated by a Second Article mentality.' " But the document then down-played the dominance: "It must also be recognized that we can be dominated by a First Article mentality or by a Third Article mentality."[33] Both Reformation enthusiasts and contemporary charismatics sought to describe the Spirit's person and work independently of Christ. This was—and is—problematic for Lutherans. Clearly, a christological focus is preferable.

This christological focus, however, does skew things trinitarian. The first person of the Trinity is not dependent on the second person in the same way that the Holy Spirit is dependent on Christ. An implicit subordination is present. The Spirit is sent by the Son: this is how Lutherans have traditionally understood the person of the Spirit and the *filioque* clause. Further, the word of God in Scripture describes and defines the work of the Spirit. Scripture is what has to do with Christ (*was Christem treibet*). This is how Lutherans have traditionally understood the work of the Spirit.

Both old controversies and new ones are forcing Lutherans to reassess the relationship between christology and pneumatology, between the second and third persons of the Trinity, between Son and Spirit.

The Trinity. Luther's explanation of the creed is oriented toward the work and not the person of the Father, Son, and Spirit. God's presence within the creation is critical to Luther, but he focuses on *how* God is present, rather than *that* God is present. For Luther what God *does* is more important than who God *is*. The Lutheran designation

---

[33]Appendix B: The American Lutheran Church and Neo-Pentecostalism, in Opsahl, p. 248.

for the persons of God is revealing: creator, redeemer, sanctifier. One could perhaps more accurately render this: God creating, God redeeming, God sanctifying.

Less attention has been given to who Father, Son, and Spirit are. Less attention has been given to the various relationships that obtain between each. As Lutherans reassess the relationship between Son and Spirit, as they grapple with problems such as the *filioque* clause, they will be thinking not simply about what God does—what the creatures can "expect and receive from God," as the Large Catechism put it—but who God is. This may well be the next reformation within the church that is always undergoing reformation.

Pneumatological Issues in American Presbyterianism

RICHARD LOVELACE

INTRODUCTION

THE FOCUS OF THIS CONSULTATION makes it doubly serviceable to the ecumenical cause. It is centered on a major block of issues which divide the Eastern Church from the West. And since those issues have to do with the Holy Spirit and his renewing work in the body of Christ, we are also dealing with a dimension which is crucial for church unity.

Both the World Council of Churches, in its inception, and the Second Vatican Council built their hopes for a unified church on the hope for renewal, for spiritual revitalization of the existing structures. Since the time of Count Zinzendorf, one of the main architects of modern ecumenism, it has been taken for granted that the renewing work of the Spirit, Christian unity and effective mission ar vitally interrelated and mutually reinforcing factors.[1]

The W.C.C. Memorandum, "The Filioque Clause in Ecumenical Perspective," in calling for the restoration of the original form of the Niceno-Constantinopolitan Creed as normative in all communions, has taken an obvious practical step in promoting greater unity between Orthodox Christians and others. But it is especially significant and gratifying that the Memorandum's first recommendation deals with the need for a greater development of a trinitarian lifestyle in all the churches, and particularly "a new sensitivity to the person and work of the Holy Spirit."

---

[1] See A. J. Lewis, *Zinzendorf the Ecumenical Pioneer* (London, 1962).

The root concern of Orthodox theologians, today and in the past, has not been confined to securing the correct technical expression for the procession of the Spirit. It has always moved beyond this to seek the Church's experience of *theosis,* the Orthodox tradition's analogue for Western formulations of spiritual renewal, brought about through the *energeia* of the Holy Spirit. We can hope that Eastern and Western Christians alike will not move too easily toward a merely formal unity by resolving the *filioque* issue, without giving continued attention to the enlarging of the Church's theology of the Holy Spirit, and also its experience of his work, which is to actualize the power of Christ's resurrection among the whole people of God.

The Eastern Church, by the accidents of history, has had its theological attention arrested and fixed on pneumatology. Whether or not they have been in grave technical error in their doctrine of the Spirit, Western Christians have too easily been able to evade studying his person and work. This may be because the related section of the Creed, rising out of historical controversies focussed on the second person of the Trinity, is relatively terse in its handling of the Spirit. The position he has been given in our theologies is greatly inferior to the treatment of his ministry in the New Testament.

In our actual historical experience, every part of the Church has developed practical emphases and components of life and teaching which try to make up for this lack. The Methodist tradition, as Donald Dayton points out in his paper for this consultation, has its doctrine of sanctification and its practice of spiritual deepening through small group meetings for mutual confession and prayer. Roman Catholicism has the mystical tradition, with its tacit but important pneumatological assumptions.

In the same way, the Reformed tradition which I represent has dealt with pneumatological issues at crucial points in its development. Issues involving the Holy Spirit's person and work are very much alive in its current experience. I want to devote the majority of this paper to tracing out these pneumatological elements in American Presbyterianism, both in past history and in the present. But first, as has been requested, I will comment on the volume edited by Lukas Vischer which provides a central focus for the consultation.

RESPONSE TO *SPIRIT OF GOD, SPIRIT OF CHRIST*

This work is especially helpful as an introduction to the more sharply delimited issues in the *filioque* controversy. While the same ground is inevitably covered many times, the reader gains an increasing appreciation of the current mood in the East and West.

It becomes apparent that the situation in the West has turned around since the Councils of Lyons and Florence, that the historical case for the elimination of the *filioque* clause is admitted, and that there is little theological zeal for its retention. Whatever remaining concerns there are seem to be diplomatic in nature. If the *filioque* is to be dropped, as Garrigue indicates, it must be recognized that the theological interpretations of it held in the West have been legitimate and orthodox, however imperfectly expressed.

In the East, on the other hand, the imposition of the *filioque* is still a painful memory, and the whole tradition developed in reaction toward it is a matter of vital interest. It is difficult for Protestants to empathize with the intensity of this concern.

If Reformed observers might agree with Vladimir Lossky[2] that there are connections between the "depressed area" in Western thought and experience related to the Holy Spirit, and many deformities in the Church's structure and historic functioning, we would have to admit candidly that those deformities appear in Protestantism as well as Roman Catholicism — and add that they may be present in Orthodox church life also. Again, it may be questioned whether these effects of defective spirituality are strictly and entirely traceable to an inadequate formulation of the procession of the Spirit.

The clarifying theses of B. Bolotov, distinguishing between dogmas, theologoumena, and opinions, and relegating much of the controversy to the second and third categories, seem helpful in resolving this question (and perhaps many others as well).[3] The objections of Dumitru Staniloae[4] seem to concern points which are not really at issue, since Western theologians admit the monarchy of the Father and never meant to contest this by their use of the *filioque*.

If the range of opinion in this volume is representative of the whole Church, there should be little difficulty in eliminating this doctrinal block to convergence between the East and West—provided that Eastern Christians will accept in good faith what Westerners say about what they meant by the formula they are now willing to retire from

---

[2] Lukas Vischer, ed., *Spirit of God, Spirit of Christ* (Geneva, 1981), pp. 71-72.

[3] Vischer, p. 135.

[4] Vischer, p. 175.

use. Then both can work together on improving the Church's pneuma-tological foundations, both in clarifying the narrower issue of the Spirit's procession (perhaps along the lines suggested by Moltmann), and in the larger concern for developing a practical theology which better insures response to the Spirit's ministry throughout the Church. Unless these continuing tasks are addressed, the effort to unite East and West will founder almost as rapidly as it did in the thirteenth and fifteenth centuries.

The NCC study, "Towards the Common Expression of the Apos-tolic Faith Today," should encourage the use of the original text of the Creed, without the *filioque,* among its member communions. It should offer a relatively brief historical and theological basis for this change, endeavoring to indicate the sensitivity of the issue for Orthodox Chris-tians, without going into too much detail. Beyond this, the N.C.C. needs to give much more attention to the first recommendation in the W.C.C. Memorandum, addressing the question of how we may encourage the growth of a vigorous trinitarian spirituality among Protestants.

As a Presbyterian, I would recommend that the P.C. (U.S.A.) follow the same approach as it takes stock of its doctrinal heritage and for-mulates a new confessional statement for this newly reunited church.

THE HOLY SPIRIT AND AMERICAN PRESBYTERIANISM

Handling of the Filioque Clause

As Dietrich Ritschl indicates, Reformed thinking about the delimited question of the *filioque* clause has been content to copy the Western tradition. This is especially true of American Presbyterianism, which has engaged in little creative reflection either to interpret or to transcend the received position.

The Old Princeton theology, the result of a mixture of scholastic Reformed theology with Scottish Common Sense Realist philosophy, bears out this generalization. Reflecting Calvin's reserved attitude toward metaphysical speculation, Charles Hodge wants to limit theologizing on the matter to stating biblical data: "Paternity, therefore, is the distinguishing property of the Father; filiation of the Son; and procession of the Spirit. It will be observed that no at-tempt at explanation of these relations is given in these ecumenical creeds . . . The mere facts as revealed in scripture are affirmed."[5] Hodge faults the fathers for going beyond scripture to assert the

---

[5] Charles Hodge, *Systematic Theology* (Grand Rapids, 1952), 1, p. 461.

monarchy of the Father,[6] and comments, "The Reformers themselves were little inclined to enter into these speculations."[7]

Hodge is uneasy even with much talk about the eternal generation of the Son: filiation could mean "derivation of essence," but
it could also simply mean sameness of nature, equality, likeness or
affection, which are also qualities in the father/son relationship.[8] As
for the Holy Spirit, Hodge simply reasserts "the common church doctrine" that the Spirit proceeds "equally from the Father and the Son,"
noting that "the Church in calling the relation, thus indicated, a procession, does not attempt to explain it"; for in fact it is "incomprehensible, and therefore inexplicable."[9]

A. A. Hodge provides a more explicit citation of the Hodges'
favorite theologian, Francis Turretine, who follows the *filioque* into
perilous waters:

> The Son emanates in the way of generation, which affects not
> only personality, but similitude, on account of which the Son is
> called the image of the Father, and in consequence of which he
> receives the property of communicating the same essence to
> another person; but the Spirit, by the way of spiration, which
> affects only personality, and in consequence of which the person
> who proceeds does not receive the property of communicating
> the same essence to another person.[10]

The biblicism which A. A. Hodge shared with his father prevented
him from adopting this explicit subordination of the Spirit:

> . . . In order to make the method of the divine unity in Trinity
> more apparent, theologians have pressed the idea of derivation
> and subordination in the order of personal subsistence too far.
> This ground is at once sacred and mysterious. The points given
> by Scripture are not to be pressed nor speculated upon, but re-
> ceived and confessed nakedly.[11]

---

[6] Hodge, 1, p. 465.
[7] Ibid. p. 466.
[8] Ibid. pp. 468-69.
[9] Ibid. p. 477.
[10] A. A. Hodge, *Outlines of Theology* (Grand Rapids, 1972), p. 190.
[11] Ibid.

It seems apparent that the Princeton theologians did not accurately understand the Fathers on the meaning of filiation and procession, and also that their positivist biblicism was unable to penetrate behind the economic Trinity to make statements about the ontological Trinity. A position as reticent as this has difficulty distinguishing the Spirit from the Son, since both manifest equality, likeness and affection with respect to the Father. Nevertheless, the concern to avoid metaphysics and *theologia gloriae* which the Hodges display is probably characteristic not only of them, but of many American Presbyterians before and after their time.

The Old Princeton theology was displaced from mainline Presbyterianism by Neo-Reformational theology in the 1930s, although it continues to be dominant in several smaller Reformed communions, exerting a strong persisting influence within the larger contemporary Evangelical Movement. The strong residual attachment to the Westminster Confession in these circles gives the *filioque* a tacit continuing support, though the issue is hardly discussed.

It is questionable how much Karl Barth's defense of the *filioque* has really captured the theological mind of recent mainline Presbyterianism. George Hendry did not follow Barth here, as Alasdair Heron points out.[12] Many Presbyterians during the period of Neo-Orthodox dominance (1930s—1950s) were trained in theology using Emil Brunner's clearer and more concise texts, and Brunner seems to dismiss rather than discuss trinitarian theology at this level.[13] The wilder strains of secular theology during the 1960s were even less amenable to such questions.

Among more recent American theologians whose thought is impacting Presbyterianism in this country, my guess is that most would surrender the *filioque* rather quickly in order to facilitate unity with the Orthodox—but not always for reasons which would please Orthodoxy. I have sent out some enquiries to Presbyterian theologians, and may have more to report on this at the consultation.

Broader Pneumatological Issues in the Presbyterian Tradition

There is a common stereotype of Calvinism as rationalistic and spiritually cold. This is, however, supportable only from selective

---

[12]Vischer, p. 113.

[13]Emil Brunner, *The Christian Doctrine of God* (London, 1949), pp. 226-27.

evidence: the Reformed scholasticism developing after Beza; those who continue to hold unmodified forms of this; and parts of the Dutch Reformed community which are reacting against any emphasis on Christian experience because of the roles this played in Liberal theology, or in the Puritan/Precisionist movement in Holland.

Calvin's own thinking has been characterized as a theology which gives prominence to the role of the Holy Spirit. The Augustinian emphasis on the sovereignty of God and human depravity leads inevitably to a stress on the work of the Spirit in prevenient grace. Calvin's Augustinianism is also practically focussed on spiritual issues in the life of the believer. At its outset it confronts the reader existentially and experientially: self-knowledge can only be found in knowing God, and this comes only as we perceive ourselves *coram deo* in a vision which has been spiritually illuminated. The stress on the experience of encountering God in repentance is continued in Calvin's careful reconstruction of the doctrine of sanctification through the mortification of sin, regrounded on the Protestant understanding of justification. Calvin's pneumatology is not centered in theoretical definitions connected with the Trinity, but in a concern for the average believer's practical appropriation of the Holy Spirit's distinctive ministries as described in the text of Scripture.

This practical experiential concern is even more pronounced in the Puritan Calvinism which mediated the Reformer's thinking in England and America. Puritanism, first through Perkins and Ames and later through Jonathan Edwards, was the dominant theological strain in American Presbyterianism prior to the rise of the Princeton theology in the nineteenth century. In order to appreciate the extraordinary depth of pneumatological concerns in this theological movement we shall have to look at its development also in the context of Congregationalism, since the boundaries of church polity are largely irrelevant to the currents of theological cross-pollination in these two Reformed communions in the seventeenth and eighteenth centuries.

Puritanism was essentially an effort to continue the Reformation impulse, not simply in purifying the church of Romanist elements in its liturgy and polity, but above all in producing whole congregations of "visible saints" who would exhibit not only sound doctrine but holy lives. Challenged by Counter-Reformation piety and depressed by cheap grace among Protestants, the Puritans worked hard to construct a genuinely Protestant spirituality.

It is important to note that in the process they immersed themselves in patristic literature. In many Puritans there are many more references to the Fathers than to Reformation authors or later Calvinists. It is no exaggeration to say that Puritan theologians lived in the same spiritual atmosphere that the early Fathers breathed, since those responding to Puritan spirituality find the same qualities attracting them in the Greek and Latin patrologies.

Following Calvin's lead, English Puritans developed an elaborate emphasis on sanctification, reattached to a Reformation base. There is, however, a distinctive enlargement of regeneration, the first stage of sanctification, in their thought and practice. The Puritans are the origin of all later "born again" movements. Most of them practiced infant baptism, but they were extremely reserved in what they attributed to its meaning. Conscious conversion, for Puritans, was judged an essential sign of the reality of regeneration by the Spirit.

Later Puritans like Cotton Mather allowed for great diversity in the timing and manner of conversion, and were really looking for a vital current experience of the Holy Spirit rather than for a datable crisis. But all Puritans were united in the insistence that real Christians must be born of the Spirit as well as of water, and this cannot be taken for granted even among those baptized. This accounts for the strong emphasis on evangelism even among the churched in Puritan-based traditions such as modern Fundamentalism, Evangelicalism, and Pentecostalism.

It is significant that one of the ways in which believers could be assured of their regeneration was through the internal witness of the Holy Spirit, following Rom 8.16 and Gal 4.6. More "evangelical" Puritans, like John Cotton, used this pneumatological canon; others considered this approach antinomian, and stressed the inspection of works as the only objective canon of conversion, following 1 John. Luther, incidentally, might have considered both approaches legalistic, as diverting attention from the justifying work of Christ, appropriated by simple faith.

During the sixteenth century, Puritans produced an immense literature of spiritual edification. This involved a number of genres, including tracts leading the reader toward regeneration; treatises on the growth and conduct of the Christian life; and manuals of spiritual warfare (categories paralleled in the spiritual literature of the Counter-Reformation). The titles of some of the major works give the flavor of this practical biblical spirituality: Lewis Bayly's *Practice of Pietie*;

Robert Bolton's *A Comfortable Walking with God*; and Thomas Goodwin's remarkable Protestant version of *The Dark Night of the Soul, A Child of Light Walking in Darkness.*

In the whole pattern of the Christian life as the Puritans conceived it, the Holy Spirit played many crucial roles. He mediated the application of Christ's saving work in regeneration; in assurance of salvation; in enabling prayer; in the illumination of Scripture and doctrine to produce "the power of godliness" rather than a formalistic, "notional" orthodoxy; in bearing witness; and in facilitating a constant walk of communion with God.

Thus it is not surprising that through theologians like Richard Sibbes and John Owen, Puritanism produced the largest body of literature on the Holy Spirit in Anglo-American theology. Owen produced four monumental works on the subject: the *Pneumatologia; Of Communion with God the Father, Son, and Holy Ghost; A Discourse of the Work of the Holy Spirit in Prayer;* and *The Grace and Duty of Being Spiritually Minded.*

The characteristic effort of Owen, and of the many other Puritans who wrote about the Holy Spirit in shorter works, is not to inculcate correct theory about the person of the Holy Spirit, but to evoke vigorous practical response to his ministry as it is described in the text of Scripture. Puritans, like Wesleyans, were concerned that lay Christians would have orthodox opinions about the faith. But they were even more concerned that average believers would be exercising faith, and thus enjoying communion with the Holy Spirit in al his ministries as described in Scripture.

The Puritan movement, and the movements of evangelical awakening which carried forward its essential thrust in the eighteenth and nineteenth centuries, were not content even with a broad-scale catechesis of the laity along pneumatological lines, something which is much beyond us today. They would not settle for anything less than personal confrontation of individual believers with biblical directives indicating what the Holy Spirit should be doing in their lives, followed by appropriate responses of faith and obedience.

There was, of course, one area of biblical pneumatology which was off limits to the Puritans: the Lukan texts dealing with the "extraordinary gifts" of the Spirit. The Reformers had found it advantageous, against their Catholic adversaries and the Protestant enthusiasts of the Left Wing, to limit the charismata of 1 Cor 9 to the apostolic age. Even so, visions and prophetic revelations had a way of spilling over into Puritan experience, and lurk not far under the surface of the literature.

And Cotton Mather, an omnivorous reader of the fathers and practitioner of ascetic piety, developed another pneumatological strand which went back to Joachim of Fiore and had resurfaced in Puritan spirituality: the notion of a coming "age of the Spirit." After a night-long vigil interceding for the whole of Christ's body, including the Eastern Churches, Mather struck notes which are significant both for later revivalism and for the modern Charismatic Renewal:

> We can do very Little. Our Encumbrances are insuperable; our Difficulties are infinite. If He would please, to fulfill the ancient Prophecy, of pouring out the Spirit on all Flesh, and revive the extraordinary and supernatural Operations with which He planted His Religion in the primitive Times of Christianity . . . and fly thro' the World with the everlasting Gospel to preach unto the Nations, wonderful Things would be done immediately; His Kingdome would make those Advances in a Day, which under our present and fruitless Labours, are scarce made in an Age . . . I concluded with a strong Impression on my Mind; /These times /are coming! They are coming! . . . They will quickly be upon us; and the World shall be shaken wonderfully![14]

This diary entry of 1716 marks an enlarging dimension of Puritan pneumatology. Experience of the Spirit was no longer focussed simply in the growth of mystical piety in the individual saint. Now it is acquiring a corporate dimension, in a context like that of the second chapter of Acts: the outpouring of the Spirit to turn congregations into garrisons of believers equipped for extraordinary tasks in mission.

This brings us to the brink of the Great Awakening, and to the theology of Jonathan Edwards, both of which were critical factors in the future of American Presbyterianism. As Leonard Trinterud has ably documented, the Presbyterian Church in this country was literally forged in the fires of the awakening movement of restored Puritan spirituality during the 1730s and 40s. British Calvinism was lapsing toward scholastic formalism. The Synod of Philadelphia was willing to settle for "notional" professions of faith in the doctrinal formulae

---

[14]Cotton Mather, *Diary* (New York, 1957), 2, pp. 365-66.

of the Westminster Confession, and was indifferent toward assurance of personal commitment to Christ. William Tennent and the graduates of his Log College awakened congregations by reasserting the categories of Puritan spirituality, including regeneration and vital experience of the Spirit.

Trinterud comments that spiritual awakening was achieved here not by detouring dogma, but by applying doctrine to the laity in terms they could understand.

> One of the striking aspects of the preaching of the Log College men was its heavy dogmatical approach and content. It might have been expected that at least during the revival their preaching would have been more popular and topical, and cast in terms of their hearers' interests, fears, hopes, and needs. Instead, these men faced the problems of their day and analyzed them dogmatically. In their preaching they erected before their auditors the heavy structure of the Federal theology, and then, so to speak, stood between it and their people to reason and plead. To their hearers they argued that this dogmatic structure gave a true picture of the relations between God, man, and the world.[15]

Much literature about the Awakening has obscured the fact that it was in no case the product of novel doctrinal or methodological additives. It appears simultaneously, wherever basic doctrine is being practically focussed on Christian living: in Germany, in Zinzendorf's "Moravian" movement which is really a rebirth of Lutheran Pietism; in England, in the Wesley's Arminian redaction of Puritan spirituality; and in American Calvinism, restoring its Puritan roots. (Ironically and typically, the "Old Lights" who resisted the Awakening were really modernists who had forgotten their Puritan origins, while the "New Lights" were the real conservatives.)

The theologian who rose out of the Awakening controversy to dominate American Presbyterianism between the 1740s and the 1830s happened to be a Congregationalist. Jonathan Edwards restates and sums up Puritan spirituality in the way that Bach epitomizes the Baroque era. But he is also a great innovator and an original mind, and he continues the development of Calvinism toward a fullblown

---

[15]Leonard Trinterud, *The Forming of an American Tradition* (Philadelphia, 1949), p. 177.

theology of radical dependence on the Spirit.

Edwards' practical theology is dominated by its focus on the difference between theoretical orthodoxy and the spiritually illuminated vision of faith. His concern for his well-catechized but spiritually inert parishioners, whose ultimate concern was not God but success in business, was that the Spirit would illuminate their minds with "a divine and supernatural light," producing "a true sense of the divine and superlative excellency of the things of religion; a real sense of the excellency of God and Jesus Christ, and of the work of redemption, and the ways and works of God revealed in the gospel."[16]

Edwards' famous sermon evades his real text, which is Ephesians 1.17-18: "I keep asking that the God of our Lord Jesus Christ, the glorious Father, may give you the Spirit of wisdom and revelation, so that you may know him better. I pray also that the eyes of your heart may be enlightened in order that you may know the hope to which he has called you." As Edwards comments, "It is not a thing that belongs to reason, to see the beauty and loveliness of spiritual things; it is not a speculative thing, but depends on the sense of the heart."[17] This restates the core of Puritan spirituality. It is not anti-intellectual pietism, because what Edwards means by "the heart" is not emotion, but the fusion of the mind, will and affections at the core of personality. What it describes is an orthodoxy which has come to determine the thoughts, words and actions of an individual, because the Holy Spirit has transformed concepts into ultimate concerns, through the experience of union with Christ.

The significance of this combination in Edwards' theology is that he did not simply insist, as all Puritans did, that each Christian should become a practicing mystic, cultivating a personal relationship with the indwelling Spirit. Edwards went beyond this to assert that all Christians should unite to pray for a worldwide outpouring of the Holy Spirit to renew the Church, so that it would constitute a Messianic people which would transform society and culture even before the personal return of Christ. In Edwardsean theology the reign of the Spirit through a renewed Church anticipates the millenial rule of Christ, introducing justice and a unified world society through what might be called a "realized pneumatology."

---

[16]Jonathan Edwards, "A Divine and Supernatural Light," in *Works*, ed., Serone E. Dwight (Edinburgh, 1974), 2, p. 12.

[17]Edwards, p. 16.

The resulting theology gave New School Presbyterianism a re-markable spiritual dynamism undergirding the social dynamism which sought the abolition of slavery and other reforms. The individual and corporate dimensions of experiencing the Spirit were generally foun-dational to the reform movement, although Charles Finney feared that enthusiasm for reform would outrun revival.

At this point we need to note that the Protestant efforts at social transformation through spiritual renewal were a multitraditional af-fair, like the first Awakening. Wesley's perfectionism had one set of dynamics which aided the reform movement; Edwardsean Calvinism had analogous elements; and even Lutheran Pietism overflowed its theological container to impact society. The common element which united all these traditions in a united front working for individual and social conversion during the eighteenth and nineteenth centuries was a focussed concern for spiritual vitality, and a pronounced de-pendence on the Holy Spirit.

This synthesis, which in its Reformed expression is traced by H. Richard Niebuhr in *The Kingdom of God in America*, and George Marsden in *The Presbyterian Mind and the New School Experience*, began to break up with the emergence of Finneyan revivalism. In a pat-tern which has become depressingly familiar, Charles Finney united bad theology about the Holy Spirit's work with strong promotion of the Edwardsean dynamism in mission. The Princeton theology, on the other hand, maintained scholastic accuracy on doctrine while mov-ing steadily away from the emphasis on the Spirit which characterized its founders, leaders like Archibald Alexander and Samuel Miller. B. B. Warfield's writings are models of logical and theological clarity. But they are insensitive to the values emerging in the Wesleyan and Pentecostal movements despite their theological imbalance. And they lean away from the original pneumatological concern of American Presbyterianism in the direction of a lucid but ennervated rationalism.

During the early twentieth century this scholastic Reformed syn-thesis was opposed in American Presbyterianism, first by forms of Liberal theology, and later by the Neo-Reformation theology of Barth and Brunner. In the 1930s J. Gresham Machen and others continu-ing the Old Princeton tradition seceded from mainline Presbyterianism to form the Orthodox Presbyterian Church, after establishing West-minster Seminary to continue the line of Warfield and the Hodges. The parent church was thus left in the control of Neo-Orthodoxy and Neo-Liberal theologies along the line of Paul Tillich.

None of these twentieth-century Reformed variants preserved much of the pneumatological emphasis of early Presbyterianism. The Westminster theology was virtually allergic to practical pneumatology, since it associated experiential Christianity with Liberalism and existentialism. Westminster was increasingly influenced by Dutch theology in the school of Abraham Kuyper. But while Kuyper's movement had risen out of the *Reveil,* the Second Evangelical Awakening in Europe, his descendents were reacting against the experiential excesses of Dutch-based fundamentalism.

In mainline Presbyterianism, meanwhile, Barthians replayed this theological objectivism in another key. Despite its merits in other areas, Neo-Orthodoxy largely ignored both practical and theoretical concerns in the area of pneumatology. During the 1960s, the theological center of Presbyterianism began to break up into Neo-Liberal variants which had little resemblance to the Reformed tradition in either their theological shape or pneumatological focus. Confronting the Death of God emphasis and other forms of secular theology, James McCord, President of Princeton Seminary, complained that Presbyterian theology had become "a shambles." Other critics complained of "theological amnesia" in the mainline Presbyterian community.

John Mackay, who preceded McCord as President of Princeton, had already begun to investigate what Henry P. Van Dusen called the "Third Force" in world Christianity, Pentecostalism, through his friendship with Dr. David DuPlessis. By the 1970s it seemed that Mackay had transferred his hopes for both renewal and reunion to the spiritual resurgence appearing among Charismatics and Evangelicals. Indeed, if we are looking for trinitarian theology lived out daily in a practical manner, laypeople in these movements may be the best examples in current Protestantism. They understand in a very personal way the role of the Son in redemption, and they know more than most Christians about the Holy Spirit's work as defined by Scripture, despite their weakness in the area of social concern.

It may be, however, that real trinitarian balance is not present in the life-experience of any current network of Christians. There may really be at least three "ecumenical movements" in the world today: "The Church of the Father," which is Conciliar Ecumenism with its characteristic concerns for justice and proper rulership of Creation; "The Church of the Son," which is the Lausanne Movement with its concern for proclaiming Jesus Christ in evangelism; and "The Church of the Spirit," the Pentecostal/Charismatic world fellowship, with its effort to make up for the lack of pneumatology in the rest of the Church. It would be cheering if we could define Roman Catholicism and Orthodoxy as "churches of the Trinity." But these communions often seem to need cross-pollination from other sectors in order to gain full vitality in the use of their distinctive gifts. Perhaps none of us can live out trinitarian theology except as we more toward trinitarian unity.

Returning to the Presbyterian scene: in the 1970s and 1980s new theological currents emerged which could be fruitful for fresh pneumatological insights. Whether liberation and process theologies will actually develop pneumatologically still remains to be seen.

Meanwhile, there are evidences that mainline Presbyterianism is seeking to find its way back to the Reformed tradition of spirituality. Influenced by the Lilly Foundation's study of spiritual life on seminary campuses, the United Presbyterian Church set up s series of forums on Reformed Piety in its related seminaries. Dr. McCord called for historical study of the spiritual climate of Presbyterianism during its great eras of missionary expansion, and an effort to translate conclusions from this study into the modern situation.

Two theological streams in the church, converging somewhat on one another are reemphasizing Reformed spirituality. One is a new conservative impulse which Thomas Oden, a Methodist theologian, has called "Post-Modern Orthodoxy." As Neo-Orthodoxy sprang from a rediscovery of the Reformers, Post-Modern Orthodoxy emerges from a broader look including the Reformation tradition but reaching back into the patristic era, and responding both to the theology and spirituality of the fathers.

The other theological current is a post-Fundamentalist evangelicalism which is also quite catholic in its tastes and influences. A good example of this strand is Donald Bloesch, a U.C.C. theologian from a German Reformed background teaching in a Presbyterian seminary. Bloesch's theology is grounded in Luther and Calvin; the Puritans and Pietists; Barth, Thielicke, Forsyth and other conservative modern thinkers; and patristic authorities like Augustine and Irenaios. Bloesch is deeply concerned about the church's need for creedal formulations defining the limits of the pluralism which has been the ethos of mainline Presbyterianism since the Fundamentalist-Modernist Controversy.

The *Confession of 1967*, produced by a committee headed by Edward Dowey, attempted to apply Barthian theology to current social problems, centered around the doctrine of reconciliation. It did not have a large pneumatological component. Since the reunion of the United Presbyterian Church and the Presbyterian Church in the United States, a committee has begun to work on a new doctrinal statement for the reunited church. The chances are that any document produced by this committee will not penetrate into new ground in pneumatology or in other areas, but will restate the core of Reformed theology within a short compass, in order to function as theological cement binding the reunited church.

Meanwhile, sectarian Calvinism in the smaller Presbyterian churches is developing larger social and cultural concerns, in common with the larger Evangelical Movement in which it is a main strand. The influence of Abraham Kuyper is strong here. Kuyper's doctrine of Common Grace and his quite developed pneumatology supply spiritual dimensions which are missing in most modern Reformed expressions of social concern. Whether any of the Reformed strains visible today will develop the spiritual dynamism of Edwardsean Calvinism, however, remains to be seen.

The Role of the Holy Spirit from a United Methodist Perspective

ROBERTA BONDI

AT VARIOUS TIMES from the early days of the Church until the present the doctrine of the Holy Spirit has been a stumbling block to Christian unity. Disagreement over the doctrine still trips us up or at least causes us to stub our toes in two areas: first, at the formal point of division between the Eastern and Western churches, with respect to the *filioque,* and second, among those Christian groups who emphasize the extraordinary gifts of the Spirit, such as tongues, healing, prophecy, and so forth, and those who emphasize the presence of the Holy Spirit in all of Christian life from the time of baptism. Among those who emphasize the extraordinary gifts of the Spirit are the Pentecostal denominations which began at the start of the century, on the one hand, and the various neo-pentecostal or charismatic groups that may cut across denominational lines, in Orthodox churches, the Roman Catholic churches, and various Protestant churches, on the other. Though the *filioque* is not a live issue in United Methodism, the debate over special and ordinary gifts of the Spirit is. Surprisingly bitter feelings divide many congregations and surely are undermining Christian unity within the denomination, much less outside of it.

In this paper I will try to say what I am able to with respect to what might be said to be the United Methodist perspective on the Holy Spirit. This is not an easy enterprise, however. United Methodists recognize four sources of religious authority: Scripture, tradition, reason, and experience. Insofar as we have explicitly spelled out doctrinal standards, they consist of John Wesley's *Forty-four Standard Sermons* and his *Notes on the New Testament,* and what is contained in the modern *United Methodist Discipline.* Nevertheless, we recognize ourselves to be a church which allows for a great deal of theological diversity, and we value that diversity, for

> the ethical fruits of faith concern us more than systems of doctrine. . . . The freedom we foster in this regard has been a function of our larger sense of belonging to the whole People of God.[1]

This means that constitutionally as a United Methodist, delineating a doctrine of the Holy Spirit is difficult. Nevertheless, there is so much pain in so many United Methodist congregations on this question that, even apart from the ecumenical needs for a statement, we need together to look again at the whole question of our own tradition concerning the role of the Holy Spirit in the life of the Church. For this Wesley in a particular way, but also the rest of Christian tradition and Scripture are resources, along with our own experience and our rational thought processes. In all of this Wesley has a special place: not the most important place, of course, for that place is reserved for Scripture. But Wesley has a special place as the one who originally interpreted Scripture and tradition to give modern United Methodists the broad shape of the way we experience and understand the Spirit, and in many respects, it is out of a Wesleyan theology that we enter into ecumenical dialogue.

Much water has flowed under the bridge since Wesley's eighteenth century, however, and only the exceptionally educated United Methodist would know what Wesley taught. Nevertheless, I would contend that a good deal of what makes modern-day United Methodists who they are is a memory of Wesley's doctrine of the Spirit that is in our genes, and it is out of this modern identity that we can begin finding healing in the Spirit for our own wounds as well as being able to enter into ecumenical dialogue. I intend, therefore, to try briefly to do three things in this paper: (1) to look at Wesley's own doctrine of the Spirit, which would constitute in some sense the "official" United Methodist position, (2) to try to see how this position is manifested at the congregational level today, and (3) to suggest ways in which we might enter the larger conversation on the Spirit with the rest of the Church.

---

[1]*Discipline* (New York, 1984), par. 69, p. 74.

JOHN WESLEY

John Wesley was born in 1703 in Epworth, England, the son of a High-church Anglican clergyman and an exceptionally well educated woman from a Nonconformist background. He was educated at the Charterhouse in London, and then at Christ Church, Oxford. At Oxford, he read voraciously in the Christian spiritual classics. In 1726 he became a fellow of Lincoln College, Oxford. In 1729 he joined in Oxford a group his brother had founded for "Bible study, mutual discipline in devotion, and frequent Communion. This group had developed a keen interest in the ancient liturgies and the monastic piety of the fourth century 'desert fathers.' "[2] Though the Church in its first centuries was only one source among many for Wesley's theology, Wesley's deep understanding of the heart and soul of this early Christianity, and especially of early monasticism, underlies the whole of his thought. His own doctrine of the Holy Spirit must surely owe a substantial debt to the *Makarian Homilies,* which he abridged for the first volume of his Christian Library. His wide and serious reading and incorporating of much from the Eastern patristic writers, along with his study of Western spiritual classics, Anglican, Roman Catholic and Reformation writers, related United Methodism theologically at its roots in some way to large segments of the modern church.

The movement that came to be the Methodist Revival really got its start in 1739 when he reluctantly preached in Bristol for his friend George Whitefield. Wesley had by this time had a disastrous missionary trip to America and his reluctance to preach outdoors at Bristol to uneducated masses of people must surely be related to that disaster. Much to his own surprise, once he actually did preach to them, he was able to communicate; he had read Jonathan Edward's account of his New England Revival and its spectacular conversions, and he found the same things happening when he preached in Bristol. People responded with great manifestations of deep emotion, and those who followed Wesley during Wesley's own time were frequently dismissed as "enthusiasts," that is, fanatics.

But Wesley had no intention of being schismatic. While the Church of England did not care for him, he placed a high value on Christian unity, and he regarded what he and his followers were about as a renewal movement within the Church of England. It was not until

---

[2]Albert C. Outler, ed., *John Wesley* (New York, 1964), p. 8.

two years after Wesley's death that Methodism broke off from the Church of England.

THE PLACE OF THE HOLY SPIRIT IN
WESLEY'S UNDERSTANDING OF THE CHRISTIAN LIFE

For John Wesley there is no human life apart from the Holy Spirit. While natural humanity is as full of sin according to Wesley's theology as it is according to Luther's, Wesley did not believe that human beings are ever to be found in that natural state. Instead, he believed that God's prevenient grace surrounds each person from their birth, so that it is only by means of the Spirit that anyone is empowered to live at all:

> I believe firmly, and that in the most literal sense, that "without God we can do nothing . . . "; that we cannot think, or speak, or move a hand . . . without the concurrence of the divine energy; and that all our natural faculties are God's gift, nor can the meanest be exerted without the assistance of His Spirit.[3]

This means that the grace of the Spirit from birth is given to each human being, activating the conscience, allowing each of us to distinguish between right and wrong and pointing us toward God to take the first steps toward our salvation, enabling repentance and allowing us to ask God for help. (Wesley is very close to the *Makarian Homilies* at this point.) This gift of the Spirit is the result of the work of Christ in the Atonement.

By means of the grace we receive through the Spirit we are able to repent of our sins, and we are given the gift of faith which allows us "to see the things of God," including our own pardon through the death of Christ, which is our justification. This justification is the beginning of our new life of salvation. It comes to us from God. It is done for us through the gift of the Holy Spirit. Only by means of the Spirit can we have the faith to experience "a sure trust and confidence that God's love and mercy in Christ's sacrifice is for me."[4] It is the Holy Spirit witnessing to our spirit that makes a theoretical knowledge of God's forgiving love into a personal inner reality.

---

[3] Quoted by L. Starkey, p. 40, *The Work of the Holy Spirit: A Study in Wesleyan Theology* from a letter of Wesley.

[4] Starkey, p. 49.

But the Holy Spirit does more. Justification for Wesley is only the beginning of the Christian life. One who is justified is not free of sin. As Wesley says, the newly justified may be tempted to think that sin in them is dead, whereas "it is only stunned." Even though justified, no one can, without the power of the Holy Spirit, resist sin and do good. Justification itself is lost without the continual presence of the Spirit.

It is sanctification, or Christian perfection, that is the goal of the Christian life. This Christian perfection is not a static goal, the culmination of a process of "doing all the right things" and "not doing all the wrong things." It is for Wesley what it was for those who lived out the early monastic tradition: perfect love of God and neighbor. He, like they, believes that the command to love God with all our hearts and our neighbors as ourselves is both a command and a promise that can be fulfilled in this life. That doesn't mean it happens often, nor does mean that, once reached, the Christian cannot fail.

Journeying toward Christian perfection is not something we do ourselves of our own effort any more than being justified is. Just as justification can occur only through the Spirit's gift of faith, so the whole process of sanctification can only come about as the Holy Spirit gives us the power to produce the ordinary "fruits of the Spirit," including love, joy, and peace.

By human effort alone we cannot fight the evil in ourselves or do any good. On the other hand, the Holy Spirit does not automatically bring us through the process of sanctification without any human effort. Only by a synergistic working of the Holy Spirit with our own spirit are we empowered to work with God in the Christian life to move toward perfect love. At this point of synergism Wesley again demonstrates his similarity to the ancient monastic tradition.

All of this is intensely personal, as the Holy Spirit and the human being continually interact. It is an interaction of which we can be consciously aware in two ways, first by the direct witness of the Spirit and second, by the indirect witness of a life that begins to show forth the fruits of the Spirit. Wesley speaks of the direct witness as

> an inward impression on the soul, whereby the Spirit of God witnesses to my spirit that I am a child of God; that Christ Jesus hath loved me, and given himself for me; and that all my sins are blotted out, and I, even I, am reconciled to God.[5]

---

[5]Sermon 10, "The Witness of the Spirit, Discourse 1," 1.7, p. 115.

In his earlier years Wesley believed that every Christian would be given this "assurance of faith"; pastoral experience taught him, however, that it does not come to every person in the same way. For some, the assurance of faith is mixed with doubt; for others, it is not. Nevertheless, for everyone salvation is only real where God is actually experienced, and this experience is not a one time thing that we reflect back on, but rather, a continuous interaction of a person with God through the Holy Spirit.

As for the indirect witness of the Spirit, presence of the Spirit within us surely guarantees that we will bring forth fruits of the Spirit. Wesley insists repeatedly that unless there is an actual change in a person's life, unless a person is moving toward holiness, the person cannot be filled with the Spirit. In his own time, people were as suspicious of "enthusiasts" as they are of religious fanatics in our own time, and Wesley was not inclined to be soft on them. He was perfectly aware of religious experiences that were in fact only the production of self-delusion. The presence of the Spirit in our heart is more than a feeling.

But the Spirit does not bring about Christian behavior without our own cooperation. The Spirit does not overwhelm us, but rather,

> the Spirit may lead [a person] as much by his head or understanding as by his heart or affections, as much by light as by heat. . . . By these metaphors Wesley means that the Spirit works in and through, and not against the whole of [a person's] personality.[6]

Any movement toward God, in fact, is with the work of the Spirit, and yet never does the Spirit overrule human will, or work without human cooperation.

Wesley did not separate the work of the Spirit from the life of the Church. The true Church itself Wesley was convinced was not made up fo those whose doctrine was pure, or who read Scripture properly, or who worshipped properly or had a genuine apostolic succession in its clergy, or the right polity. Instead, it includes

> all the persons in the universe whom God hath so called out of the world as to entitle them to the . . . character of [Christians];

---

[6]Starkey, p. 73,

as to be "one body," united by "one Spirit"; having one faith, one hope, one baptism, one God and Father of all, who is above all, and through all, and in them all.[7]

This is a broad and ecumenical vision of the Church, whose primary characteristic is its unity in the Holy Spirit. By seeing the Church in this way, Wesley does not mean to suggest that polity, doctrine, sacraments, ways of reading Scripture, and so forth, are of no concern to the Christian: probably no one in the history of the Church has ever written as many words arguing over these very issues than he.[8] Nevertheless, he never confused the need for and the presence of the Spirit with any of these components of church life.

Though God's grace may be conveyed to us however God chooses, by means of the Spirit, we receive God's grace through the ordinary means he has given us, in our private worship, but also in our life within the Church:

> The chief of these means are prayer, whether in secret or with the great congregation; searching the scriptures . . . ; and receiving the Lord's Supper, eating bread and drinking wine in remembrance of Him. . . . We allow, likewise, that all outward means whatever, if separate from the Spirit of God, cannot profit at all . . . [9]

Wesley assures us that if we make faithful use of these means, God will surely finally fulfill the promise he has made to us and grant us the gift of his grace.

Thus, according to the theology of John Wesley, there can be no life, much less Christian life, without the Holy Spirit. Every stage of the Christian life depends upon the work of the Spirit. Furthermore, the Church itself is constituted by those who have the Spirit, and it exists wherever people have the Holy Spirit, witnessing, pardoning, empowering, sustaining, bringing to completion God's work in us. The presence of the Holy Spirit is not limited to those who believe the right things, have the right religious experiences, worship in the right way, or even read Scripture properly. Wesley's understanding of the work of the Holy Spirit is broad and inclusive,

---

[7]Ibid.

[8]See, for example, sermon 14, "Catholic Spirit," where he makes it quite clear how important these things are.

[9]Sermon 12, "The Means of Grace," 2.1,2, pp. 136-37.

tolerant of the different ways God works in our midst, and convinced that the proof of the presence of the Holy Spirit must always include the fruits of the Spirit displayed in Christian life and love.

MODERN UNITED METHODIST CONGREGATIONS IN THE SOUTHEAST UNITED STATES AND THEIR UNDERSTANDING OF THE HOLY SPIRIT

The United Methodist Church in the Southeastern United States, where I come from, suffers from what afflicts it in other parts of the country. It is too successful: that is, it is one of the establishment churches. For this reason, one will often find almost no difference between the culture outside of the church and the people within. On the whole, we share the friendliness of the South, coupled with a strong sense of privacy over our deep religious feelings and their manifestations. The most conservative among us, who will often be quite close to moderate Southern Baptists, are comfortable using the language the evangelicals use. It is not at all unusual to hear people speak of altar calls, finding the Lord, or being saved. The more liberal among us may hesitate to use this language, and will be more oriented to Christian fellowship and social action. In all its strands, however, United Methodism is optimistic in its outlook, and members will frequently be reluctant to let their church acquaintances know about the seamier side of the problems most people have at one time or another with their families, or jobs, or money, or certain kinds of health problems. Perhaps this reluctance partly stems from the ancient Methodist heritage from Wesley that a person full of the Holy Spirit will be full of peace and joy and love, but partly, too, it comes from the conviction that "nice people" don't talk about these things.

In matters of doctrine, United Methodists generally "believe and let believe." Few of us have much sense of what our theological heritage contains, but we have retained Wesley's sense that true Christianity has more to do with Christian living and the presence of the Holy Spirit than it has with beliefs. In its watered down version, this translates into "it doesn't matter what you believe, as long as you're sincere." At its best, it translates into an insistence on open communion, and a genuine belief that the varieties of ways God deals with human beings is infinite. At its worst, it goes with a tendency to allow any sort of thoughts to be passed off as legitimately Christian in church life without any correction.

United Methodists in the Southeast are partly attracted to

charismatic groups for reasons having to do with the above description of many United Methodist congregations. That is, they usually feel that there is not much conviction in congregational worship. But United Methodists attracted in this direction are also responding out of another deep seated Wesleyan insight: there is no real Christianity where there is no live and personal ongoing relationship with God. Every Methodist of whatever stripe acknowledges the importance of Christian experience, and those attracted to charismatic religion seek to have a vital and ongoing experience of God that might contain more life than that which seems to flow in the politely approved channels of Methodist worship. In this they are living out their own Wesleyan tradition.

United Methodist charismatics often seek this experience by looking for what many charismatics of other denominations associate with the "baptism in the Spirit," such as tongues, interpretation, healing, and so forth, as the major gifts of the Spirit, but not all charismatic United Methodists think of the primary work of the Spirit in this way. Many intelligent and thoughtful United Methodist charismatics are fully aware of the way in which the Holy Spirit enlivens all of the Christian life in its most "ordinary" ways.

Nevertheless, there is a great deal of bitterness among the congregations, and some conferences are felt to discriminate against pastors of a charismatic bent. Each side of the split offends the other. Perhaps both sides tend to exhibit what Wesley himself calls "enthusiasm," or a kind of religious madness.[10] Certainly in a lot of places there is a terrible lack of charity.

Many non-charismatic Christians believe that charismatic Christians regard them as less than Christians if they do not have a "baptism in the Spirit" on top of their "water baptism." Indeed, charismatic United Methodists often seem to have forgotten that they have not been appointed by God to pronounce judgment upon the adequacy of their non-charismatic brothers' and sisters' religious experience, not to mention their way of reading Scripture. Often, their charismatic experience is backed up by a theology that inclines them to ignore the great social issues in their community, in our nation, and in the world. Non-charismatics who are convinced that the Christian is to witness to the gospel through acts of love in a wounded world will be offended by their neighbors' air of superiority, as well

---

[10]See Sermon 32, "The Nature of Enthusiasm."

as the suggestion that the Spirit we all received at baptism is not a motivator and empowerer of their Christian service. Furthermore, because so many charismatic groups have taken themselves out of United Methodist congregations to set themselves up as separate Bible churches, United Methodist congregations very rightly fear that where charismatics come, schism may shortly follow. On the other hand, charismatics are equally offended by being treated as slobbering fanatics by people whose real objection may have more to do with how they believe "nice people" act than anything else.

Yet, I believe, each side needs the other. We need to remember that where there is no ongoing experience of God, there is no Christian life. We also need the structure and the discipline of our community worship, and we certainly all need a new sense of *all* of the ordinary ways we experience our life in the Spirit.

ENTERING THE LARGER ECUMENICAL DIALOGUE

The charismatic renewal is itself an ecumenical movement in that it crosses all sorts of denominational lines that are otherwise hard for non-professional church people to cross, and this is potentially a great blessing for the Church. Being a lay movement, for the most part, it does not depend for its vigor on the various churches' official hierarchies: both its strength and its weakness lie here. The power of the Spirit is surely present in many different places, but many groups will find the gospel as they experience it being distorted where they are not incorporated into and tested within the individual denominations to which they belong. The need for the testing of spirits is as great now as it was in Paul's day. This process, however, will never take place until each side can learn to give up some of its pride, mistrust of and scorn for the other. Where there is no charity, surely God does not dwell.

Furthermore, the whole of the Church needs prayerfully to begin to think harder about who the Holy Spirit is, who we acknowledged in 381 at the Council of Constantinople to be full member of the Trinity. We need to search back in Scripture and within our own Christian tradition for hints as well as for overt statements.

Pneumatological Issues in the Holiness Movement

DONALD W. DAYTON

LOST AS IT IS BETWEEN the better understood evangelical and pentecostal traditions (between which it is the historical and theological bridge), the "holiness movement" was one of the most influential religious movements in nineteenth century America and has produced in the twentieth century a cluster of denominations and institutions which, with the products of their missions and other forms of international impact, constitute one of the more recent "world confessional communions" to emerge on the Christian landscape. This "holiness movement" is basically a variation within Methodism, but has in this century evolved into a distinct ecclesiastical and theological tradition represented by its interdenominational "ecumenical" agency, the Christian Holiness Association, and the related Wesleyan Theological Society. Since this movement is not well known in wider church circles and is not yet well chronicled in the studies of American religion, it is necessary to preface this study with a more extensive introduction to the movement whose pneumatology is described in this paper.

Like the evangelical revival before it and the pentecostal movement which it spawned, the holiness movement has been a complex spiritual movement with many subsidiary currents and eddies that make it difficult to describe simply. It was born in the 1830s in the confluence of recently imported Methodism and the older American revivalist traditions as they were finding current expression in the evangelism of Charles G. Finney, the so-called "father of modern revivalism." The motivating force was a reassertion of a variation on the doctrine of "Christian perfection" or "entire sanctification" that had been articulated by John Wesley in the preceeding century. Essentially it was a spiritual movement that involved a search for a deeper spirituality or a "higher Christian life" that took on many characteristics of the more recent charismatic movement. Within its broader emphasis on process and growth within sanctification, this movement expected generally a second "crisis" or "blessing" following conversion in which a high degree of consecration and sanctification took place so that the believer was lifted to a new plane of spirituality and purity of intention that permitted a life of "victory" over sin. In the formative years before the Civil War this movement gathered force, especially in the revival of 1857-58, and, like the charismatic movement of today, broke the boundaries of Methodism to become an interdenominational spiritual revival that had wide impact among Presbyterians, Congregationalists, Episcopalians, Baptists, Quakers, and others. This interdenominational impact and growing tensions within Methodism led eventually to new sect formation and a process of realignment and new denominational configurations still in the process of taking shape.

The vanguard of this new configuration was in two splits within Methodism during the antebellum period. Both groups antedated the denominational formation of the holiness movement proper, but both were efforts to preserve themes of original Methodism (or at least current perceptions of what constituted the themes of primitive Methodism). Such efforts to preserve original Methodism led naturally to an emphasis on Wesley's teachings on Christian Perfection (though one must, of course, notice a nuancing provided by the optimistic — and thus perfectionist — impulse of the American antebellum experience). The Wesleyan Methodist Connection (now the Wesleyan Church by virture of a 1968 merger with the Pilgrim Holiness Church) was founded in protest against the Methodist Episcopal compromise of Wesley's anti-slavery convictions and developed a reformist platform combined with a congregationalism that reflected a corrective to a conservative episcopacy that had tried to suppress Wesleyan dissent and abolitionist activity. Similarly the Free Methodist Church emerged as a protest against the *embourgeoisement* of classical Methodism and its assimilation into traditional church life, especially the adoption of the "pew rental" system that Free Methodists felt hampered Methodism's historic relationship to the poor and forms of worship that minimized congregational participation in music and liturgy — as well as the concern shared with the Wesleyans about Methodist compromise on slavery. Both churches, as we have suggested, emphasized doctrines of "Christian perfection" and with the rise of the holiness movement proper and under its influence moved toward identification with the larger movement.

The holiness movement proper, especially in its more Methodistic wings, tends to look back to the work of Phoebe Palmer and her doctor husband Walter C. Palmer. Phoebe was known especially for her widely imitated "Tuesday Meeting for the Promotion of Holiness" that took the shape of a parlor "house church" meeting somewhat akin to some facets of the more recent charismatic movement. This movement had wide impact among the leadership of Methodism and eventually broadened its impact as church leaders and educators in a number of denominations came into the experience of "entire sanctification." Methodist preachers identified with the movement founded just after the Civil War a National Campmeeting Association for the Promotion of Christian Holiness, the precursor of today's Christian Holiness Association. The movement spread through independent camp meeting associations, local and state "holiness" associations, independent mission societies carrying the message, innumerable rescue missions, and various other institutions spread across the continent and around the world in a very loose but identifiable network. By the end of the century tensions with Methodism had increased with the traditionalists accusing the holiness folk of a new "specialty" or "hobby" that upset the delicate balance of classical Methodism while the holiness advocates accused the Methodists of losing touch with both the teachings (especially the Wesleyan emphasis on sanctification but also more generally a broader defection from classical Christianity) and disciplines of early Methodism. The expulsion/departure of holiness advocates from Methodism, the increasing interdenominalization of the movement, and a weakening of national holiness leadership producing a form of scattered seeding in which the fragments of the holiness network were spread across the North American continent to contribute to the rise of innumerable new denominations.

The first of these denominations to emerge in the wake of the holiness revival was the Church of God (Anderson, Indiana), which in the early 1880s combined the Wesleyan/Holiness soteriology with a Campbellite ecclesiology which hoped to transcend the sects and denominations as the new "Church of God." Like the Campbellite

Disciples of Christ, this vision led in some cases to an ecumenical concern illustrated in the extended involvement of the late John Smith in the NCCC Faith and Order Commission. Its distinctive ecclesiology, however, led the Church of God to stand aloof from other denominations and thus interdenominational agencies like the Christian Holiness Association with which it nonetheless cooperates.

More typical of the holiness movement and its largest denominational product has been the Church of the Nazarene which took shape at the turn of the century in an agglutinative process by which various fragments of the broader holiness movement have coalesced to form a new denomination. This denomination, while proud of its interdenominational origins, has felt the strongest loyalty to the more conservative and more Methodistic leaders of the National Campmeeting Association and reveals in its life and ethos the profound influence of the campmeeting culture. At the same time the radicals of the period (here so-called because of their affinity with doctrines of divine healing and the rising tide of premillennialism — topics forbidden on the platform of the National Campmeeting Association) tended by a similar process to gather into what became the Pilgrim Holiness Church, a major tributary of the present Wesleyan Church. Many other similar groups were also founded at the turn of the century, but some of these moved on into Pentecostalism and others have tended to maintain a more isolated existence.

Perhaps the best known product of the holiness movement has been the Salvation Army. William Booth was converted under the evangelistic ministry in England of Phoebe Palmer's pastor, and his wife-to-be Catherine Mumford felt called into public ministry under the influence and example of Phoebe Palmer during her several years of evangelistic tours of England in the wake of the Revival of 1857-58. In a pattern reminiscent of similar developments in America, the Booth's concern for the disenfranchised and the downtrodden led to tensions with a Methodism rapidly moving into the middle class and a separate organization incarnating the polemic against bourgeois church life. The identification of the Salvation Army with the Holiness Movement has been particularly strong in the United Stated where the army has been active in the Christian Holiness Association and has produced in the twentieth century spiritual teachers of broad influence within the larger holiness movement.

The intense piety and disciplined Christian lives of the holiness advocates had a special affinity with the Anabaptist and Quakers of

the nineteenth century, especially those groups that felt the influence
of revivalism. Holiness revivalism had great impact on certain year-
ly meetings of Quakers (especially in Ohio, Kansas, the Rocky Moun-
tains, and the Pacific Northwest). These holiness Quakers have recently
come together in the Evangelical Friends Alliance and many of them
have found identity in the broader holiness movement. Similarly the
Mennonites and "Dunkers" felt the influence of the holiness revival,
especially among the various antecedents of the present Missionary
Church and the Brethren in Christ with their roots among the
"Dunkers."

The twentieth century has also seen the emergence of a certain
dynamic which has swelled the ranks of the Christian Holiness Association with new denominations that have found a "holiness" identity
without being strictly products of the holiness revival as such. Along
the lines of the fundamentalist/modernist controversy that has divided
many Protestant denominations along more conservative and more
liberal lines, there have emerged in the present century various conservative Methodist bodies who by their appeal to a form of classical
Methodism have often preserved original Wesleyan teachings on sanctification and have thus tended to identify with the holiness churches. Illustrative of this current would be the Evangelical Methodist
Church and more recently the Evangelical Church of North America
which represents largely congregations of the old Evangelical United
Brethren who refused to join the 1968 merger to form the United
Methodist Church. Other examples could be given.

In addition to these separate denominational groupings, one needs
to give attention to the large pockets of the holiness movement that
have remained within the United Methodist Church. The most influential of the these would be the circles dominated by Asbury College and Asbury Theological Seminary (both in Wilmore, KY), but
one could speak of other colleges, innumerable local campmeetings,
the vestiges of various local holiness associations, indepedent holiness
oriented missionary societies and the like that have had great impact within United Methodism. A similar pattern would exist in
England with the role of Cliff College within Methodism in that
context.

The holiness spirituality has also had a diffusion through many
other denominational contexts, especially in a more moderate form
known as the "Keswick" or "victorious Christian life" piety. American
holiness teachers like Asa Mahan and Hannah Whitall Smith were

determinitive in the Oxford and Brighton Holiness Conventions that climaxed in the annual summer conferences held in Keswick in England's lake district. Keswick spirituality had been profoundly influential among Anglican Evangelicals and was reintroduced into America in close association with the revivals of D. L. Moody. Because of the impact of evangelists Finney and Moody American revivalism has been largely suffused with holiness teachings — so much so that holiness spirituality of the Keswick variety is the dominant piety of American revivalistic evangelicalism and the various "faith" missions associated with it from the China Inland Mission to the present. The extent to which this is still true is clear in the writings of such evangelists as Billy Graham and Bill Bright, as well as in the books on the Holy Spirit by such prominent evangelicals as Harold Lindsell and Harold John Ockenga.

One other facet of the holiness constellation deserves mention. As already hinted above, the Pentecostal movement is best understood as an offshoot of the radical wing of the holiness movement; from the holiness perspective it was in a sense a "holiness heresy" that was largely repudiated by the holiness movement in spite of its paternity. As a result of this relationship, many themes of the holiness movement and its piety and spirituality are carried along into Pentecostalism. A large block of the pentecostal movement is also decidedly holiness in doctrine and piety while most of the rest advocates the more moderate Keswick form of the holiness spirituality. More attention will be given to this question below, but Pentecostalism needs to be clearly listed here as one of the currents arising from the holiness revival.

As can be seen from the above effort to delineate the major products of the holiness revival, the movement is very complex and includes many facets that make easy generalization very difficult. In this paper I am attempting to speak in general for as much of the movement as possible, though I will speak most directly out of that aspect of the tradition which has found identification with the Christian Holiness Association. This perspective sets both the Keswick spirituality and Pentecostalism somewhat off to the side as related but not strictly "holiness" traditions.

The Holiness Movement and the Filioque Controversy

The assignment for this paper includes the reviewing of the WCC discussions on the *filioque* controversy as reported in Faith and Order paper No. 103 edited by Lukas Vischer under the title *Spirit of God, Spirit of Christ.* This is very difficult to do from the perspective of the holiness movement — for a variety of reasons, but basically because I have not been able to find much literature that speaks directly to this issue. The collected works of Wesley reveal no comment on the *filioque* issue and only a couple of casual references to Nicea, basically in the context of Wesley's Anglican affinity with the church fathers and a special fondness for the Antenicene fathers which he considered especially authoritative in view of his conviction of a radical decline in apostolic faith and piety after Constantine.

On the other hand, it seems clear that Wesley would have followed the Western tradition and affirmed the *filioque.* His abridgement of the Anglican thirty-nine articles of religion into the Methodist twenty-five includes 4. "Of the holy Ghost": "The Holy Ghost, proceeding from the Father and the Son, is of one Substance, Majesty and Glory, with the Father and the Son, very and eternal God." One is not sure what to make of this appropriation of traditional language, but Wesley's commitment to the *filioque* is made clear in his *Explanatory Notes on the New Testament.* In commenting on John 15.16, he suggests

> that he [the Holy Spirit] proceeds from the Son, as well as from the Father, may be fairly argued from His being called the "Spirit of Christ" (1 Peter 1.11), and from His being here said to be sent by Christ from the Father, as well as sent by the Father in His name.

But the situation is complicated interestingly enough by the fact that Wesley dropped the Nicene Creed from the Anglican communion service when he revised it for the American Methodists. It is not known whether Wesley had any reason for this excision other than the fact that the morning prayer service, which he expected to be used with the communion service, already included the Apostles' Creed. Wesley surely used the Nicene creed regularly in his own Anglican worship, and as far as I know, made no critique of its use. At any rate, the Nicene creed was not restored to American Methodist worship until the twentieth century merger of the Northern and Southern churches, long after the holiness departures from Methodism.

A similar situation obtains for the classical systematic theologies of Methodism that the holiness movement has treasured and the twentieth century expositions of holiness theology. These include occasional references to the *filioque* controversy, but typically in historical sections on the development of the doctrine of the trinity without entering into any discussion of the issues as a live debate. They seem satisfied to live within the Western tradition confessionally.

Within the holiness movement proper the question does not rise with regard to the use of the creed because of the accentuating of the Methodist tendency away from creeds and confessions as normative for church life or a usual part of the liturgy. It is not common for even the Apostles' Creed to be used in holiness worship, though this is changing in some contexts, and the Apostles' Creed is contained, for example, in the Nazarene hymnal and in the latest (1976) revision of the joint hymnal of the Wesleyan and Free Methodist Churches. But the use of the Nicene creed would be as far as I know unheard of.

It could be argued that this reluctance to use the creed is principial, at least in the holiness ethos, which has, if anything, amplified Wesley's tendency to find continuity with "apostolic faith" in terms of spirituality and piety. For Wesley, the "apostolic faith" is to be lived and experienced rather than confessed; it is a matter of the "heart" rather than the mind and propositions. On the other hand, it could be argued that because of the "classical" and "orthodox" character of Wesleyan and holiness thought, it has no real objection to the Nicene creed and could well accomodate it into theology and worship. From this angle the "soteriological" focus of Wesleyan and holiness thought shifts attention away from speculation about the internal life of the trinity to the *opera ad extra,* especially the work of redemption, and views the Holy Spirit primarily in that context. From this perspective one could argue that holiness thought assumes and applies classical trinitarian formulations — that its contribution to trinitarian reflection is practical rather speculative.

This difficulty could lead one in several directions. One might affirm the continuity of Wesley and the holiness tradition with the classical Western tradition and suggest that it so far has no significant contribution to make to trinitarian reflection. Or one might argue that its contribution to the discussion is to raise the fundamental question of whether the "apostolic faith" is basically a matter to be "confessed" — whether in the Nicene creed or otherwise. Or one might argue, somewhat along the lines of Rahner, that one cannot separate the immanent and economic trinities, and that in the practical and soteriological focus of the Wesleyan tradition certain moves are made that when raised to the level of theological articulation do have implications for the discussion at hand. I have the feeling that when these issues are fully sorted out, elements of all three of these positions will find a place in the discussion, but since I myself am new to these issues and have no history of textual discussion on which to rely, I am reluctant at this point to speculate about what might emerge as a normative position on the issues raised in *Spirit of God, Spirit of Christ*, especially with regard to the *filioque* controversy directly.

On another level, however, the Wesleyan and holiness tradition finds itself drawn into the wider issues of the discussion as they go beyond the question of the *filioque* clause itself. Here we enter debated territory where I am not competent to make an independent judgment, though I am inclined with Yves Congar and others not to attribute the major differences between East and West so exclusively as some to the *filioque* difference. But *if* there is any truth to the thesis of Vladimir Lossky, a surprising result emerges with regard to the holiness movement. In *Spirit of God, Spirit of Christ* Andre De Halleaux summarizes the supposedly fatal consequences for Western ecclesiology of the *filioque* — as discerned by Lossky: "the subordination of charisma to the institution, of freedom to power, of the prophetic to the legalistic, of mysticism to sholasticism, of the laity to the clergy." (pp. 71-72). Again, *if* there is truth in this thesis, there would be a strong tendency in the Wesleyan and holiness tradition toward the "eastern" tradition in spite of apparent acceptance of the "western" *filioque* formulations.

If so, this might be another illustration of the Wesleyan and holiness tradition tendency to break the usual categories of intepretation. It has been a common observation that Wesley attempted a synthesis of the Protestant doctrine of grace with the Catholic vision of sainthood. Albert Outler has argued repeatedly what Wesley represents a sort of "third alternative" to Protestantism and Catholicism:

> a Protestant doctrine of original sin minus most of the other elements in classical Protestant soteriology, *plus* a catholic doctrine of perfection *without* its full panoply of priesthood and priestcraft.[1]

---

[1] Albert C. Outler, *Theology in the Wesleyan Spirit* (Nashville, 1975), p. 33.

This argument can be continued in the way that Wesley has affinities as well with the disciplines of the radical reformation and its critique of the magisterial reformation while remaining within the "catholic" Anglican tradition.[2] The point is that Wesley was so "catholic" in his sources that he represents a subtle synthesis that breaks most categories of interpretation. He was both Catholic and Protestant, established and radical in his view of the church, and so on. In a similar way he transcended some of the differences between East and West.

It is clear that the Wesleyan and holiness traditions are deeply dependent on sources outside the Western experience. The Wesleyan tradition has always been profoundly ambivalent about the Augustinian tradition of the West. While it has its affinities (especially in the doctrine of original sin), it has always resisted the implications for election and soteriology as they were mediated by the reformed tradition within Protestantism. Wesley, moreover, thought Pelagius a great saint much maligned by Augustine. A close examination of Wesley's sources (often abridged in his extended *Christian Library*) reveals that among the most determinitive were Makarios the Egyptian, Ephraim of Syria (for Wesley the "most awakened" of the early church), Clement of Alexandria, and interestingly the Cappadocians, especially Gregory of Nyssa, according to Outler the most significant source of Wesley's theology of perfection so often misinterpreted because it has been read in the Western rather than the Eastern context.[3]

As far as I know, these connections have not been pursued as fully as they deserve. They remain one of the highest priorities on the agenda of holiness scholarship. A start has been made in the most recent study of the Wesleyan sources by Paul Bassett of the Church of the Nazarene. He suggests that the holiness views of perfection came close to finding full expression in Gregory of Nyssa, but that the Wesleyan position is essentially a "unique fusion of a genuinely Augustinian perspective with the perspective of Eastern Christianity in the unique context of the thought and worship of the Church of England."[4] If these

---

[2]Cf. Howard Snyder, *The Radical Wesley and Patterns for Church Renewal* (Downers Grove, IL, 1980).

[3]Cf. the famous, provocative footnote 26 in Albert Outler, ed. *John Wesley* (New York, 1964), pp. 9-11.

[4]Paul M. Bassett and William M. Greathouse, *The Historical Development,* "Exploring Christian Holiness, Volume 2" (Kansas City, 1985), p. 108.

undeveloped hints are correct, and I am inclined to think that they are, then perhaps the Wesleyan tradition will find itself at the center of broader efforts to reconcile the Eastern and Western perspectives — if not precisely at the point of the *filioque* controversy — and we may find in the Wesleyan tradition a significant ecumenical bridge between them.

One final point deserves comment. The "Memorandum" produced by the WCC dialogue suggests that the relevance of the *filioque* is to be found in two "warnings": the danger of separating the Spirit from Christ in such a way as to allow a "Christologically uncontrolled 'charismatic enthusiasm' " on the one hand and the danger of too radical a subordination of the Spirit to Christ on the other so that the Spirit becomes a mere "power" or "instrument." If this is to be understood as the meaning of the *filioque* controversy, then we are immediately into the most essential and profound question of the holiness movement — and the greatest ambiguity in its pneumatology. This question will be developed more fully in the next section.

Holiness Pneumatology

Here we are immediately beset with difficulties that need some mention. As will already be clear in the earlier part of this paper, there is a fundamental ambiguity in the holiness movement that makes it difficult to determine what might constitute its normative expression. It has two formative moments — the eighteenth century evangelical revival expressed in the work and teachings of John Wesley and the nineteenth century holiness revival expressed in a variety of strands and teachings. In an earlier era the nineteenth century holiness reading of Wesley was accepted within the movement uncritically. With the more sophisticated scholarship of the last couple of decades the differences between the eighteenth and nineteenth centuries have become more apparent. As a result the holiness movement is now engaged in a very complex theological and hermeneutical struggle at precisely this point: will Wesley be interpreted through the nineteenth century developments or will Wesley be allowed to correct the nineteenth century. The pneumatological issues are at the center of this struggle, and the final results are not in. I am, moreover, a partisan in these theological debates with some preference for the formulations of the eighteenth century, and readers may wish to take account of this possible bias.

A second problem is the difficulty of interpreting Wesley. His thought is so "catholic" (some might say eclectic) and so subtle a synthesis of apparent opposites (or at least having a tendency to conjunctively relate what many other traditions have disjunctively separated) that few of his successors and interpreters have maintained the same balance and catholicity. Wesley, moreover, has become something of a mirror, in which many interpreters have found enough of their own concern in Wesley that in pursuing that theme have ultimately given a reading of Wesley that reflects back the image of the interpreter. Thus Wesley has been claimed by both sacramentalist and campmeeting preacher, Protestant and Catholic, liberal and conservative, etc. Wesley cannot be all of these; yet he has something in common with each.

I myself am inclined to interpret Wesley as basically a soteriologically and practically oriented theologian. His thought includes, of course, other communal, word-transforming elements and so forth, but these are organized around and rooted in an individual soteriology. This, of course, can be said of much of Protestantism, especially the more "evangelical" versions of that tradition, but there are significant differences in Wesley that deserve attention. In the first place, it should be noticed that Wesley's soteriology works with organic and therapeutic metaphors. That is, the intention of God is to put the world back together, and Wesley is rather optimistic about the extent to which this can be done under grace within history — both personally and socially. The Wesleyan traditions of theology are as a result very leery of the Protestant traditions that cultivate too exclusively "forensic" categories of justification and salvation that do not include "actual" or empirically verifiable transformation. While Wesley learned much from Luther, for example, and incorporated much of his thought on justification into his own thinking, he insisted on pushing beyond these themes to a genuine doctrine on sanctification that becomes in many ways the organizing principle of his thought.

Another way of making the same point is to notice the moral/ethical axis around which Wesley's thought revolves. Wesleyan theology shares much of the critique of Protestantism that the radical reformation, Catholicism and other critics have made at various points — the danger of "cheap grace." For Wesley love rather than faith is the chief theological virtue; faith for him was clearly instrumental to love. Wesley's thought often seems to be organized around the motif of "love." What was lost in the fall is the ability to love, the essence of sin is the lack of love, what is restored by grace is the ability to love, the goal of the Christian life is "perfect love," and so on. This shift of emphasis is crucial, I believe, to understanding the inner dynamic of the Wesleyan tradition and the shape of its theological reflection. It is no accident that the magisterial reformation left great confessions of faith as its major legacy to the Christian world and the Wesleyan tradition has left instead a trail of acts of mercy and love, including great campaigns against social evil.

Such a position obviously leads to the questions and problems of "perfectionism." At this point Wesley is often described as having a "pessimism of nature and an optimism of grace" that brings into this life what other traditions have reserved to life beyond the grave. From one angle Wesley has a form of "realized eschatology" that conceives of "salvation" primarily in terms of what it means for this world — or perhaps better, that whatever salvation may be in the other world is continuation of the processes begun, and to a great extent achieved, in this world. This may be seen by contrasting Wesley's thought with the Puritanism of his time by which he was so deeply influenced. Both had elaborate schemes of the *ordo salutis* that detailed the progress of the soul from the first promptings of grace through conversion, justification, sanctification, and the Christian life to eschatological themes of glorification. Both traditions agreed on the necessity of "entire sanctification," but Puritanism reserved this for the moment of death and made it a part of "glorification." Wesley wondered why this experience could not be a part of human life and take place this side of the grave. This lead eventually to the claim that "entire sanctification" was a blessing to be expected in this life.

But the doctrine of "entire sanctification" must be seen in this larger context, as a point along the long and continuous path toward glorification. It is both preceded and followed by growth in grace and continued sanctification. It is not "sinless perfection" in the strong sense if by that one means being beyond the possibility of sinning. It is a perfecting of the ability to love according to one's capacities at a given point in one's life pilgrimage — a purifying of intentions and a focusing of the will. The Wesleyan tradition has all too often been interpreted by those assuming and importing into the discussion a foreign concept of an absolute "perfection." Here is the significance of interpreting Wesley in terms of the Eastern tradition rather than the Western tradition. It is also possible to discern in these teachings of Wesley certain echoes of the Eastern doctrine of *theosis*.

Wesleyan pneumatology needs this background because for Wesley the Holy Spirit is to be understood primarily as the instrument by which this whole process of salvation and sanctification is achieved. Though this perspective would be disputed by some, I am inclined to read Wesley very much at this point in the classical Protestant tradition in which the Holy Spirit is the spirit of Christ. I think that it is striking that Wesley does not devote extended attention to the Spirit as such. His treatments are buried in larger discussions, and are, at least according to my reading, very Christocentric in character. For example, Wesley's sermon on "Scriptural Christianity," based significantly on the text "and they were all filled with the Holy Ghost" (Acts 4.31), describes the purpose of the coming of the Spirit in these terms:

> It was, to give them (what none can deny to be essential to Christians in all ages) the mind which was in Christ, those holy fruits of the Spirit, which whosoever hath not, is none of His; to fill them with 'love, joy, peace, long-suffering, gentleness, goodness' (Gal v.22-24); to endue them with faith (perhaps it might be rendered, *fidelity*), with meekness and temperance; to enable them to crucify the flesh, with its affections and lusts, its passions and desires; and in consequence of that inward change, to fulfil all outward righteousness; to 'walk as Christ also walked,' in the 'work of faith, in the patience of hope, the labour of love' (1 Thes 1.3).[5]

The tendency of Wesley to conceive of the work of the Spirit in almost exclusively sanctification terms is also seen in perhaps his clearest short summary of his teaching on the Holy Spirit, found in his letter "to a Roman Catholic":

> I believe the infinite and eternal Spirit of God, equal with the Father and the Son, to be not only perfectly holy in Himself, but the immediate cause of all holiness in us; enlightening our understandings, rectifying our wills and affections, renewing our natures,

---

[5]Wesley, "Spiritual Christianity," preface, section 4.

uniting our persons to Christ, assuring us of the adoption of sons, leading us in our actions, purifying and sanctifying our souls and bodies, to a full and eternal enjoyment of God.[6]

But there is in Wesley another theme that breaks this pattern to a certain extent. It was his doctrine of "assurance" or "the witness of the Spirit" that so often got him into trouble and caused the epithet of enthusiast to be applied to him in his own time and since. Twenty years later Wesley quotes himself and indicates that he has no reason for retracting his definition of this experience:

> by the testimony of the Spirit, I mean, an inward impression on the soul, whereby the Spirit of God immediately and directly witnesses to my spirit, that I am a child of God; that Jesus Christ hath loved me, and given himself for me; that all my sins are blotted out, and I, even I, am reconciled to God.[7]

I have not studied the role of this doctrine within Methodism in any detail, but some have attached great importance to it as the real key to the growth and impact of Methodism. On the other hand it has had less consistent cultivation in the Wesleyan and Holiness traditions than the doctrine of sanctification. It has not been a major theme in my experience of the holiness movement, though I must remain open to correction at this point.

At any rate, these two themes (a Christologically oriented doctrine of sanctification and a more directly pneumatologically oriented doctrine of assurance) indicate some of the ambiguity in Wesley's thought. The issue can be focused somewhat by raising the question of in what sense Wesley might be appropriately called a "theologian of the spirit." Many have made this claim. For example, Clare Weakley paraphrased some key texts of Wesley under the title *The Holy Spirit and Power*[8] for modern charismatics. But the title does not sound like Wesley to me; the language is more characteristic of the charismatic movement than the Wesleyan tradition. And the content

---

[6]Wesley, *Letters,* Vol. 8, also cited in Robert Burtner and Robert E. Chiles, *A Compendium of Wesley's Theology* (New York, 1954), p. 91.

[7]Wesley, "The Witness of the Spirit, Discourse 2," part 2 section 2.

[8]Weakley Clare, *The Holy Spirit and Power* (Plainfield, NJ, 1977).

of the book is primarily about the experience of salvation and includes little direct exposition of teachings about the Holy Spirit. There are similar problems in a thesis by Norman Kellett on "John Wesley and the Restoration of the Doctrine of the Holy Spirit to the Church of England in the 18th Century" (Ph. D dissertation, Brandeis University, 1975). Upon closer examination it appears that this is actually a study of Wesley's orientation to Christian experience. It may be that any heightening of Christian experience involves an intensification of a pneumatological orientation, but I am still inclined to argue that one may be experientially oriented in both a Christological mode and a pneumatological mode. If this distinction can be sustained, then I think it is quite clear that Wesley falls in the former camp, though one must grant that this impulse toward a stronger pneumatological orientation is always present in the Wesleyan tradition. Again, at least in my reading, Wesley maintains here a delicate balance that was not always sustained by his followers. The work of the Spirit is firmly rooted for Wesley in the work of Christ and is essentially the application of his benefits to the human soul, but this is a real and active application through the Holy Spirit that cannot be reduced or naturalized to a mere "influence."

This question, however, sets up the problematic that would trouble the next century within Methodism and the holiness movement, and the issue was raised even within Wesley's time by a proposal by the man that Wesley hoped would succeed him as the leader of Methodism, but who unfortunately died before Wesley, the saintly John Fletcher. By the 1770s the pattern of expecting the "second blessing" of "entire sanctification" was well established, and several figures around Trevecca College (the center of the Calvinistic wing of Methodism under the Countess of Huntingdon) began to speak of this moment as a "baptism of the Spirit" to be understood along the line of Pentecost. Fletcher especially was inclined to see in the Scriptures a pattern of history that he felt should be replicated in the life of each believer. This involved a trinitarian division of history into the ages of the Father (basically the Old Testament era), the age of the Son (the Messianic age of the presence of Christ), and the age of the Spirit (basically the age of the church, ushered in by Pentecost and climaxed in the return of Christ). This corresponded quite well to the division of the Christian life into three stages that was emerging in the Wesleyan tradition. Fletcher suggested that pre-Christian existence corresponded to the state of the race in Old Testament times, that Christian discipleship before entire sanctification corresponded to the ambiguous status of the disciples of Christ before the full empowerment of Pentecost, and that Pentecost should be understood as the moment of entire sanctification of the disciples. It seems to me, at least, that this scheme of Fletcher involves something of a revision of the classical Protestant pattern. In the older way of thinking we remain in the "dispensation" or "covenant" of Christ — though administered by the Holy Spirit. In the new scheme there is a heightened emphasis on the Holy Spirit — we are now in an age of the Holy Spirit that is a different "dispensation" (Fletcher's term) from that of Christ. But whatever we are to make of Fletcher's thought, it is clear that Wesley objected to this scheme on the grounds that it tended to separate the bestowal of the Spirit from conversion or the beginning of the second stage. In this concern Wesley clearly expresses his identification with the classical Protestant tradition on this question, and by force of his leadership managed to suppress Fletcher's position within Methodism — though it always remained in the background and Wesley and Fletcher remained always conscious of this difference in their thinking.

More was at stake in this difference than either realized. During the period of early Methodism, especially in the British context, Fletcher's exposition of Wesleyan soteriology continued to carry the Christocentric and moral transformatory themes of the Wesleyan exposition. But it had the potential of moving in the direction that Wesley feared — to give more autonomy to the Holy Spirit in such a way as to separate the work of the Spirit from the work of Christ and to separate the coming of the Spirit in the life of the individual from initiation into Christian life. At the very least it involved a subtle shift of axis for theological thinking. This can be seen most clearly in the nineteenth century writings of Asa Mahan, the first president of Oberlin College, who wrote books articulating the holiness doctrine in both the style of Wesley and the style of Fletcher. In *The Scripture Doctrine of Christian Perfection* Mahan was careful to insist that the Holy Spirit was merely the administrator of the work of Christ. In the *baptism of the Holy Ghost* the orientation had so shifted that he was anxious to make the point that even Christ was dependent upon the Holy Spirit, the great facilitator of all spiritual life.[9] This shift in theological axis also in-

---

[9] I am preparing an edition of these two texts by Asa Mahan which will appear (in 1987?) in the new series, "Sources of American Spirituality," being published by Paulist Press.

volved a subtle shift in exegetical foundations. Wesley had tended to ground his doctrines of soteriology and sanctification in the Johannine and Pauline texts of the New Testament. Fletcher's scheme worked better as an exposition of the Lukan texts, especially the book of Acts. But the Lukan texts lead more naturally to an understanding of the "baptism of the Spirit" in terms of empowerment for witness, service, prophecy and even miracles in a way that moves away from the distinctively Wesleyan soteriology. This struggle was played out in the background of Methodism over the next century.

Wesley's patterns of thought dominated early Methodism in America. There is a debate about whether themes of entire sanctification tended to be suppressed during this period before the holiness revival. I am inclined to think so. It is also clear that the writings of Fletcher, however, began to gain circulation during this period — and his formulations were also in the background. They tended to surface briefly in the late 1830s among the theologians of early Oberlin College, the Congregationalist center of Finney's revivalism that by this time had adopted essentially Methodist theology with regard to sanctification. The American holiness reformulation of entire sanctification tended to mechanize the process of its reception and move the event from goal to precondition of the Christian life. These tendencies accentuated the event-like character of "entire sanctification" and moved in the direction of Fletcher's formulation. Fletcher's formulation gained acceptance especially in the years just before and after the Civil War. After the Civil War, the holiness movement increasingly moved in the direction of the doctrine of the "baptism of the Spirit" as the way in which to articulate Wesleyan themes of "entire sanctification" while Methodism more and more dispaired of the whole issue and tended to move away from the themes of perfection that were so fascinating the holiness movement.[10]

The Holiness Movement and Pentecostalism

It should be obvious by now that we are now discussing the

---

[10]These developments are treated in much more detail in my dissertation, "Theological Roots of Pentecostalism" (Ph. D. dissertation, University of Chicago Divinity School, 1983), to be published as *Theological Roots of Pentecostalism*, forthcoming (1987) in the series "Studies in Evangelicalism," published by Scarecrow Press and Zondervan.

theological history that led to the emergence of Pentecostalism. The interpretation of Pentecostalism has often so focused on the distinctive practice of speaking in tongues that the underlying theological substructure has been obscured. My own analysis of early Pentecostal documents has led me to the conclusion that Pentecostalism is best described as a gestalt of four regularly recurring theological themes: conversion (as understood in the revivalist tradition); baptism in the spirit with the evidence of speaking in tongues (the evidence aspect of this doctrine is diluted in the charismatic movement and is debated now within classical Pentecostalism); divine healing; and an emphasis on the second coming of Christ. Late nineteenth century holiness theology had moved in all of these directions. The primary shift is the pneumatological one that we described above toward the formulations of Fletcher and the doctrine of the "baptism with the Holy Spirit." This led to a series of new themes — an increased emphasis on the "empowerment" of the Holy Spirit (and the consequent theological problem of how to relate this to the themes of sanctification that had been the hallmark of the holiness movement); a greater emphasis on "prophecy" and speaking under the influence of the Holy Spirit, increased concern about "impressions" (or direct dealings with the Holy Spirit in guidance, etc.). By the late nineteenth century the holiness movement was immersed in these themes, had adopted doctrines of divine healing and had shifted from a post-millennial eschatology to a premillennial eschatology. All that was needed for the emergence of Pentecostalism was the addition of the evidence doctrine. This might well be seen as a resurfacing of the Wesleyan doctrine of "assurance" which had served the same function in the preceeding century. At any rate a biblical search for the evidence of the "baptism of the Spirit" in the book of Acts in a small Bible College outside of Topeka Kansas led to the final articulation of Pentecostal theology and the separation of the holiness movement into those who resisted the practice of glossolalia and attempted to freeze the theology of this trajectory at its pre-Pentecostal stage and those who followed out the trajectory and became the Pentecostal movement.

This split led to a tremendous struggle in which the holiness movement built strong barriers to Pentecostalism and became probably the strongest critic of Pentecostalism in the Christian world. On one level this antipathy must be seen in terms of a struggle over turf. Large segments of the holiness movement were torn down the middle

by the struggle; whole conferences were swept out of holiness churches and into Pentecostalism. The holiness movement (and large
segments of revivalistic evangelicalism in the Keswick tradition)
repudiated Pentecostalism and moved to disassociate itself from the
new movement. One of the most striking signs of this was the movement in the (then) Pentecostal Church of the Nazarene to strike the
word "Pentecostal" from the name of the church to avoid any con-
fusion. And the Church of God (Anderson, Indiana) began to empasize
in its name the location of its headquarters so that on all church signs
it would be clear that this group was *not* Pentecostal in contra-
distinction to the many Pentecostal denominations bearing the name
"Church of God." This historical position of the holiness movement
has been largely maintained into the present. Entering into charismatic
experience (especially speaking in tongues) has meant more or less
instant excommunication in many holiness denominations, particularly
for the clergy, though in some cases closeted charismatics or sym-
pathizers have found a role in holiness leadership.

This phobia of Pentecostalism has had its impact theologically
and exegetically on the holiness movement. Most exegetes in the
holiness movement deny that glossolalia, as it exists in modern
Pentecostal and charismatic experience, can be grounded in the New
Testament. They tend to take the Pentecost account as normative
and use it to interpret Paul to claim that "speaking in tongues" is
a supernatural "missionary gift" of speaking in other "unlearned"
(but not "unknown") tongues for the purpose of witness to the gospel.
Similarly there is in the holiness movement a certain ambivalence
about any stress on the "gifts of the Spirit." When the theme is addressed, it is often with great warnings and caution about the dangers
of this emphasis. The popular way of expressing the holiness position is to say that the holiness movement places the emphasis on the
"fruits" of the Spirit rather than the "gifts" of the Spirit — and
that this is basically the thurst of Paul in 1 Corinthians 12-14. This
basic line is, however, not without its dissenters. Howard Snyder, for
example, has argued that these concerns have distorted holiness ecclesiology so that the movement has difficulty recognizing the appropriate senses in which the church must be understood to be
"charismatic" and in which one may appropriately speak of "gifts
of the Spirit."

Genuine theological issues are, of course, at stake in this discussion — ones that have troubled the holiness movement for a century

now. I reveal my own sympathies with the classical holiness movement when I prefer the sanctification motifs and the holiness emphasis on "fruits" and "love" — an emphasis which I believe best
captures the thrust of the Wesleyan tradition and the concern of Paul
in the key text in Corinthians. The major question that the holiness
movement faces theologically, in my view, is whether these themes
can be preserved in the late nineteenth century "Pentecostal" formulations. I am inclined to think that the Pentecostals do a better
job of reading the key Lukan texts than recent holiness exegesis and
more appropriately work out the logic of a pneumatological orientation theologically. But I am, of course, strongly opposed in these positions, and the questions are intensely debated within the movement
at the present time. Only time will tell what the final resolution will
be, and hopefully what will emerge from these discussions is a new
and more subtle synthesis of all the biblical themes that need attention.

Holiness Social and Political Concern

These theological debates within the holiness movement have implications as well for the shape of the holiness social and political
witness. History reveals a very complex intertwining of themes that
cannot be fully explored here. But it is very significant — and deserv-
ing, I believe, of wider ecumenical notice — the extent to which the
holiness traditions have been carriers of a quite profound and consistent witness on a series of important social questions that have
bedeviled the church over the last century and a half. In fact, nearly
every facet of the holiness movement has had a significant social issue
at the heart of its emergence, though this has not received the attention that it deserves from outside the movement and has often been
forgotten inside the movement. I have tried to explore this in more
detail in *Discovering an Evangelical Heritage* (New York, 1976), a
study of the social witness of American evangelical traditions when
they were more under the sway of the holiness ethos. Let me merely
mention three themes of this history of social witness and attempt
to make pneumatological correlations wherever possible.

(1) Deeply influenced by the civil rights movement during my college years in the 1960s, I have been fascinated with and explored
more fully the question of the interrelationship between the holiness
movement and abolitionism in the antebellum era in the United States.
Wesley, of course, had been profoundly opposed to slavery and had

great impact on Wilberforce and the British abolitionist movement. Early Methodism in the United States attempted at first to maintain this anti-slavery witness, but soon gradually qualified it when it began to hinder growth, especially in the South. The early antebellum vanguard of the holiness movement — in part by virtue of its claim to represent the "original" thurst of Methodism — was largely abolitionist and may even be said to have intensified this original thurst of Methodism. The American optimism of a new nation born in the midst of enlightenment visions of human perfectability led to much social experimentation in this period — and holiness themes of perfection were easily assimilated into this larger vision and led to a broadbased "reform" platform within the early years of the holiness movement. Such reform (abolitionist, temperance, peace activism, etc.) was seen to play a role in the inauguration of the millennium whose imminence was widely contemplated in the period. (The rise and fall of this reform vision is closely tied to the rise of an intense "postmillennial" eschatology during this period before a decline under the rising influence of the fundamentalist premillennialism.) Even the perhaps excessive moral scrupulosity of the holiness movement heightened the stakes by denying the classical doctrine of the *adiaphora* — the morally neutral practices that for some Reformed theologians of the time included not only smoking and drinking, but also slavery and political despotism. For the holiness folk nothing was morally neutral; a determination had to be made about everything, including slavery; and if a practice was determined to be sinful, it had to be immediately denounced and put away — thus immediate abolitionism. The cumulative effect of these factors was an intense abolitionism that appears among the Wesleyans, the Frees, at early Oberlin College under Evangelist Finney and President Mahan, and within Methodism among the early editors of *The Guide to Christian Perfection.*

It is fascinating to read this literature after a century and a half. Contrary to what many would expect, this abolitionist vision was grounded in an intensification of piety rather than in its dilution. Finney was to argue that resistance to reforms was a sign of a vapid piety and to insist that taking the wrong position on a question of civil rights was a "hindrance to revival" that could stop the work of the Spirit in a church or community. The Wesleyans were proud of the conjunction of "piety and radicalism" in their midst. In fact, I have become increasingly fascinated with the parallels between these movements and contemporary liberation theologies. Some of these are on the structural and methodological level: the Methodist prax-eological and ethical orientation; the expectation of a form of salvation within history; the similar function of perfectionism and millennialism in the earlier period and utopianism (whether Marxist or not) in the more recent movements; the consequent impatience with "realist" thinking in both periods, and so on. Other parallels relate to a common content: a preferential option for the poor that characterized Wesley and much of the holiness movement; the understanding of God as a deliverer of the oppressed, and so on. The struggle against slavery led in some similar paths of radicalization. What began as a sympathy for the slave and a conviction that slavery was a sin led to acts of civil disobedience through the underground railroad and other acts of resistance to fugitive slave laws and finally to a defense of a form of "just revolution" that defended John Brown's raid on Harper's Ferry and the impending Civil War. These parallels are just beginning to be studied and understood, but there is suprising receptiveness to making many of these connections in the modern holiness movement.[11]

(2) As has always been suggested, Methodism has always had a special relationship to the poor. Much of the power of early Methodism was its turn to the unchurched poor more or less untouched by the Church of England. Wesley's own struggles with field preaching and his own turn to the miners and other workers required a profound resocialization for this Oxford don. But Wesley came to understand that Methodism was called to the poor and argued that her spiritual vitality was bound up in keeping this task at the center of her vision. Historians are still trying to sort out the role of the Methodism in the modernizing of English society and the rise of the trade unions in the nineteenth century. The holiness movement arose in the period

---

[11]A significant beginning to such discussions may be found in Theodore Runyon (ed.), *Sanctification and Liberation* (Nashville, 1980), the proceedings of the sixth Oxford Institute of Methodist Theological Studies, July 18-27, 1977, which was also noteworthy for bringing together in a common arena theologians of both the holiness movement and classical Methodism. Articles arguing that Wesley was a sort of "liberation theologian" may be found a short-lived periodical *The Epworth Pulpit* founded largely by students and faculty of the Nazarene Theological Seminary in Kansas City.

of Methodism's emergence into the middle class and into traditional church life — and largely in response to that dynamic. It is becoming clearer that nearly every facet of the holiness movement incarnated in its origins some form of a "perferential option for the poor." In antebellum America this was closely tied up with the anti-slavery struggle. The Free Methodist Church was especially articulate about this theme in its struggle against the pew rental system that was increasingly adopted within Methodism to finance the more expensive churches that were being built. Founder B. T. Roberts proclaimed these principles in the founding editorial of his journal *The Earnest Christian*, arguing from the Lukan texts that are so much used today that Christ's own turn to the poor was the crowning proof of his messiahship and that following the model of Christ was of the *esse* rather than the *bene esse* of the church. In his words, "There are hot controversies about the true church. . . . It may be that there cannot be a church without a bishop, or that there can. There can be none without a gospel, and a gospel for the poor."

Phoebe Palmer, who represents in many ways the mid-century dilution of social reform in the holiness movement (especially the more radical anti-slavery struggle) and a turn to a more privatized and experiential "parlor" version of sanctification, was nonetheless also a carrier of this theme. She was deeply involved with the "ladies of the mission" in transforming the "Old Brewery" into an inner-city mission that became the model for much Protestant urban ministry in New York City. Part of the explicit rationale for the adoption of the "campmeeting" in mid-nineteenth century was that it was a form adapted to maintaining contact with the "masses" that Methodism was perceived to be losing touch with. The Salvation Army is, of course, the epitome of this impulse and a continuing symbol of the churches' identification with the poor. Similar themes dominated the formation of late nineteenth century holiness churches. In early years many of these churches were little more than a loosely affiliated string of rescue missions in various American cities. The event that precipitated the founding of the Church of the Nazarene was the request of Phineas Bresee that he be "located" so that he could work with an inner city mission in the Los Angeles area while the Methodists were anxious to have his skills in building large churches. The founders of the Pilgrim Holiness Church were proud of the fact that they were willing to go into the "darkest jungles" as missionaries and into the heart of the cities as mission workers. The illustrations could be multiplied indefinitely — as could the appeals to the fourth chapter of Luke so popular today in defending a "preferential option for the poor."

This theme deserves further analysis. In the later era of the holiness movement the call to "preach good news to the poor" was especially attractive because of its pneumatological grounding in Luke 4.18 ("The Spirit of the Lord is upon me, because he has anointed me to preach good news to the poor") and took primarily the form of evangelism — but an evangelism that breaks many of our stereotypes. While it was not a direct form of political and social action, it often led in that direction. The act of moving to be with the poor often led to a new awareness of their physical condition and often to a political radicalization. It is too easy today to over-look the radical side of even the temperance movement with its effort to transform the debilitating environment in which too many poor people were reared. And the tendency to see the Salvation Army today as illustrative of the forms of Christian "relief" that need to be transcended by direct political action fail to understand the broader political commitments of the Army in the profundity of its wholistic involvement and fail to grasp the radicality of its vision in its own time. Obviously these issues need fuller exploration than can be given here. My basic purpose at this point is to draw attention to a significant witness to a form of a biblically grounded "preferential option for the poor."

(3) In view of the debates about the question in the churches today, it is perhaps worth noting the consistency with which the holiness movement has been committed to the ordination and the ministry of women. Again this practice was foreshadowed in Wesley's time by his openness to a more informal ministry of women. Methodism in American struggled with the question throughout the nineteenth century but did not proceed with the full ordination of women until the middle of the twentieth century. It was, however, the holiness movement that competes with Unitarianism perhaps for the honor of first opening up the ordained ministry to women. It is amazing the number of events in the rise of feminism and the ministry of women that are associated with facets of the holiness movement; so much so that the history of this question will never be fully understood until this fact is taken into account — and much current historiography on this question is vitiated by its failure to do so.

The first woman to be ordained was Antoinette Brown, who though she later became a Unitarian was originally a follower of Finney and educated at Oberlin College. Oberlin was the first co-educational college and for that reason educated many of the leaders of the nineteenth century feminist movement. The preacher of Antoinette Brown's ordination sermon was Luther Lee, a founder of the Wesleyan Methodist Church. The first Woman's Rights Convention in 1848 was held in the Wesleyan Church in Seneca Falls. Antoinette Brown was ordained in 1853 and the Wesleyans began to practice of ordaining women soon thereafter. B. T. Roberts, founder of the Free Methodist Church, wrote *Ordaining Women* (1891) and other defences of the practice, but his church did follow his advice until the mid-twentieth century. Many agitators for the ministry of women in other contexts, such as Frances Willard within the Methodist Episcopal Church, were persons who had fallen under the influence of the holiness movement during this period.

Historians have noticed the close linking of abolitionism and feminism in the nineteenth century and the civil rights movement and feminism in the twentieth. In the last century it was natural to extend the anti-slavery hermeneutic to women, and Galatians 3.18 seemed to provide an abvious rationale for doing so. The holiness commitment to abolitionism led many to take this path and defend in the antebellum period a strong doctrine of sexually equality that was supported by other holiness theological themes. While some traditions found in Genesis 3.16 a curse that prescriptively determined an inferior status of women for all time, the holiness movement was more inclined to see a description of the sinful state out of which we are being redeemed. As grace effects its transformation of persons and the world, women are restored to equality with men as the new "Eve." And even if Paul may be proved to have opposed the ministry of women (a doubtful claim in the first place to much of the holiness movement), grace is so much at work that this is not the same world, and what may have been inappropriate then might very well be appropriate now. And as has often been the case, the turn to religious experience in Methodism and the holiness movement proved to be a great leveller that took religious authority out of the hands of the privileged and the educated and put it in the hearts of those who respond to the grace of God.

This openess to the ministry of women was, if anything, radicalized by the holiness turn to pneumatological orientation in the late nineteenth century. After all, the account of Pentecost proclaimed that "in the latter days . . . your sons and your daughters shall prophesy."

And if one were not convinced by the antebellum arguments for the ministry of women, it was now clear that this new practice was a sign of the "latter day" outpouring of the Spirit of which the holiness movement was the harbinger. Very significantly Phoebe Palmer's book, *The Promise of the Father* (1859) was both one of the first to fully adopt the pneumatological exposition of "entire sanctification" and also essentially a defense of the ministry of women — required, of course, by her own practice. We have indicated the impression that Phoebe Palmer made on Catherine Booth about this time, but one result was that the Salvation Army became arguably the most consistently egalitarian Christian organization to date. At any rate, with the rise of the pneumatological language came increasing commitment to the ministry of women — so that by the end of the century the practice was a hallmark of the movement. In some groups, such as the Church of the Nazarene and the Pilgrim Holiness Church, the percentage of women achieved was about one third earlier in this century. Interestingly enough, with the not unexpected decline of intense pneumatological focus and the twentieth century *embourgeoisement* and assimilation of the holiness churches to more traditional forms of church life, the ministry of women, while still largely accepted, has declined — though there is renewed commitment today to the practice as a hallmark of the holiness movement.

Other illustrations of the resulting social commitment of the holiness movement could be given, but these illustrations should suffice to indicate something of the subtle interaction of the Wesleyan soteriology and holiness pneumatology with these issues to produce, so it seems to me, a series of models of Christian social witness worth much more exploration.

Reflections on Pneumatology in the Church of the Brethren Tradition

LAUREE HERSCH MEYER

We believe in the Holy Spirit . . .

CONTEMPORARY PNEUMATOLOGY DISCUSSIONS
SINCE 1927, ECUMENICAL CONVERSATIONS have been characterized by hope and tension. As communions opened our lives to one another and reached toward common understandings in our search for visible unity, we found our differences painful, indeed faithless. So we sought *common* understandings, guideposts to help us negotiate the rugged terrain which seemed to threaten our pilgrimage together.

Yet our effort to establish common understandings can also misserve us. Tension in ecumenical life is heightened when the *terms* of conversation are meaningful and appropriate for some communions, while being constrictive and alien to the center of other communions' life.

Its terms set the limits within which conversation is appropriate. So *how* we carry out discussions on pneumatology constitute the terms, the limits within which we are open to the Spirit about whom we speak in conversations about pneumatology.

In earlier days, often spoken of as the era of comparative ecclesiology, the Faith and Order movement made less effort to speak normatively than to come to know other Christians. More recently, and especially visible in drafting the current version of the *BEM* document, we have sought to formulate a normative text in which all

[159]

communions might find themselves, and about which all could confess that the text was both faithful and adequate.

Brethren believe we are today in an epoch where neither comparative ecclesiology nor normative texts adequately serve communions as members of Christ's living Body. Many contemporary Christian voices cannot be heard or understood from within our inherited perceptions. Brethren believe the sociological expression of Christology occurs when members of Christ's Body relinquish "our" place and open ourselves to the incarnate experience of others' places and contexts, to thought that seems alien or offensive to us.

Comparative ecclesiology and normative theology both address faith's *content*. Theologians embody our Christology in the decision how to engage one another. The choice to genuinely hear and come to know one another bears witness to conviction that we belong together and can identify commonality more basic than our division. The decision to sculpt a common content of faith bears witness to already agreed on presuppositions or contexts of faith. The choice to open ourselves to one another as radically diverse members of Christ's Body, bears witness that we receive and offer faith incarnately, content-in-context. *As* Christ-ian, incarnate con-ver-satio, we give ourselves to, receive, and enter one another's lives, turning together until satisfied.

The context we assume centers and limits any text. When speakers and hearers share one context, their similar contextual presuppositions co-interpret the words. Those with similar contexts rarely think about how their presuppositions co-interpret their confessions. But when those of different contexts come together to draft a text, dissent often lodges in the different significance identical words have in the drafters' varying contexts.

For generations, Anglo-academic theologians were in close enough conversation to have rather homogeneous presuppositions regarding the appropriate ways to inquire into and express faith. Not infrequently, theologians' inter-ecclesial and inter-national homogeneity was felt to be in painful tension with members of their particular ecclesial bodies. The ecclesial bodies' predominantly local context, while understood, was often felt to be restrictive and inappropriately limited. The "translocal" context of world communions, ecumenical life, and academic theological reflection seemed more faithful precisely in that it transcended the confines of particular faith expressions.

In both local and translocal contexts, most *public* voices were those of free, white, Anglo men who owned property, were able to travel, and conversed with other public figures in the "foreign" contexts they visited; that is, "alien" public life was open to them and ideas informed by their "home" context were received seriously by others. In both local and translocal contexts, men were generally able to speak or even dissent openly on political, religious, or ethical matters without losing life or property. As public figures, such men were granted respect and a serious hearing when they spoke their minds. It is therefore hardly surprising that the Euro-North American ecclesial and academic male community shared similar theological perspectives. No less surprisingly, women, Blacks, Hispanics, Asians, Africans, and others whose voices had never become part of this public life and conversation found it difficult to engage in ecumenical life in the terms of conversation basic to their contexts.

The Brethren Context

Children of the radical reformation, Brethren never recited creeds. The historical *filioque* debates were followed more with academic than confessional investment. As persecution of our forebearers was justified by citing creeds, Brethren radically embraced the reformation view of Scripture, stating that "we have no creed but the New Testament, our authority in all matters of faith and practice." Brethren affirm the great ecumenical creeds' content and value their place in forming and directing Christian faith. We would surely profit by their use in worship and Christian education, and may be ready for such a step.

Our existential concern for the Holy Spirit does not center in agreement over explicating the third article of the creed so much as in discerning how our various communions are enlived by God's Spirit. We see from the richness of Scripture and contemporary experience that the reality of God's Holy Spirit exceeds what our explications embrace. We know God is not bound to our understandings. So when Brethren inquire into the work of God's Spirit, we turn to Scripture to see how variously God has worked. Correspondingly, in contempary faith life, we are more prone to trust embodied and confessional witness to the Holy Spirit than the analytic and conceptual statements about the Spirit.

Brethren identify as having pneumatological dimensions one matter often addressed as a concern for social justice or according to theological ontology. We believe God's Holy Spirit calls all believers

into both the royal priesthood, and into the Church's ordained ministries. We consider it a basic theological matter whether Christian
life is ordered by the affirmation that the Holy Spirit calls into the
full range of its life and ministries all, or only some, as those created
in God's image. We are not surprised to find conflict among believers
on this matter in our day. In Paul's day, similar conflict surrounded
the theological and ethical understandings of the ontological status
granted Christ-ians who ate meat and failed to practice circumcision.

We believe communions' formation and historical contexts effect
our perception in such questions. The form of Christian confession
is rooted in, while not identical with our theological anthropology,
our socio-historical context. There is doubt about the public place
of women (and males of color and non-European origin) as significant public, ecumenical voices in the Church's life and thought; it
remains unclear whether the Church believes God's Spirit calls all
anthropoi or only the males among *'adam* into its full public life and
ministries.

Contemporary Conversations on Pneumatology

To address *God's* Spirit calls us to receive what God has in store
for us: not to defend the coherence of what we believe, but to offer
it to one another, opening ourselves beyond the limits of any communion's context, concepts, and understandings. God is the life and
understanding of all Christians. We know we do not "capture" God's
Spirit with texts, doctrines, teachings, and confessions. Yet in formation, ministry, and teaching, each communion needs and uses them
all. Just as public ecumenical con-ver-sation yielded a shared context more able to draft a text acceptable and useful to all, so common texts useful to all communions will form local Christians with
similar as well as disparate contexts. Common texts are basic as we
seek to manifest Christ's unity in our life together. Indeed, our desire
for trustworthy common texts leads us to offer one another the deeply
particular texts which reflect our diverse contexts and often conflicting convictions.

Contextual variances among ecumenical voices may remind us
that, and how, Christ is everywhere present. It is difficult to receive
witness alien or perhaps offensive to us; it feels like an assault upon
our faith. Like Jews and Gentiles who both confessed Jesus as God's
Christ after Pentecost, we may find that some of our most cherished
religious inheritance is a tutor *others* need not obey as we learn to

manifest unity in Christ Jesus.

In consultations on the apostolic faith, Christians seek more than simple agreement on a text; we seek mutual correspondence as members of Christ's Body. Then we shall be one. Inasmuch as *how* we discuss the apostolic faith embodies our confession; it "is" part of our documented faith.

Since Babel, humans are prone to seek unity in our own strength. God's answer then, and forever, is to call us into the promise of a fruitful, fulfilled, and fulfilling future amidst our fragmentation. God's promise of fulfillment is crowned in the last promise to Abram immediately following Babel: that Abram's descendents, Israel as a particular community of faith, shall be a blessing to all peoples. In Jesus Christ, Christians confess God's fulfillment of the promise of salvation to all creatures.

In order for God's whole people to speak together, we open ourselves to God's promise; we offer to one another as a blessing the rich inheritance each has been given, and we receive from others the blessing of fulfillment God gave them. We give thanks that this remembrance is our participation in the new covenant of Christ's Body, broken for us. And we look forward to God's life and salvation for each new generation and all creation, making one in Christ's risen Body all the peoples of God's earth.

The Contribution of Spirit of God, Spirit of Christ

This volume embodies meaning-filled conversation between communions long separated by history, context, and presuppositions. The *filioque* clause of the Nicene Creed, long a major church-dividing historical controversy, was addressed in such a way as to identify in what contexts Eastern and Western Christians understood that form of the creed each used. As a result, leaders of communions long placed under one anothers' anathemas now affirmed their common faith with those whose formal creedal content still differed.

This volume presents diverse creedal texts as living witnesses to the same Christian faith by attending to the content, history, and living confessions of differing traditions. When in earlier debates the historical perspectives of East *or* West defined the conversation, theologians moved to defend their particular faith expressions. Debate where each used, but did not engage, the terms of their content resulted in debates which pitted particular expressions of faith against one another.

The power of this volume is that, while the ancient church-dividing differences are sharply addressed, they are shown in context, and found to be less differences of faith than of faith's contextual presuppositions. *Spirit of God, Spirit of Christ* shows how the teachings of both Eastern and Western Christianity were understood and received not as Truth, but as true witness to the Church's faith in their time and place.

That churches may overcome a historical chasm as deep as that over the *filioque* clause gives hope that other church-dividing matters, if addressed in the contexts which informed faith, may also lead us to deeper unity in the midst of our diversity.

In this hope, Blacks, women, Hispanics, the evangelical and free churches, peoples of Central and South America, of the Pacific, of Africa and Asia — all come to ecumenical conversation giving voice to experiences and expressions of faith whose terms only rarely define the perimeters of serious ecumenical conversation. Seen logically, confessional differences call for resolution into uniformity. But seen in faith's embodied contexts, differences may bear diverse witness in various places and ages to the same Lord.

CHURCH OF THE BRETHEREN REFLECTIONS
ON THE HOLY SPIRIT

Introduction

Brethren have always searched scripture to measure our experience and direct our understanding on matters which concern us. More recently, we have become aware how carefully we attend to Christian voices from the Brethren tradition, and from other ecclesial traditions. Our awareness that the early Church wrote the New Testament, "our guide in matters of faith and practice," further heightens our awareness that, when we attend to Scripture, we are guided by both Scripture and tradition. Our enlarged terrain of faith is God's gift to us, given as the Church's ecumenical life has enriched us. Even so, we refer to it with words from our tradition, saying we listen with brothers and sisters in the faith to God's living voice addressing the whole household of faith throughout all ages and places.

Brethren have learned from Christian brothers and sisters in other communions, contexts, and ages that it is important to attend simultaneously to faith's content, context, and dynamics. Content, faith's expression of normative truth, may be experienced as "mere" dogma when it is disembodies from context. Context, the places in all ages

God indwells, may be viewed as "mere" phenomenon when addressed apart from faith's content. Dynamics, God's empowering presence, may be viewed as "mere" relationships when viewed apart from content and context. In discussions on the Holy Spirit, Christians may address only the content, context, or dynamics of God's Spirit. But attention from any single perspective will truncate our understanding.

As Brethren characteristically look to Scripture to inform and illumine our understanding, I look broadly to Scripture to reflect as Brethren upon the Holy Spirit.

Biblical Witness to God's Spirit

Less systematic than narrative, Scripture bears enormously diverse witness to God's Spirit. Scripture records the Spirit's actions more than understandings about it. I lift up three particularly characteristic expressions of God's Spirit visible in the New Testament, in Hebrew Scripture, and in our communions today: God's Spirit forms community; God's Spirit enlivens community; God's Spirit is the believing community's truth and life.

God's Spirit Forms Community

Paul attributes to God's Spirit the creation into one community all peoples who believe in Jesus Christ: Jews and Gentiles, slave and free, male and female. Moreover, in Paul's witness, God's Spirit not only *creates* community; it also calls forth those persons (Paul, as a prime illustation) with the leadership gifts needed to form of those who believe in Jesus a church, a body of believers.

In Hebrew scripture God's Spirit also creates community. So in its post-Jordan diversity, Yahweh's Spirit "came upon" judges and prophets able to form Israel's tribes into one people. Israel remembered this time when God gave it leaders able to create of many tribes one people as God's fulfillment of the promise to Abraham that Israel would become a great nation.

In the understanding that God's Spirit forms community, narrative accounts emphasize God's activity and initiative which makes of diverse peoples one people of God. God-appointed leaders have a prominent place as midwives who help direct exclusive tribal or particular loyalties toward mutual loyalty to the same God. Communal doxology, liturgical celebration, and instruction in the faith are central to communal faith life, while rarely discussed in the texts characteristic of this terrain.

By analogy, churches today long for unity in Jesus Christ.

Communions nevertheless fear that we might not be led to fulfillment and salvation in God's Spirit, but alienated from God's heritage and promise which has been our life and truth from the beginning.

God's Spirit Enlivens Community

Central to Luke-Acts is an understanding that God's Spirit enlivens community. God's Spirit is that dynamic power by which God's people are empowered with new insight; the authority of God's Spirit directs radical personal and institutional change. Reduced from enlivening change to directive instruction in James, the Spirit's visible role is diminished even more in much non-canonical literature, until the community virtually measures its faith by its practice(s).

In Hebrew scripture, the understanding that God's Spirit gives life is particularly visible among the prophets. God's life-giving activity regularly calls for deeper congruence with, or radical change from, earlier expressions of faith. So Samuel resisted Israel's call for a king, yet was led by God to anoint both Saul and David. Even when desolate in exile, God's Spirit enlivened silent hearts to sing where they had been frozen with alienation.

God's Spirit as life-giving emphasizes God's creative activity able to re-form for changing contexts a people whose history and tradition led them to understand themselves as God's people. Narratives of empowerment and transformation which record the life-giving work of God's Spirit often bristle with awe and theophany.

By analogy, Christian communions who today seek visible unity, long to be enlivened as one, holy, catholic, and apostolic people of God. Communions confess that all are changed as unity becomes manifest; all will be transformed. We know *we* cannot do the Spirit's transforming work. Yet we who know "creation itself will be liberated from bondage" long for visible unity as God's people, as God's incarnate sign of renewal for all creation.

God's Spirit is the Believing Community's Truth and Life

John's gospel presents Jesus as God's Word, Life, Truth and Spirit. Believers abide in God by remembering Jesus. John's remembrance pneumatology is deeply akin to his Christology in that faithful communal memory mirrors that perfect union of human with divine life known in Jesus Christ. God's initiative is the basis on which God's people can remember Jesus Christ who, as God's life and truth for us, is also our life and truth with God. We remember and enact our communal identity and memory; we "wash one anothers' feet"; we "eat bread and drink the cup" in remembrance of Jesus. In remembrance, we are restored to life; and Jesus' Truth is extended to the next generation.

Similarly in Torah, as God "remembered" Israel and then went into action to call Moses to deliver Israel, so claims upon Israel's obedient service and action are introduced by words of remembrance: liturgies recounting their identity as those who *have* life only as it stems from God's claim upon and fulfillment of them. Likewise, whether traced through national kingship or messianic geneologies, salvation is assured through David's line to all who remember from generation to generation that God is their life, even when nations fall and leaders fail.

This understanding of Spirit features God's active, embodied presence in which the believing community is invited to "abide" that it may endure. The Spirit creates between God and God's people the kind of union known in Jesus who was fully human and fully God. Believers whose life and truth *is* God, who remember and abide in God, live by or are indwelt by God's Spirit. Such remembrance constitutes union with God, the result of which is a people internally and externally God's own people.

The narratives surrounding this understanding direct believers' attention to appropriate enactment of their memory: for example, the passover meal with sacrificial blood visibly smeared, its roasted meat eaten in haste with unleavened bread, and all leavings burned; or Jesus' passover/last supper before crucifixion with various instructions regarding footwashing and bread and cup. The person and office of leaders fit to carry out the community's memory are not directly addressed. But in Jewish, as in early Christian tradition alike, remembrance acts were carried out in household and intimate local gatherings. God's Spirit as truth and life re-members us to life by redeeming life-threatening events such as Israel's post-exodus experience of being no people, or abandoning our Lord to crucifixion, that what threatened us with death may bear us in life.

God's Holy Spirit in Life Contexts

Scripture is clear that God is present with us in each life situation. From the beginning when God accompanied Adam and Eve from the garden, God seeks out, is present to, remains with, restores, and enlivens God's people in whatever condition we find ourselves. We may know *about* God apart from awareness of our contexts and conditions. But in confessing that Jesus is God's incarnate Messiah, we confess that all human knowledge *of* God is incarnate; it reflects the form, condition, context, and limits of believers' lives.

We have our treasure in earthen vessels. Because God addresses believers incarnately, Christian understandings of God's Spirit reflect communions' diverse and enfleshed social fabrics. Our social, national, religious, political, economic, racial, gender, and ethnic expressions become enmeshed with our faith. We are prone to condemn as not-of-God what God did not give *us*. Throughout scripture and the life of the Church, we believers confuse our God-given treasure with the earthen vessels in which it is given us. And, as in scripture, believers today bear witness through our diverse contexts and experiences to the height and depth and breadth of the Holy Spirit's work among us.

In faith which celebrates God's life and work incarnately present among us, we are not surprised to find significant correspondence between an ecclesial tradition's socio-cultural experienced and its dominant understanding or doctrine of the Holy Spirit. (By "understanding," I refer to dynamics visible in the narratives people tell that show God's Spirit is their life. By "doctrine" I refer to concepts about God's action and "nature.") I want to explore tentatively how understandings of God's Spirit visible in scripture and communions today may correspond to traditions' socio-religious formation or experiential contexts. Several assumptions are present throughout:

> In Scripture as in contemporary experience, the understanding that God's Spirit forms community has doxology as its center; the understanding of God's Spirit as enlivening community is concerned for right behavior, rightly embodied faith; and the understanding of God's Spirit as God's very truth and life calls us to rightly remember God's life for us through liturgy and teachings which have proven themselves life-giving.

> All communions experience each of these understandings of God's Holy Spirit in our lives, even if our doctrinal explications about the Holy Spirit are at home primarily in one terrain.

1. *Doxology* characterizes the life of a faith community whose formation is rooted in celebrating God's life-giving it life. Doxological language may be examined to determine its orthodoxy, but believers life-context amid doxology is worship and praise. Faith-life primarily centered in doxology forms believers by leading them more to praise than to understand God.

Doxology loses its power if worshipers sense no vital connection between the liturgical drama of blessing and praise, and events of their daily existence. Doxology which fails to form Christians is more apt to be inert than idolatrous. Nevertheless, when Christians examine the content and object of doxology, we distinguish between doxology that is and is not faithful.

2. Emphasis on right *behavior* may result from faith's passion to embody doxology or as a corrective to "empty" words. Rooted in an understanding that God's Spirit enlivens community, concern for right behavior issues a call to con-form personal life with God's words so believers embody what they confess. Believers are responsible to seek integrity between outward behavior and what is hidden in the heart. Experientially, "good" words or actions which contradict the spirit in us, is deadly. So those who murmured in the wilderness after making covenant with Yahweh were stricken, as were Ananias and Sapphira, whose words also misrepresented their hearts.

Concern to rightly embody God's Spirit tempts Christians to precisely identify right behavior: as in the *Haustafeln* and James. Teachings about right behavior, like the content of doxology, may be examined to see what faith is embodied. But assessing behavior provides no norms by which believers can separate those who do from those who do not belong to God. We recall the early Church's struggle to decide whether believers must be circumcised or would be permitted to eat meat offered to idols. Christians today face similar quandaries over behavioral questions. Contemporary "issues" debates remind us how deeply contextual is any explicit understanding of faith and heresy in this understanding of God's Spirit.

3. *Remembering* God's Spirit as our truth and life is basic to both doxology and right behavior. Israel knew, as John reminds Christians, that believers "become" one with whatever memory indwells us. We are literally re-minded, re-membered into the one who is our life. As we remember the Spirit of God, God's Spirit comes to and is the Spirit in us. As each generation "becomes" Israel by remembering Torah, we "become" Christian by continuously re-membering ourselves to Christ's life, truth, and way. Deeply theological in character, the experiential context for this pneumatology is embodied, interpreted liturgy which meaningfully illumines how God's life with and for us is present in all our human experiences.

As priests struggle with doxological irrelevance, as prophets and disciples struggle with idealized behavior, so theologians struggle with conceptualized truth. Concerned to explicate and illumine right thought, thinkers may treat as a universal norm truth known enmeshed in context.

Contemporary and scriptural understandings of God's Holy Spirit are rooted in and illumined by communions' living contexts of faith. Christians respond to the work of God's Spirit today, as from earliest memory, in doxology, with responsible behavior, and learning who we are by remembering whose we are. Christians may consciously be guided more by one than another understanding of God's Spirit. Like God's people Israel, the apostolic Church, and the Church throughout all ages, we experience and find in our traditions various understandings of God's Holy Spirit. In ecclesial conversations on pneumatology, the content significance of statements is known in confessors' contexts. Thus how we address and receive one another both co-interprets our understanding of God's Holy Spirit and constitutes our openness to how God may answer our prayers for unity.

The Nicean Creed, Filioque, and Pentecostal Movements in the United States

GERALD T. SHEPPARD

INTRODUCTION

AN ATTEMPT TO DESCRIBE pentecostal movements can be ventured only after admitting that no definition of "pentecostals" will satisfy all groups claiming that name. For our purposes I prefer an inclusive definition of pentecostal churches, namely those who advocate some form of "Spirit" baptism replicative of what the disciples received at the first Pentecost described in Acts, chapter two. "Speaking in tongues" or *glossolalia* may or may not be required by these churches as a sign of such a Spirit baptism, though it usually is, and, in any case, *glossolalia* is not forbidden. Usually a restoration of other apostolic gifts is more important than *glossolalia,* especially healing and testimony of experiencing the sanctifying power and presence of God. The focus of this paper will be on the classical pentecostal movement associated with an emphasis on *glossolalia* which gained public notoriety during the massive revivals of the early twentieth century. I am fully aware that many of my generalizations will not satisfy other pentecostal interpreters. Such a complex set of movements make any sweeping overview precarious. At most, I can draw an empathetic scenario for various groups which deserve more participation among us and much more historical research.

"Ecumenicity" and the Christian Confession among "Pentecostals"
    From the classic pentecostal point of view, an assessment of pentecostal "theology" or doctrinal statements invites misunderstanding

at the outset. On the one hand, movements of pneumatic enthusiasm, such as those associated with contemporary pentecostal and charismatic groups, are predicated on only a few slim points of doctrinal agreement, putting more emphasis on an ecumenicity inherent in the common experience of lives realized and secured in the power of the Holy Spirit. A well-known British pentecostal spokesperson, Donald Gee, expressed this dimension when he wrote,

> When we "came out" for Pentecost we came out not merely for a theory, or a doctrine: we came out for a burning, living, mighty *experience* that revolutionized our lives. The Baptism in the Spirit which we sought and realized was a *reality,* even though we probably understood little of the doctrines involved at the time. How different, then, from the purely doctrinal and theoretical issues involved in this matter.[1]

The excitement of overcoming denominational barriers and of setting most doctrinal nuances aside in an experience of common affirmation pervades the earliest pentecostal testimonies. The tabloid published during the Azusa Street revival (considered by many the true beginning of twentieth-century pentecostal identity) is entitled appropriately for our present concern: "The Apostolic Faith." At the beginning, a succinct, *ad hoc* summation of faith affirms the beliefs of the participants,

> *The Apostolic Faith Movement.* Stands for the restoration of the faith once delivered unto the saints—the old time religion, camp meetings, revivals, missions, street and prison work and Christian Unity everywhere.

At the end of a statement regarding "justification . . . of God's "free grace," "sanctification," "The Baptism with the Holy Ghost," and "seeking healing," we find the assurance,

> We are not fighting men or churches, but seeking to replace the dead forms and creeds and wild fanaticisms with living, practical Christianity. "Love, faith, Unity" are our watchwords . . . [2]

---

[1] "Tests for 'Fuller Revelations,' *The Pentecostal Evangel,* February 14, 1925.

[2] *The Apostolic Faith* 1/1 (1906) p. 2.

On the other hand, the repetition of the phrase "we 'came out' " in the above mentioned statement by Donald Gee betrays the utopian dimension typical of such an optimistic ecumenicity of the Spirit. There is inevitably a divisive element to the testimony by a group which claims to have been the recipient of a divine visitation, gift, realization, or fulfillment—no matter how ecumenically diverse the backgrounds of those in the group. Either everyone else from those backgrounds joins the movement and "comes out" also, or dramatic political transformations must take place allowing for a highly diverse degree of doctrinal options. For this reason, I think that the Roman Catholic scholar, Donald L. Gelpi, correctly locates "pentecostalism" in church history as part of a whole series of periodic movements of the Spirit known for their "divisive enthusiasm."[3] If, for a brief moment, racial, doctrinal, class, regional, denominational, and sexist barriers seemed to have disappeared in the pentecostal "outpouring" at Azusa Street under the tutelage of a Black Holiness preacher, William J. Seymour, the "unity" of this galvanizing moment in the formation of American pentecostals quickly dissipated.

In the place of a unified congregation of Christians "baptized in/with the Spirit" there arose a plethora of independent churches, new denominations, and movements frequently divided by either some of the traditional barriers of race, class, and creed or by new differences over leadership, church order, practical aspects of ministry, or doctrinal positions.[4] Later, a massive, somewhat less divided Hispanic pentecostal movement arose in the 1930s, often considered a mission church of the Assemblies of God, nurtured by some remarkable hispanic leaders, such as Mexican-born Francisco Olazabal. The pentecostal call for the "unity" of all Christians, regardless of denominational affiliations, found justification in their sense that God had revivified the essence of apostolic faith "in these last days." Pentecostals often tried to overcome disunity among Christians by discrediting what they perceived as divisive creeds. They saw themselves as the fulfillment of an eschatological promise, as the leaven

---

[3] *Pentecostalism: A Roman Catholic Viewpoint* (New York, 1971).

[4] Cf. Grant Wacker, "Primitive Pentecostalism in America: A Cultural Profile," in *Problems in the Pentecostal-Charismatic Movement,* ed. Harold D. Hunter (Cleveland, TN, 1983). For a provocative discussion of ecumenical attitudes within the Assemblies of God, see Cecil M. Robeck, "Name and Glory: The Ecumenical Challenge," ibid.

in the lump that would help bring about a single united Christian Church. Their thwarted hopes echo today in the continued refusal of many large organizations of churches (e.g. the Assemblies of God) to recognize themselves as constituting "denominations," despite the external trappings of general council meetings and rules for ordination and ministry. Pentecostal groups have responded in various ways to other types of ecumenical opportunities among Christian churches—Caucasian and Hispanic pentecostals have generally sided with "evangelical" associations against the NCCC; Black pentecostal churches find racism still a barrier to any ecumenical endeavor, including the white spin-off of evangelical coalitions: The Pentecostal Fellowship of North America.

Ambivalence Toward the "Nicene Creed"

Before addressing the specific issue of the *filioque* controversy, the pejorative assessment of the Nicene Creed among many pentecostal churches must be directly confronted. As should be evident from the above quotations, pentecostals generally regarded creeds as signs of "formalism," denominationalism, spiritually dead recital, and unsanctified confession. People who acquired the "new" pentecostal experience felt that they had transcended centuries of neglected apostolic faith through the recovery of a Christian gift, experiencing now just what the disciples received in the Upper Room. Stanley Frodsham, one of the earliest editors of a pentecostal periodical, expressed this dimension well:

> This same year (1908), the Lord filled the writer with the Spirit, making no difference between him and those at the beginning (at the first-century Pentecost). He was soon awakened to the fact that he was one of a large, worldwide fellowship. There were Baptists, Methodists, Presbyterians, Congregationalists, Episcopalians, Holiness people, Christians from every denomination and from no denomination, who had received a like experience.[5]

Frodsham's pentecostal identity rested on his personal testimony and had been prompted by the teaching of William Seymour, who affirmed that,

---

[5] *With Signs Following,* rev. ed. (Springfield, MO, 1941), p. 7.

when any one receives the Baptism in the Spirit according to the
original pattern, he will have a similar experience to that which
the disciples had on the day of Pentecost, and speak in tongues
just as they did on that occasion.[6]

From the perspective of these "pentecostal" believers, with their
newfound sense of the power of God in and through their lives, came
the view that, sometime after the Apostolic Age, the Christian Church
had failed to treasure what God had chosen to reestablish "in these
last days." Pentecostals commonly cited the prophecy of Joel 2.23
to the effect that there would be a "former" and "latter rain." The
former they identified with the first Pentecost of the Apostles, and
the present manifestation was seen as the " 'Latter Rain' outpouring," a sign of the end of this age and the imminence of the Second
Coming of Jesus Christ.

Consequently, for most pentecostals, creeds indicated a departure from apostolic faith for two reasons: a) because of their lack of
concern with practical Christianity, emphasizing formal doctrine instead, and b) because of their origin in and support for an episcopacy alien to the priesthood of believers and detrimental to foster-
ing the kind of intimacy in the Christian community reported from
the apostolic period. By the first criticism pentecostals challenged
other Christians who no longer hoped for the occurence of miracles,
healings, *glossolalia,* and other indications of the Spirit commonplace
in early Christianity. Faith expressed through creeds seemed idealized, a set of bloodless abstractions, divorced from the reality of God's
presence in everyday life. Pentecostals insisted that many Christians
who knew how to talk to God, had ceased to walk with God. Correct
or not, they saw in the "mainline" denominational churches an ane-
mic, pious repetition of "creeds," lacking in evidence of dynamic
testimonies, of lives empowered by the same spiritual resources available to the first Christians. They preached that apostolic Christianity could now be "recovered" through a fresh pentecostal experience
and that the need for denominations defined by differing creeds should
cease to exist.

The second argument against creeds saw them as the product of
an apostate church, often associated with the episcopacy of
"Romanism." I will cite one fairly detailed example of this criticism,

---

[6] Frodsham, p. 31.

partly to illustrate how the question about the significance of creeds gained serious attention. At an address on the occasion of the Eighth Annual Assembly of the Churches of God (Cleveland, Tennessee), Brother Spurling epitomized their view of church history: "The Church from its state of virginity drifted into Roman Catholicism."[7] He made an analogy between the Church and a locomotive, with John the disciple as the "civil engineer." God intended this train to ride upon the two golden rails of loving God and loving one's neighbor as oneself. The power of Pentecost provided the fuel. However, both Roman Catholics and even the protestant Reformers (who "failed to reform from creeds"[8]) had prolifereated various creeds, based on their "glimpses of truth," which represented "side tracks." Early in church history opposition began to grow when the train began its move ahead:

> Satan now sees that at that rate he would soon be left with no people so he set about a plan to derail the engine.

> About 320 A.D. Alexander and Tiranos, two great leaders, met at Constantinople and formed a creed from which the many different man-made creeds have had their origin.

> Here in this division they left the golden rails of the law of love and made their own rails of wood upon which the heavenly train could not run as they were narrow gauge.[9]

Later, at the Tenth Annual Assembly in 1914, the General Overseer contrasts what he considers to be a divinely ordained "theocratic" government enacted by the apostles with the later "episcopal form of government" in the second and third centuries inaugurated by those who later adopted the Nicene creed. The events at Nicea are portrayed in pejorative terms:

> ... there was much discussion with no regulations by the exercise of any external authority. The Arian party made an effort to submit the draft of a creed which called forth violent disapprobation and was literally torn in pieces by the excited

---

[7] *Book of Minutes: A Compiled History of the Work of the General Assemblies of the Church of God* (Cleveland, TN, 1922), p. 98.

[8] Ibid. p. 137.

[9] Ibid. p. 99.

assemblage. When this failed to pass, Eusebios produced a confession of faith which he had been taught in his youth as the faith of the church of Palestine. This also failed to meet the approval of the orthodox faction so it was dismissed. Finally, however, a creed was produced by the opposers of Arianism that was received and the announcement was made that the creed of the Church was settled.

This action resulted in the disruption and division of the Church. At that very moment it ceased to be the Church of God, for God's Church has no creed.[10]

These strong objections to the Nicene Creed grow out of a yearning for "apostolic order" and a unified Christianity. Some pentecostal groups, like the Churches of God, thought that fresh biblical study would yield the proper "Bible plans of (church) order."[11] Moreover, a new realization of the Spirit would accompany this exegetical task so that "when the final decision is reached the Holy Spirit will so set His approval on it that there will scarcely be a whisper of dissension."[12] By this example, I wish neither to defend this assumption nor to imply that all pentecostals thought in exactly these same terms. At a minimum, such views were not unusual among pentecostal groups; despite their divergent forms, pentecostals shared—like their counterparts in the first century—a utopian vision of a unified Christianity on the edge of the Eschaton. The darkened glass was surely clearing in a manner that ought to allow all Christians to see both where

---

[10]Ibid. pp. 163f.

[11]The anxiety over time of this search surfaces verbally at places in the *Minutes*. In his annual address of 1912, the General Overseer remarked, "Beneath the folds of that Book, somewhere, is the perfect plan for setting forth and ordaining ministers, and if it is not found and put into practice God will let us make shipwreck, and will raise up others that He can trust with His business. This is a subject of too great weight and importance to be lightly esteemed. Every member of this assembly should humble himself and earnestly seek God for a special revelation of His Word and will, so that, if mistakes have been made in the past in regard to the plan we have practiced, the correction should be made here and now, and this convention should not be dismissed until the Bible plan is ascertained and preparation made for the practice of it hereafter." Ibid. p. 58.

[12]Ibid. p. 165.

Christian history had gone astray from its true foundations and how to recover the original "apostolic faith."

Though Nicea became associated with a perjorative view of a hierarchical apostolic succession and the episcopate of priests, this criticism did not mean that pentecostals were in principle opposed to statements of doctrine. They would occasionally admit even to some value served by creeds. One of the first systematic approaches to theology was written by a highly respected pentecostal teacher, Myer Pearlman, who writes positively about "formulations of dogmas, that is, interpretations which define the doctrine and 'fence' it against error."[13] As an instance, Pearlman refers to the Athanasian Creed and reproduces this post-Nicean statement verbatim for his readers. Aware that some pentecostals may raise objections, he notes:

> This statement may appear dry, involved and hair-splitting to us, but in the early days, it proved an effective means of preserving the correct statement of truths that were precious and vital to the Church.[14]

Most pentecostals understood well that the gifts of the Holy Spirit could only *confirm* what was *taught* as doctrine by the apostles.[15] Correct doctrine could be established, as in the first century, only by an appeal to apostolic tradition, that is, the testimony of prophets and apostles later preserved for us in Scripture. The maturation of the pentecostal movement, with its own experience of doctrinal controversy, led to increasingly stronger *ad hoc* statements of faith looking very much like creeds. The impulse to show that "speaking in tongues" and other related gifts are found throughout church history has, also, allowed many groups to make a more positive assessment of the intervening centuries between the "former" and the "latter" rain of the Spirit. Most importantly, rather than thinking of themselves as innovative theologians, pentecostals considered their views of the Trinity unoriginal and simply orthodox. The exceptional situation of a minority of "Jesus Only" pentecostals provides the only self-consciously idiosyncratic proposal which, for the limited purposes of this paper, I cannot discuss in great detail.

---

[13]*Knowing the Doctrines of the Bible* (Springfield, MO, 1937), p. 71.

[14]Pearlman, p. 72.

[15]*What Meaneth This? A Pentecostal Answer to a Pentecostal Question* (Springfield, MO, 1947), p. 80.

Filioque Clause and Pentecostal Understandings of the Trinity

At the outset, pentecostals have made only passing reference, if at all, to the "*filioque* clause" in their surveys of church history. It played no significant role in any pentecostal discussion, to my knowledge. Its citation may be described as an endeavor to mark any occurrence of positive church statements about the Holy Spirit. Minimally pentecostal appeals to church history confirm a deep ambiguity within their own ranks—church history can serve both to document the loss of true apostoloc faith after the first century or it may attest to the normal Christian character of pentecostal religious experience by confirming precedence of the same in favored figures (e.g. Tertullian) and confessional expressions (even creeds) throughout Christian history. One might mention the *filioque* as one of those latter "places in the sun" for pentecostals who were concerned to refute charges that they might be historically unorthodox, abnormal, or fanatic.

Nevertheless, many of the underlying issues at stake in the historic controversy over the *filioque have been* of great interest to pentecostals, even though most pentecostals have yet to realize that fact. The pentecostal restorationist view of Christianity inevitably destined them to "re-play" certain aspects of church history, complete with the shaping of doctrinal statements in response to perceived "heresy." Within a decade after the galvinizing Azusa Street revivals of 1906, both Black and Caucasian pentecostal groups were divided over a trinitarian controversy, called the "Jesus Only" movement. In its extreme form, some "Jesus Only" pentecostals argued that the idea of the "Trinity" had been forced upon the Church at the Council of Nicea by the bishop of Rome. Biblical texts were used to support the idea of convert baptism in the name of Jesus alone, instead of the trinitarian formula. This "new issue" grew essentially out of an attempt to follow a "Bible order" in baptism.[16] Many "Jesus Only" pentecostals held that the one person of the Godhead was Jesus Christ, for whom terms like "Father" and "Son" are merely labels, while others advocated more of a dynamistic modalism associated with an economic view of the Trinity. Reacting against the "new issue," most pentecostals found themselves confessing a view of the Trinity remarkably similar to or borrowed from the Nicene Creed, which they

---

[16]Vinson Synan, *The Holiness-Pentecostal Movement in the United States* (Grand Rapids, 1971), pp. 154f.

may have previously portrayed in entirely negative terms. Against their idealism, most pentecostal groups were forced to nuance their doctrinal statements and sharply distinguish themselves from the "Jesus Only" movement which had attracted some prominent early leaders along with many of their church members and led to new, independent churches and separate pentecostal movements.

Reading the early pentecostal trinitarian statements, a church historian will be struck by the admixture of formulae and phrases which "trickle down" from standard Christian creeds alongside original expressions designed to eliminate a "Jesus Only" possibility. Still, pentecostals tried to retain an emphasis on affirming the mystery of the three-in-one with its biblical support. In statements of the Black pentecostal Church of God (Memphis, Tennessee), one is reminded that, "The conception of the divine trinity may only be apprehended through revelation"; that is to say, one comes to "know that this One being consists in the three persons, of Father, Son, and Holy Ghost, as he finds this stated and portrayed in Holy Scripture."[17] In the Assemblies of God a lengthy statement on "The Adorable Godhead" was added in 1916 in response to the "Jesus Only" controversy. Admitting that the terms "Trinity" and "Persons" are "not to be found in Scripture," the statement asserts, nonetheless, that these "words are in harmony with Scripture." The statement emphasizes "the distinction of Persons in the Godhead," though acknowledging that "this distinction and relationship, as to its mode is *inscrutable* and *incomprehensible,* because *unexplained*" in scripture. Lest the impression be left that pentecostals are entirely ignorant or could care less about these issues, the next two articles found in the 1916 Assemblies' Statement of Fundamental Truths refute that assumption:

Unity of the One Being of Father, Son and Holy Spirit

Accordingly, therefore, there is *that* in the Son which constitutes Him *the Son* and not the Father; and there is *that* in the Holy Ghost which constitutes Him *the Holy Ghost* and not either the Father or the Son. Wherefore the Father is the Begetter, the Son is the Begotten, and the Holy Ghost is the one proceeding from the Father and the Son. Therefore, because these three persons in the Godhead are in a state of unity, there is but one Lord God

---

[17]O. T. Jones and J. E. Bryant, *Manuel of the Church of God in Christ* (n.p., 1936), pp. 8f.

Almighty and His name one. John 1.18; 15.26; 17.11,21; Zech. 14.9.

Identity and Cooperation in the Godhead

The Father, the Son and the Holy Ghost are never identical as to *Person*; nor *confused* as to *relation*; nor *divided* in respect to the Godhead; nor *opposed* as to *cooperation*. The Son is *in* the Father and the Father is *in* the the Son as to relationship. The Son is *with* the Father and the Father is *with* the Son, as to fellowship. The Father is not *from* the Son, but the Son is *from* the Father, as to authority. The Holy Ghost is *from* the Father and the Son proceeding, as to nature, relationship, cooperation and authority. Hence, neither Person in the Godhead either exists or works separately or independently of the others. John 5.17-30, 32,37; John 8.17,18.

One must be careful still not to assign too much weight to every nuance in any of these pentecostal statements, because they were written for the purpose of solving particular problems. The appearance of the *filioque* clause in this last one is in the form of a simple repetition of what is perceived to be an orthodox position and plays no central role in later pentecostal discussions of the Trinity or the role of the Holy Spirit. For instance, when the Assemblies teacher Myer Pearlman treats the Trinity, he refutes the heresy of "Sabellianism" and offers the following view against "sharp distinctions" drawn between the trinitarian persons:

> The Father is preeminently Creator, yet the Son and the Spirit are described as cooperating in that work. The Son is preeminently the Redeemer, yet God the Father and the Holy Spirit are described a sending the Son to redeem. The Holy Spirit is the Sanctifier, yet the Father and the Son cooperate in that work.[18]

In these and other expressions pentecostals sought to confess the three-in-oneness in a balanced manner without confusing the economic roles of the three persons; the *filioque* clause pointed in this direction but was not definitive nor necessarily understood. Certainly the controversy behind it remained unknown. Their affirmation of the "mystery" of the Trinity cautioned them against employing too freely extra-biblical terminology beyond what they perceived to be biblical warrants.

---

[18]Pearlman, p. 69.

The Present World Council Debate and Pentecostal Self-Interest

As I understand the present discussion in the World Council of Christian Churches, surrounding the possible use of the Nicene Creed as a statement of apostolic faith and the role of the *filioque* clause in it, pentecostals have much to benefit from it and their voice deserves to be heard in this debate. Certainly, many of the issues in the present controversy are cast in philosophical and/or theological terms foreign to twentieth-century pentecostal history. My response can only point toward a potential which I think and hope is realistic. Before addressing the larger scenario of how the Nicene Creed can be a statement of apostolic faith, some brief consideration may be useful regarding the stake pentecostals should have in the question of *filioque* and the Nicene Creed.

Pentecostal interests in this present controversy must necessarily be at a high level of generality. In practical terms, the debate may appear to pentecostals as a classic confrontation between the churches of East and West. The position of the West seems most concerned to link the Spirit immanently with Jesus Christ lest movements of the Spirit minimize the corrective of the Word of God in Christ. Conversely, the East sees a danger in the response of the West, perhaps due in part to the nature of the West's confrontation and triumph over gnosticism. However, as Photios and subsequent Eastern Orthodox theologians have argued, the creedal formulations in the West may seem to treat the Holy Spirit as an inferior member of the Trinity. Pentecostals would pose a similar challenge to the Western church. Though little informed about Eastern Orthodoxy, pentecostals share the anti-"Romanism" from the Puritan Reformation. However, they realized that the Reformers dismissed or condemned Anabaptist and charismatic groups within the so-called "Radical Reformation" as well. Hence, in their view, the Reformers, "not reformed from [Roman Catholic] creeds" of the West, still perpetuated an atrophied understanding of the importance of the Holy Spirit in daily Christian life. Though pentecostals did not foresee problems in the Reformers' affirmations of the Trinity, they often felt that the reformation creeds paid inadequate attention to either practical Christianity or the significance of the Holy Spirit in the Church Age. Consequently, when pentecostals proffered their own trinitarian statements (as above), the expressions often attempted a fuller explication of the role of the Spirit within the Trinity than was familiar from the Nicene Creed, with or without the *filioque* clause. My suspicions are that, given a fair hearing, pentecostals would find the Eastern Orthodox critique foreign in language but more familiar in content than that of the West.[19]

Pentecostals generally have been much less concerned with theories about the immanent Trinity than with stating a position which in practical terms precludes the unorthodox views of tritheism, dynamistic modalism, or unitarianism (with the exception of the minority "Jesus Only" pentecostals). At the same time, the Trinity remains a mystery revealed through Scripture. Pentecostals concentrated their trinitarian reflection more explicitly on the economic activity of the Trinity in salvation, sanctification, and the filling with the Holy Spirit. Only in this area of trinitarian discussion do most pentecostals feel that they have something to preserve in apostolic faith and to contribute to the Church at large. The particular problem for pentecostals concerns the ambiguity of the phrase "the baptism of the Holy Spirit," a phrase popular in the Holiness movements of the nineteenth century and articulated attractively in America through the works by Asa Maham and R. A. Torrey. In economic terms, pentecostals needed to discern differences in the role of the Holy Spirit in various peak Christian experiences associated with salvation, sanctification, and spiritual empowerment.

This was the issue that preceded the genesis of what we think of today as the pentecostal—"tongues speaking"—movement of the twentieth century. For example, at the turn of the century, Arthur T. Pierson published a provocatively bold book entitled, *Forward Movements of the Last Half Century: A Glance at the More Marked Philanthropic, Missionary, and Spiritual Movements Characteristic of Our Time.* He devotes a chapter to something called, "The Pentecostal Movement," best exhibited in contemporary revivals in Uganda. Pierson justifies his use of this label to describe the success of that mission work by explaining in Keswick-like fashion that the Bible teaches a difference between the conversion of Jesus' disciples by which they had the Holy Spirit "*with* them" and the experience at Pentecost when the Spirit was revealed as "*in* them." In the latter

---

[19]Cf. *Spirit of God, Spirit of Christ,* ed. Lukas Vischer (London, 1981). Many of the Orthodox concerns over the *filioque* would be shared by pentecostals. The Old Catholic response by Kurt Stalder, however, concurs with pentecostal suspicions that the Creed needs to say more in order to fully reflect apostolic faith. As Stadler observes, " . . . the form of the Creed without the *filioque* which we regard as the ecumenical one and advocate ourselves does not seem to us to meet all requirements." Ibid. p. 109.

case, one obtained a post-conversion experience of "the power of the Holy Spirit' which is the "last and greatest gift of God"; Christian neglect to seek the fullness of this "gift" in modern times means that those now receiving "in our day *come into an entirely new experience by the enduement of the Holy Spirit.*"[20]

The "pentecostals" of the twentieth century, though often equivocal in their understanding of sanctification, have continued to distinguish the role of the Spirit at conversion from that of a subsequent empowerment associated with the apostolic pentecostal experience. The phrase "baptism of the Holy Spirit" might wrongly imply that pentecostals minimize the working of the Spirit in the lives of those converts lacking a subsequent, empowering experience. Since Christians are all baptized "of the Spirit," the difference between conversion and sanctification/empowerment needed clarification. Most pentecostal groups resolved this problem by noting the ambiguity of the genitive preposition "of" in the expression, "baptism of the Holy Spirit." Was it a subjective or objective genitive? Was one baptized *by* the Spirit at Pentecost or *in* or *with* the Spirit? The prevailing pentecostal solution is to argue that the Holy Spirit baptizes us *in Jesus Christ* at conversion, while after conversion the resurrected Lord baptizes us *in* or *with the Holy Spirit* as at Pentecost.[21] Though these matters do not directly touch on the question regarding the "procession" of the Holy Spirit within an intrinsic formulation of the Trinity they do convey the concern of pentecostals in any discussion of matters of practical Christian experience and the need to articulate how the Holy Spirit can be appreciated as an essential person in the cooperative work of the Trinity through Christian faith and praxis. Without the Spirit our praxis may fail to accompany the knowledge of the Word of God in Christ; without the Word of God in Christ the Spirit might empower only our mystical (I-Thou) sense of God's presence among us.

An Ecumenical Future

Pentecostals have much to learn from the current ecumenical

---

[20](New York, 1901), p. 141.

[21]E.g., Ralph M. Riggs, *The Spirit Himself* (Springfield, MO, 1949), pp. 42-61; P. C. Nelson, *Bible Doctrines* (Springfield, MO, 1948), esp. pp. 86f., cf. "note" on p. 86.

controversy regarding the *filiioque* clause and the Nicene Creed. Recent Vatican sponsored dialogues between pentecostals and Roman Catholics have already helped to dispel some prejudices pentecostals inherited from the Puritan ethos of North America. More familiarity by pentecostals with the Orthodox Churches and the arguments of the Greek Fathers could expose other significant points of resonance, particularly on the doctrine of the Holy Spirit. There was a time when pentecostals could write a testimonial history of their movement under the title: *Suddenly From Heaven.*[22] While other denominations celebrated their particular founders, pentecostals themselves claimed to have no human founders at all. A more mature sense of history has slowly dispelled this myth of how things began and pentecostals have steadily been forced to become more modest about their place in church history, without abnegating the special place they justly deserve. The process of education and discernment continues throughout these churches at a quickening pace. The number of seminarians and graduate students from pentecostal backgrounds has increased exponentially within the last decade. Until the recent past, a number of large pentecostal groups have looked to fundamentalism and evangelicalism for norms of "orthodoxy" in matters outside of pentecostal distinctives. The pluralism of contemporary seminary experiences among pentecostal pastors and teachers will undoubtedly complicate this picture in the decades ahead. How pentecostals will respond to the gifts and the seductions of modernity, as well as to the guidance and betrayal of "historic" Christian churches, remains an open question.

Currently, pentecostals have shown little interest in how the so-called "mainstream" denominations solve the differences over the *filioque* clause, but pentecostals should be involved and, given more opportunity, will be. More critical reflection by pentecostals on the role of church creeds is inevitable, and the Nicene is a good point of departure, because of its significance in the present ecumenical debate. Attitudes toward the Nicene Creed and others in church history are certainly changing among pentecostals, even though most would hold it to be at best an inadequate and at worst a distorted expression of apostolic faith among Christians. In general, confessions about the economic Trinity remain more pertinent to pentecostals than statements about the immanent

---

[22]The title of an early pentecostal history by Carl Brumback.

Trinity.[23] How God in three Persons is actually present in the practical life of faith is far more important than specifying precisely what hypostasies distinguish the mysterious inner working of the Persons of the Trinity. Pentecostals may seem to be cruelly egalitarian when they speak of the Godhead. Each Person of the Trinity must be experienced as a real, transforming presence or face of God if the Church is to know God fully within the limits of God's self-revelation. While the Nicene Creed may state well *some* apostolic faith which pentecostals need to learn more about, it fails to state, for pentecostals, the faith, or the "Full Gospel," of the apostles. This dilemma—whether the Nicene Creed is merely inadequate or thoroughly distorted due to episcopacy—is a serious one for pentecostals who have traditionally yearned for the visible unity of the Church.

-----

[23]Pentecostals may find a better avenue into the ecumenical discussion when the debate over the Trinity is cast in doxological and economic terms of Christian faith. Such an orientation is, in my opinion, one of the many strengths in the various works of Geoffrey Wainwright. See his chapter on "Church and Spirit," pp. 19-30, *The Ecumenical Moment: Crisis and Opportunity for the Church* (Grand Rapids, 1983).

The Holy Spirit Consultation:
A Summary Statement

ON OCTOBER 24-25, 1985 a consultation was held at Holy Cross Greek Orthodox School of Theology, Brookline, Massachusetts to consider the similarities and differences among the Christian churches concerning our faith in the Holy Spirit. The consultation used the Klingenthal Memorandum "The *Filioque* Clause in Ecumenical Perspective," Klingenthal, 1979 (*Spirit of God, Spirit of Christ,* Faith and Order Paper No. 103, Lukas Vischer, ed., [Geneva, 1981]) as a reference point for its work. To many in the ecumenical movement, this memorandum appears to open new pathways toward resolution of the *filioque* question.

The papers prepared for the consultation addressed the place of the Holy Spirit in the trinitarian theology and life of various Christian traditions. Those of us who participated in the consultation represented an ever-wider diversity of Christian traditions. We were some fifty-five people, from the following Christian communions: Baptist, African Methodist Episcopal Zion, Brethren, Eastern and Oriental Orthodox, Episcopal, Holiness, Lutheran, Mennonite, Moravian, Pentecostal, Presbyterian/Reformed, Quaker, Roman Catholic, Swedenborgian, United Church of Christ and United Methodist. We met in the hope that, while dealing with our historic divisions and contemporary differences, we might recognize common areas of experience and thought concerning the Holy Spirit and also might serve the contemporary needs of the whole Christian Church which seeks ever anew to give authentic witness to the Holy Spirit.

Three main areas of concern emerged in the discussions of the consultation: a) the *filioque* question, b) the naming of God, and

c) the dynamic polarity between apostolic doctrine (creed) and apostolic life (experience). What follows, including the recommendations, is a summary of these discussions representing central issues raised by the papers, key points of discussion, and individual opinions. It is offered neither as an agreed statement nor as an expression of a consensus on any major issue, but rather as a contribution to the ongoing ecumenical conversation on the apostolic faith and life.

A. Filioque

1. The theological use of the *filioque* in the West was directed against any form of Arian ontological subordination of the Son to the Father and in this perspective is fully valid according to the theological criteria of the Eastern tradition.

2. In the West the *filioque* has been used to stress a) the consubstantial unity of the Trinity, b) the divine status of the Son, and c) the intimate relationship between the Son and the Spirit.

3. These points are also integral elements of Eastern trinitarian theology anchored in the Cappadocian teaching of *perichoresis* ("mutual indwelling") of the Persons of the Trinity. This teaching is reflected in the Nicene-Constantinopolitan Creed which professes an equal worship and glorification of the Persons of the Holy Trinity.

4. A fundamental and wide agreement exists between Eastern and Western trinitarian doctrine affirming the complete reciprocity and mutuality of the Son and the Spirit in their eternal relations (immanent Trinity) as well as their manifested action in creation, Church and society (economic Trinity).

5. Christ is both the bearer and the sender of the Spirit. The Spirit of God is in every way also the Spirit of the Son.

6. The Eastern tradition has long affirmed the teaching on the "monarchy"of the Father, that is, "the Father is the sole principle (ἀρχή), source (πηγή) and cause (αἰτία) of divinity." (Klingenthal Memorandum)

7. The Western tradition has historically wished to show itself as much attached to this principle as the East. In affirming the *filioque* the Western tradition never thought that the "monarchy" of the Father was called in question.

8. However, the Eastern tradition has viewed the *filioque* as unintentionally compromising the "monarchy" of the Father, a doctrine which is enshrined in the Cappadocian teaching and reflected in the Nicene Creed which declares that the Spirit "proceeds from"

or "goes forth out of" (ἐκπορευόμενον) the Father.

9. The Eastern tradition has seen its its own trinitarian approach as more consistently biblical and personal, with careful avoidance of any modalistic tendencies which compromise the uniqueness of each of the divine Persons.

10. Many contemporary Eastern theologians have felt that the *filioque* subordinates the Spirit to the Son, and thereby depersonalizes the Spirit.

11. Contemporary Eastern theologians have often pointed out what they consider to be consequences of the *filioque*: authoritarianism, institutionalism, clericalism, etc. One is hard pressed to demonstrate that such conditions actually are the result of the *filioque*. The very same patterns can be found in most churches, with or without the *filioque*. Nonetheless, a feminist theologian from the West thought that the critique of the *filioque* in this perspective by the East was essentially correct.

12. In the Western tradition the *filioque* was intended to indicate that the Son was involved in the procession of the Spirit, though only in a secondary manner, leaving the "monarchy" of the Father intact. Anything the Son contributes to the procession of the Spirit he receives from the Father. Western theologians have maintained that the Nicene Creed's concern in declaring that the Spirit proceeds from the Father was not to determine the relationship of origin but the divinity of the Spirit.

13. Eastern trinitarian thought as expressed by Gregory of Nyssa, Gregory the Cypriot and Gregory Palamas, conceives of the Son as *mediating,* but not *causing,* the Spirit's procession from the Father. On this nuanced difference hangs the whole weight of centuries of controversy between the Eastern and Western churches. This is also the reason why the Orthodox cannot accept the conjunction "and" in the *filioque* clause ("from the Father *and* the Son") which signi-fies a joint cause in the procession of the Spirit.

14. The opinion from among the Orthodox was expressed that the specifically Augustinian approach implicit in the *filioque,* namely tha the Son is in some sense a cause, would have to be recognized as doctrinally erroneous because it compromises the doctrine of the "monarchy" of the Father.

15. According to one Western opinion a considerable segment of Eastern theologians have recognized the integral relationship of the *filioque* to Western theological systems. According to this same

opinion within that system the preservation of the *filioque* is an acceptable position. The truth and the intent asserted in the *filioque* has been held by the West since the fourth century. To transfer the *filioque* out of the theological culture of the West and insert it into the Eastern framework, is a violation of the integrity of the Eastern theological culture.

16. Photios, Patriarch of Constantinople, who is recognized as a saint in the Orthodox Churches, proposed the formula "the Spirit proceeds from the Father alone." Yet this difference in teaching over against the *filioque* did not cause the breaking of communion between the Eastern and Western churches.

17. The question was asked whether the churches of the East and West would not be able to live together in a united church while the West retains the *filioque* as an authentic part of its theological identity. But others raised the question whether or not this approach would imply an avoidance, not resolution, of the *filioque* question.

18. The Klingenthal Memorandum gave a number of suggested formulations which might bridge the differences between East and West, among them "the Spirit proceeds from the Father of the Son," and "the Spirit proceeds from the Father through the Son." These formulae would safeguard the "monarchy" of the Father while at the same time affirming the active participation of the Son in the eternal procession of the Spirit from the Father.

19. It was noted that there is no possibility for some of the churches to promote the use of an alternate text of the Creed as long as there is a demand that the *filioque* be recognized as theologically erroneous.

20. Fruitful for further study are the specific implications of the Augustinian and Cappadocian approaches to the Trinity and theology in general, that is, the practical implications for the role of the Spirit in creation, the Church and society today.

21. On the agenda of both East and West is the integration of the "full and constant reciprocity of the Incarnate Word and the Holy Spirit" (Klingenthal Memorandum) into theology, catechesis and preaching.

22. The warning not to carry too far the distinctions between the economic and immanent Trinity, or between the temporal mission and eternal procession, is well taken.

23. The differences between the East and West in the matters of the *filioque* do not constitute a "great divide." Together East and West confess the Holy Trinity, and share broad agreement regarding

the work of the Spirit. These commonalities are embedded in the liturgies and theological traditions of both communities.

24. Moving beyond the question of the *filioque,* the churches should give attention to enlarging the Church's theology of the Holy Spirit. The churches should manifest an openness to the experience of the Spirit, which could lead to actualization of the power of Christ's resurrection among the whole people of God.

B. The Naming of God

1. A series of questions were posed: How do we name God? Are there limits in the language of faith? How do we recognize and then overcome such limits? How does one understand the overwhelming masculine nature of the image conveyed in naming God "Father, Son and Holy Spirit"?

2. The Puritan tradition has spoken of God in anti-analogical fashion. Therefore, if God be King, then let there be no earthly kings or dominions. Under such a God creaturely life is life among a commonality of equals.

3. An analogical fashion of speaking would assume that if God be King, then earthly kings and dominions are archetypes of the heavenly superior. Under such a God, creaturely life would take on structures of subordination and superordination.

4. The *imago Dei* language presumes an analogy between creator and creature. More explicitly, the *imago Dei* is the *imago Trinitatis.* The divine community forms, informs and transforms the human community and personality. The *imago Trinitatis* shapes, sanctions, and challenges a specific community. Subordination within the divine community might be analogically used to justify subordination within the human community. Similarly, equality, solidarity and mutuality within the divine community might be used to challenge human communities to be as equal, as mutual, and as supportive.

5. Gender categories constitute only one kind of language in which *imago Dei* is expressed. Personal language for God need not be sexual; when it is, however, it should be balanced: male and female, masculine and feminine.

6. Many Western theologians felt that feminine ways of naming God should be accessible to all. The use of feminine names for God could be liberating both for men and women within various communities.

7. The triune God both embraces and extends beyond our categories of male and female.

8. The question was raised whether language about God could be anything but analogical? What about the form of address: "the God beyond knowing . . . whom we call Father"?

9. The names given God describe "person," that is, who God is, but also "relation," that is, how God is, both within the Godhead and in acting toward creatures.

10. Communions give varying weight to the names of God and their valence in identifying person or relation. Gregory of Nyssa and Gregory the Theologian maintain that all names of God describe activities of God, while the titles "Father" and "Son" have a different status signifying the eternal Persons of the Father and the Son.

11. Some churches name God in terms of what the creature can expect from God.

12. Feminist theologians of various confessional allegiances emphasize the relational significance of the titles. Insofar as the begetting function of God is the chief content of the name "Father," God may be named "Mother."

13. A suggestion was made that the real issue of language is not creed but Gospel.

14. Also of concern is how God names us in relation to the triune God, within the community of the faithful, and before the whole of creation. The relationship between who God is and who we are is dialogical. In communication with God we discover both who we are and who God is. This discovery forms our bearing toward God, ourselves, our communities, and our world.

15. All theological language is provisional and a mere human attempt to grasp the mystery. While formed and informed by tradition, theological language is also shaped by context. There must be a dynamic interaction between scripture, tradition, and context. The problem is to adjudicate among the possibly competing claims of each. The issue finally is one of discernment: which names are inspired by the Spirit? Which are not?

C. Creed and Experience

1. We recognize that the difficulties inherent in the *filioque* cannot be reduced simply to the conceptual. What is at issue is also the experience of the Spirit. Here experience is understood both as personal and ecclesial. This experience takes place within the context of a specific theological culture which differs from other authentic theological cultures. While recognizing the plurality of such cultures,

we also want to affirm the large area of shared faith in the Spirit.

2. If one proceeds from experience, then the *filioque,* and the larger trinitarian question, becomes increasingly problematic for large segments of the population, female but also male. Increased recognition of women's experience, and the unacceptability of a God presented in purely male categories, or in two-thirds male, one-third female, will help defuse a highly charged atmosphere in many churches.

3. Taking experience as a point of departure and looking at creedal statements such as the *filioque* some classical Pentecostals would regard creeds as expressions of "sectarianism," and "formalism," whether orthodox or not. Nevertheless, most classical Pentecostal churches have statements of faith, many of them borrowed from the historic creeds.

4. Some Pentecostal churches see their experience of the Spirit, including "the baptism in the Holy Spirit," as a significant ecumenical event, an invitation for the walls of sectarian denominationalism to fall.

5. Though classical Pentecostalism is no longer identified simply with the lower socio-economic groups (it now touches all classes), the presence of so many classical Pentecostal churches among the oppressed classes and ethnic minorities poses the question: has the experience of the Spirit of these groups been given the kind of theological and ecumenical attention it deserves.

6. The experience of the churches from the Holiness tradition contains elements which are typical of classical Pentecostal churches, such as an orientation to social justice issues, and a more gradual or growth approach to spiritual maturity. Like the classical Pentecostals, they are concerned that the agreement on the *filioque,* and on the broader issue of the Nicene Creed, will not adequately state the implications of life in the Spirit as viewed from their experience.

7. The presence of the charismatic renewal in so many of the historic churches has raised questions. There is recognition that charismatic groups within the historic churches have added to the quality of that church's spiritual experience. They have also posed a question to the churches about the nature of spiritual formation which the groups need to take seriously, even while it is recognized that such groups have at times been divisive.

8. Some charismatic Christians and some classical Pentecostal churches are impatient with the discussion on the *filioque* because they fail to see that there is anything experiential at stake. Therefore

they are inclined to see this particular discussion as too narrowly focused, an ecclesiological dispute from the past without the hope of it contributing to a richer understanding of God's presence among us now. Yet they would welcome reconciliation between the historic churches on this divisive issue.

9. It is known that many of the debated formulae in the doctrine of the Trinity and affirmations about the Holy Spirit were worked out in the midst of ecclesiastical and socio-political controversies. Trinitarian theology is the foundation for Christian anthropology and ecclesiology. Ecclesiology includes a normative theory of how God wants humans to live together in community. Thus it has implications for how Christian life is to be ordered in social, political, familial, and cultural communities.

D. Reflections and Recommendations

1) Participants were in general agreement that reception of the Klingenthal Memorandum and its recommendations by the churches represents the most hopeful path toward resolution of the *filioque* question.

2. What we share in regard to the trinitarian faith is greater than what divides us. East and West share a trinitarian faith which is expressed in the Nicene Creed, used by many of the churches.

3. Both East and West recognize that the Trinity is a mystery which exceeds all of our conceptual tools. Given the common faith of East and West excessive precision is to be avoided. There has been, since the fourth century, a general understanding that the specific quality which distinguishes the generation of the Son from the procession of the Spirit eludes us. We live with the lack of precision here. We are even warned against prying (Gregory the Theologian, *Fifth Theological Oration*, 8: "What, then, is procession? Do you tell me what is the unbegottenness of the Father, and I will explain to you the physiology of the generation of the Son and the procession of the Spirit, and we shall both of us be frenzy-stricken for prying into the mystery of God. And who are we to do these things, we who cannot even see what lies at our feet, or number the sand of the sea, or the drops of rain, or the days of eternity, much less enter into the depths of God, and supply an account of that nature which is so unspeakable and transcending all words.") Could not the same kind of imprecision be accepted with regard to the way the Son is involved in the procession of the Spirit from the Father? This is posed as a question to the churches rather than a demand.

4. The *filioque* question should not be isolated from its proper context, which is trinitarian doctrine. It should be seen that the doctrine of the Trinity is not a matter of heavenly metaphysics, but of the presence of the Father through the Son in the Holy Spirit touching history and the Church. Beyond the scriptures the roots of trinitarian doctrine are Christian experience, piety, and liturgy. If trinitarian doctrine returns to these primary sources of Christian experience, and re-experiences the development of trinitarian doctrine in history, much will be done to bring the *filioque* question out of its isolation. The study project of the National Council's Faith and Order Commission is promising in this regard.

5. A renewal of trinitarian piety and theology will demonstrate that issues raised by the *filioque,* far from being an academic question, touches the deepest roots of theological formulation, liturgical practice, and pastoral life.

6. The churches need to look again at the way Christ and the Spirit (christology and pneumatology) stand in a relation of mutuality and reciprocity.

7. In approaching the *filioque* no attempt should be made to transfer what is proper in one theological culture to a different theological culture to which it is quite foreign.

8. It is the view of some that a more stringent and narrower agreement should not now be demanded than the chief participants at the time of the break up of the communion between the East and West were prepared to live with.

9. The West needs to recognize that the unilateral introduction of the *filioque* into the Creed, even given the differing ecclesiologies of East and West, was not only offensive at the time of its introduction, but continues to be so today. The West has failed to understand that this is not just to impose a Western theological view on the whole Church, but turns the Creed which has a unitive function, into a source of division. Nor do Westerners usually grasp the significance of the Creed for the East, where it plays a larger role than it has historically in the West. Further Westerners do not seem fully to grasp the offense when a liturgical text is changed without the consent of others to whom the text also belongs.

10. We recommend that the churches of the West allow their congregations, as an alternate, the liturgical use of the ancient text of the Creed before the addition of the *filioque*. This is looked upon as an interim, rather than a final, solution.

11. Both East and West recognize that there is a proper non-ontological subordination of the Spirit to the Son, as there is of the Son to the Father. What is not sufficiently realized in the West is that there is in Western theologies and piety a systematic subordination of the Spirit to the Son which does not give due respect to the mutuality and reciprocity which should exist between Christ and the Spirit. A thorough study of a wide variety of New Testament texts on the Spirit will be helpful in correcting this imbalance.

12. Both East and West need to recognize that one should not idealize one's own tradition, while caricaturing the other.

13. The Spirit is neither just an ornament of piety, nor liturgical tinsel. Attention should be given not only to relation of the Spirit to the Father and the Son, but to the role of the Spirit in creation, the political and economic orders. The Spirit should not be banished to the realm of piety, or imprisoned in liturgical formulations.

14. The issue of naming God is grave, and it touches the dignity of both women and men. No one should be under any illusion as to the deep seriousness of the issue. A solution calls for the involvement of women and men from the whole spectrum of academic and theological disciplines.

15. Though the state of the question of naming God was quite different in the fourth century, attention should be given to the norms established in the trinitarian, christological, and pneumatological controversies. For instance, Gregory the Theologian rejected the logic which says that God is male just because the vocabulary of "Father" is used. (Speaking somewhat in derision, Gregory asks, "Perhaps you would consider our God to be a male, according to the same arguments, because he is called God and Father . . . " *Fifth Theological Oration*, 7.)

16. Primary religious symbols which arise out of human experience are not unlimited and are not expendable. Therefore there is the necessity of preserving those that are central to the living tradition while at the same time purging them of oppressive elements.

17. The use of the *imago Trinitatis* as a model for naming God is to be commended. The exploration of such an avenue would be more fruitful if it were accompanied by a trinitarian ecclesiology, where equality of persons does not rule out diversity of functions and a measure of non-sexual subordination.

18. The traditional christological paradigm for ecclesiology should be set in its proper trinitarian context. Taking the trinitarian

community as a model enables one to see the pneumatological moment as co-constitutive of the Church. The pneumatological dimension does not belong to a second moment, as an energizer of an already existing structure. This more trinitarian model is also to be fostered because it provides ways of dealing with the question of authority and obedience.

19. Those from the historic churches who are somewhat new to the experiential pneumatology need to set aside preconceptions, and the supposition that the experiential can be communicated conceptually. While remaining true to their own ethos, an openness to both pre-literary and post-literary ways of approaching religious reality is to be encouraged.

20. Those from the classical Pentecostal and Holiness churches should explore ways of expanding their definition of experience. Many would find it helpful if they would communicate to other Christian brethren the wisdom they have found in the biblical hedges against an undisciplined experiential approach to God's presence in history. Their own wisdom and pastoral experience in this area is much more nuanced and sophisticated than is generally known.

21. The bearers of a more experiential pneumatology, such as the classical Pentecostals and the Holiness churches, belong integrally to the history of the Spirit. Without their presence, both formally and informally, in the theological dialogue, the ecumenical endeavor must necessarily remain truncated and impoverished.

22. The trinitarian discussions include the question of how normative ideas are related to the social fabric. Further discussion of the Holy Spirit and the apostolic faith need to include reflection on the various methodologies in dealing with this relationship, examination of the historical and social context of the formulations and the presumptions brought to the discussion by participating communions and their theologians. Ecclesiology, social theory and the basis for the political witness of the whole People of God need to be seen in their nuanced relationship to the trinitarian faith.